FOREVER FORWARD

FOREVER FORWARD

THE INSIDE STORY OF McLAREN FORMULA 1

BEN HUNT

EBURY
SPOTLIGHT

EBURY SPOTLIGHT

UK | USA | Canada | Ireland | Australia
India | New Zealand | South Africa

Ebury Spotlight is part of the Penguin Random House group of companies
whose addresses can be found at global.penguinrandomhouse.com

Penguin Random House UK
One Embassy Gardens, 8 Viaduct Gardens, London SW11 7BW

penguin.co.uk
global.penguinrandomhouse.com

First published by Ebury Spotlight in 2025

8

Typeset by seagulls.net

Printed and bound in Great Britain by Clays Ltd, Elcograf S.p.A.

The authorised representative in the EEA is Penguin Random House Ireland,
Morrison Chambers, 32 Nassau Street, Dublin D02 YH68

A CIP catalogue record for this book is available from the British Library

ISBN 9781529940992

Penguin Random House is committed to a sustainable future for our business, our readers and our planet. This book is made from Forest Stewardship Council® certified paper.

I would like to dedicate this book to my wife Hayley.
For her support, encouragement and for
remaining such a positive light in my life.
I could not have done any of this without her support.

CONTENTS

FOREWORD

BY ZAK BROWN

Winning the Formula One constructors' championship in 2024 was a dream come true for anyone associated with McLaren. This is our sport's ultimate prize and the very reason we go racing: we want to win titles, not just compete and make up the numbers.

My first association with McLaren was when I made it my favourite racing team, which was in 1988. I was an Ayrton Senna fan and he was winning with Lotus in F1, so when he joined McLaren in 1988 and won his first world championship and McLaren became so dominant, that was my first touchpoint, purely as a fan. I was hooked and McLaren were the team I supported.

The first time I met anyone at McLaren was when I picked up some paddock club passes from Ekrem Sami [CEO of McLaren Marketing and a board member at McLaren Technology Group for over 35 years, who left in 2017] in the early 2000s. I didn't make it past the front desk but I remember looking to the left and seeing the entrance and the walkway with all the cars, and I was like, 'Oh my God, I met McLaren.' I first met Ekrem because I was starting to get into sponsorships. I remember meeting Ron Dennis [former team principal and CEO of McLaren] and we became very good friends and got to know [former majority shareholder] Mansour Ojjeh, and we started doing business. So that's where my professional association with the team started, in sponsorship, before I joined as executive director of McLaren Technology Group in November 2016 and then became CEO of McLaren Racing in April 2018.

I take a tremendous amount of influence from our team's founder, Bruce McLaren. He was a pioneer, a racer, a designer, and produced a road car way back when not many teams did that. So if you look at where McLaren is today, it is the embodiment of what Bruce was trying to achieve back in the late 1960s.

Obviously, I never met him, for he died in 1970, but I have asked many people about him. People like Mario Andretti, who raced with him and won in sports cars and the Can-Am series. And McLaren's first F1 world champion, Emerson Fittipaldi, who knew him. They told me he was very humble, an awesome driver and even better person, and so bringing back the papaya colour he picked for his race cars is a nod to his history in founding the team.

The other person who I take a great deal of influence from is Gil de Ferran, the former Indy 500 champion, who passed away in December 2023 and was my friend. I've always been a fan of proper racers being part of racing teams, because they know what success looks like and they know teams work from the inside out.

Gil was wonderful to work with and very close to all of us at McLaren. He was a very humble champion and an awesome racing driver, so we talk and think about him often. His racing helmet has been reproduced on stickers and pin badges – I have a sticker on my phone and it reminds me every day that he is with us.

In terms of influence from my family, my mum was extroverted and sales oriented. She was a customer/client type of person, so I think I got that side of my character from my mum. And my dad was a single-minded workaholic. He just worked all day, so I think I got my work ethic from him – I have traits of both my mum and dad's personalities in me.

The 2024 season was an obvious high point for McLaren by winning the F1 constructors' championship but, for me, the undoubted highlight of my spell in the team has been seeing the turnaround in the team's results and culture. The speed at which we have achieved that success is unbelievable; in F1, it is unheard of. I firmly believe that it is a consequence of the power of the people in the team. Yes, we have the technology and the investments – items such as the new wind tunnel – and that has definitely helped. But we did it through the people.

The new goal has to be to stay at the top and, again, that is down to the people. We have around a thousand people at McLaren Racing and I changed only three of the more senior leaders for the change to happen, so 997, for the most part, stayed the same. It shows the power of people and how quickly things can go forward, or indeed go backwards – and I've seen both at McLaren. And it is about keeping your foot on the throttle but not getting ahead of yourself: taking it one day at a time to build a team you can rely on, with a good culture, and I believe that is what we have done at McLaren Racing and what we need to sustain.

Andrea Stella, the team principal, knows that as well. If you look at some of the teams in F1 that used to be dominant and appear to be going backwards, the reality is they aren't really going backwards: it is a function of them not going forwards while others are. Their facilities are the same and their driver line-ups are awesome, but it is hard to keep that cycle of winning going.

That is true in any sport: how do you prolong your time at the top? We are now at the top of the cycle, and it is my job to ensure we stay there for as long as possible. To do that, first I have to retain people, but also to grow and recruit to make us stronger. We know that people will retire, will move on, and we need to ensure that there is a new level of leadership that is ready to go. So that's my primary focus. Andrea thinks about today. I think about tomorrow.

Together we share a lofty vision and that is for McLaren to be the most exciting and engaged racing team in the world. So that's in Formula One, that's in IndyCar, that's in Le Mans, which is exciting in itself when you consider the McLaren team turned up at Le Mans and won on their debut in 1995, while Bruce McLaren himself won Le Mans in 1966.

We will never have the attitude that we are always going to win, but I would love to see the fans think, 'Oh, McLaren has arrived.' They know we are not going to win every weekend, but they know we will always be at the front and have that magic, whether that be in F1, IndyCar or the World Endurance Championship, motor-sport's triple crown. If we had that universal feeling then, to me, it would make McLaren the most exciting racing team in the world, if it isn't indeed already.

CHAPTER 1

ZAK BROWN

It was important for me to start writing this book from a small memorial garden nestled within the historic Goodwood Motor Circuit in West Sussex, England. Sat a few miles north of the south coast, Goodwood is now known for its hugely successful Festival of Speed and Goodwood Revival car and motorbike shows. The track itself runs around a grass runway that is still used today by light aircraft, but it served as an airfield during the Second World War. In order to prevent them from being wiped out in a single enemy bombing raid, the RAF's aircraft were scattered out strategically across the site and linked by a small concrete service road. It's rumoured that the pilots took to racing on this service road between flying missions and then, in the post-war years, it became a popular venue for car racing, largely because of its speed.

It might sound slightly preposterous, but the service-road-turned-circuit quickly became too fast. As the aerodynamic properties of the cars increased, as well as the horsepower, the machinery being used on the track effectively outgrew the circuit it was being used on. Despite repeated appeals, the circuit's owners were unwilling to invest in chicanes to slow the races down, and the track eventually closed its doors to competitive meets in 1966. It had simply become too dangerous. However, it remained a popular venue for private test days, and does to this day. It's hired out to owners, clubs or for private track days, and you can pop down to the aerodrome café and have a nosey at what is going around the circuit.

During one such private test day on 2 June 1970, the circuit claimed the life of Bruce McLaren, a 32-year-old racing driver from New Zealand, who crashed his McLaren M8D Can-Am car after the rear bodywork came loose. The loss of aerodynamic downforce sent his car into a spin and it struck a marshal post, cutting short the life of one of motorsport's great pioneers – McLaren the racing driver but also the constructor of the car he died in, bearing his now famous surname.

The tragedy is marked in the memorial garden. There is a headstone bearing McLaren's name and the words 'Engineer, Constructor, Champion and Friend' and his race team's original kiwi bird logo, representing his New Zealand heritage. The headstone here at Goodwood is a monument, for McLaren is buried at Waikumete Cemetery in Glen Eden, in his native New Zealand. He was survived by his wife, Patty, and his daughter, Amanda, who is a brand ambassador for McLaren and one of the trustees of the Bruce McLaren Trust.

It is poignant sitting in the garden. A few weeks earlier I had driven McLaren's latest road car, the 765LT, the 205mph, 755bhp supercar, around the Goodwood track, passing where he had his fatal crash. It had not been lost on me, during this specially arranged media day, that his memory was still very much part of the driving experience. For while the headstone marks the historical moment his life stopped, his vision and pioneering spirit very much live on and are baked into the DNA of the McLaren organisation we know today, competing at the highest level across multiple motorsport championships and in McLaren Automotive, their road-car division.

As we will see over these pages, McLaren's tragedy would go on to propel the team to a level of unprecedented success, inspiring the passion and determination to fight it out on track with the biggest of manufacturers. We will see that spirit in the custodians who lead the team forward in Formula One, the pinnacle of motorsport. McLaren Racing's CEO Zak Brown, the team principal Andrea Stella, and drivers Lando Norris and Oscar Piastri are charged with fulfilling Bruce McLaren's vision.

• • •

Zak Brown, McLaren's CEO, is a larger-than-life character who will be familiar to fans and viewers of *Drive to Survive*, the Formula One fly-on-the-wall series on Netflix. Born in Los Angeles in California, Brown is a racing driver turned marketeer. I remember the first time I spoke to him. It was in October 2015, ahead of the US Grand Prix in Austin, Texas, for my former job as F1 correspondent at the *Sun* newspaper. I was following up a story that Lewis Hamilton could earn around £50 million, as he stood on the cusp of winning his third world title. Hamilton's profile was growing as an F1 driver in the United States, where he was spending the majority of his time between races. He had a number of properties there, including a ranch in Colorado as well as places in New York and Los Angeles. The sport had historically struggled to attract and maintain interest from the US audience, but there was a noticeable swell in attention on Hamilton and the life he was living at the time. He was always crossing the globe and becoming increasingly famous for his fashion and music interests, and he was also rather successful. People were buying into his identity, rather than into F1, at this point.

I had reached out to Brown to ask him about Hamilton's commercial potential in the US. We chatted on the phone and I quickly realised he needed little encouragement to speak his mind. Under the headline 'Beck$ Appeal', I quoted Brown as an 'F1 marketing genius': 'Lewis is building his own brand. It is great for the sport. He has that rock-star status and appeal. He has a profile away from the track and is hanging out with the right people and celebrities. Can he be as big as Tiger Woods? I definitely think so.'

I reminded Brown of our first discussion, when we met again at the Canadian Grand Prix in June 2024. He had arrived in the paddock having had a tattoo of the Miami circuit etched on his arm the night before, to mark Norris's first F1 victory there the previous month. He had done something similar as part of a bet with former McLaren driver Daniel Ricciardo when the Australian won the Italian GP in Monza in 2021.

I asked Brown to take me back to the start of his career. Normally when you speak with team personnel at a GP, they tend to find it difficult to talk about anything but the race immediately in front of them. However, that was not the case with Brown, who took me back to the beginning of his F1 story.

'My family took my brother and me to the Long Beach Grand Prix in 1981 when I was ten,' he tells me as we sit in McLaren's hospitality unit. 'They were never into racing and they had never spoken about it. It was kind of like the circus was in town, so we went. I remember it like it was yesterday. The Williams finished one–two [Australian Alan Jones had won while Carlos Reutemann from Argentina was second] and it made a huge impression on me. I still have the race programme, which was signed by [US driver] Eddie Cheever. I met him after the race and he had finished fifth. At that point I was into everything to do with cars – Hot Wheels model cars, everything. So that is how the passion for the sport got started.'

Brown had been bitten by the bug, and then two special moments cemented his aspirations to become a racing driver. First was meeting racing legend Mario Andretti. The second was having success on the *Wheel of Fortune* TV game show, the video of which is widely available on the internet and recommended viewing.

Brown explains: 'In high school, one of my good buddies came from a family that was into racing, so I went to the 1987 Grand Prix of Long Beach IndyCar race with them, and Mario Andretti won. I then met Mario after the race with the family, who knew him. I was very intimidated, but I asked him how he got involved in racing and he told me about karting. In the race programme there was a quarter-page advert for Jim Hall Kart Racing School. I had been on *Wheel of Fortune* and won a bunch of his-and-hers watches, but what do you do with those as a 13- or 14-year-old? I went and sold them at the pawn shop. I didn't tell my parents, but I wanted to go to kart-racing school, and that's how I got started.'

He continued to draw on that entrepreneurial spirit to fund his junior racing career from the mid to late 1980s: 'My mum was a travel agent and she found someone at TWA airlines who liked motor racing, who gave me airline tickets,' he said. 'I then sold those tickets to pay for my racing. I had $100,000 of airline tickets and I would go to companies and say, "Give me $25,000 to put your logo on my car and I will give you $25,000 in airline tickets." I was about 16 or 17 at the time.'

Brown had won around 22 races before moving to Europe to follow the well-trodden route that leads to F1. 'I went to Europe because I wanted to race in F1,' he says. Despite his enterprise with flight tickets, Brown did not have enough funds to pay for a full season, yet that did not deter him. He gambled on a move to the UK to compete, in the hope of attracting sponsors when he was there and achieving a level of success that would allow him to progress with his racing career.

'I started off living in Heathfield in East Sussex driving for Eagle Racing Management and racing in the Formula Opel-Lotus Benelux Series against Jos Verstappen [Max Verstappen's father]. The team went bust halfway through the season and I finished fifth in the championship. I then moved to Sheffield to live on Richard Dean's sister's living-room air mattress because I was broke.'

Dean is a former British racing driver and Brown explained that 'Richard got me a job teaching at Jim Russell Racing Driver School at Donington Park, and I would drive at seven o'clock in the morning from Sheffield to Donington, in not-so-nice weather in January, February and March. Then I moved to Wakefield, in Yorkshire, and did Opel-Lotus again and also British Formula

Three B class, against Jan Magnussen [Kevin Magnussen's father], [IndyCar legend] Dario Franchitti and [Indy 500 winner] Hélio Castroneves. I did that for three or four years and fell in love with England, but then I got a deal to race back in the United States.'

Brown would split his schedule between racing in Europe and North America in single-seaters and sports cars but, in the mid-1990s, he found more success off track. The American created Just Marketing International (JMI) in 1995, setting himself up as intermediary between brands, brokering and advising on sponsorship deals. His background in funding his own career meant he was well placed to advise and, with little in the way of direct competition, JMI quickly became the largest and most successful marketing company in motorsport.

'I started JMI out of a necessity to earn a living,' Brown continues. 'I just wanted to do deals when I came back from Europe. A lot of people told me to stop racing, but I continued until 2000 and was doing deals at the same time.'

He had some success racing, and in 1997 he finished second in the GT2 category in the 24 Hours at Daytona with Roock Racing, driving a factory-supported Porsche 911 GT2. He also finished second in the 1997 12 Hours of Sebring in the same class.

He says: 'The racing career was going down and the business career was going up. When I stopped racing in 2000 the business went totally vertical. I sold part of it in 2008: 70 per cent to Spire Capital and Credit Suisse. I then sold 20 per cent, which was 10 per cent of my 30 and 10 per cent of their 70, to [investment group] WPP. The business at this point was just killing it, and then we [WPP, Spire Capital, Credit Suisse and Brown] sold the entire thing in 2013 to CSM, a global sport and entertainment agency who have since been sold to the Wasserman Group, a similar sports and entertainment company.' Brown was deployed across other sports, and the additional workload took him away from his true passion, motorsport.

'CSM put me in as group CEO and I hated doing it because it was a real job! And it was not within a sport that I loved, but instead sports I had zero passion for, cricket, Olympics, football – just not my thing. I had a four-year jail sentence and I got out after three years on good behaviour!'

During his booming business career, Brown would occasionally still compete, and in 2009 he also set up his own racing team, United Autosports, with the aforementioned Richard Dean. The team operates in the World Endurance Championship and the European Le Mans Series, including the 24 Hours of Le Mans race, winning the LMP2 class in 2024.

Now released from his corporate role with CSM, Brown was enlisted as an advisor for ADD Management, who were nurturing the fledgling career of Lando Norris. So, his relationship with the British racing driver started before his F1 involvement with McLaren, and it was a happy coincidence when he was eventually appointed CEO.

During our interview, Brown also reveals there was another opportunity for him to work in F1 while he was unhappy at CSM. He told me details I had never heard before about how he was asked to join the sport by the venture capital firm CVC, which had majority ownership of the sport through the Formula One Group, while it was still being run for them by Bernie Ecclestone. Brown admits these details are 'not widely known' but adds 'it is OK to know now'.

He said: 'Around 2014, under Bernie's regime, CVC offered me a role [in F1] when they were thinking of making some management changes to support Bernie.' Brown went on to reveal that, having turned down that approach, there was further courting when Liberty Media acquired their shares in the Formula One Group. There were two stages to Liberty's takeover of F1. First, on 7 September 2016 when they initially acquired the shares, and then on 23 January 2017 when they assumed authorised control after the deal was approved by the regulators. Former F1 CEO Chase Carey came in with limited authority after the first stage, but then had total authority a few months later. Brown says, 'So, when Chase was in the middle of bringing in Ross Brawn as managing director of F1, he wanted to bring me in too.' Carey would later sign Sean Bratches to the role as managing director of commercial operations, presumably the role for which Brown had been approached.

Brown continues: 'At the same time, I had Ron Dennis working to recruit me.' Dennis is the former owner, CEO, chairman and founder of McLaren Group. 'Ron is a total legend and I had a great working relationship with him from previous commercial deals, but he was the CEO and I was not that interested in being a number two, if you like. He had wanted me to work more in a commercial capacity. I loved McLaren so it did have appeal, but I had the Formula One offer going on, which was a role that had more gravitas and scope.'

However, a boardroom reshuffle saw Dennis ostracised. In November 2016 he lost a court case against his fellow shareholders that saw him suspended from his position as chairman. His contract with the company expired in January 2017 and by June he had agreed to sell his remaining shares in both the McLaren Technology Group and McLaren Automotive to the two majority shareholders, Mumtalakat, the Bahrain sovereign investment fund, and Mansour Ojjeh. His departure paved the way for Brown's arrival.

In 2017, Brown was appointed executive director of the McLaren Technology Group and was responsible for overseeing that part of the business with chief operating officer Jonathan Neale. A subsequent reshuffle saw him gain control of the racing teams while Neale was made chief operating officer of the McLaren Group. Frenchman Éric Boullier remained as the team's principal, a position he had held since 2014, reporting to Brown.

Brown says that he was overwhelmed by the opportunity to run McLaren. 'I got pursued by Mansour Ojjeh and Mohammed [McLaren Group's executive chairman, Shaikh Mohammed bin Essa Al Khalifa],' he tells me in Canada. 'They went, "Decks are clear and we can offer you a grander role."

'I started as an executive director. It was a role where you had to walk before you could run, but I had a clear path. At that point, it was, "We want you to be a boss of the business and let the racing team get on with it." And then a year later they took over after Dennis had sold his share, and I started running the whole show. The Formula One role was an unbelievable opportunity. I could hang out with drivers and be more of a racer. I can do the corporate side, going to London in a suit and tie, but once the lights go out, I am in racing mode. Also, McLaren had a history in sports cars and IndyCars, like me, and, it just felt right. And these are the coolest bosses you could possibly have, so it was the whole package.'

In an interview with f1.com in January 2017, Brown was asked about his first few days with the team, and he answered with wonderful enthusiasm. 'I'm learning all the time,' he said. 'Every new person I meet, I learn something from. The depth and breadth of experience within the McLaren Technology Centre are incredible. But I've also learned something about myself. I'm absolutely certain I made the right decision. Why? Because I'm a racer – racing is my life – and working for McLaren has made that even more crystal-clear to me than it was before.

'Here's an example. The other day I was walking from my office to the staff restaurant, and I couldn't help stopping to ogle some of the cars I was passing on my way: ex-Niki Lauda cars, ex-Alain Prost cars, ex-Ayrton Senna cars, ex-Mika Häkkinen cars, ex-Lewis Hamilton cars, et cetera, all of them world-championship winners. I don't mind telling you: it makes the little hairs on the back of my neck stand up. And, of all of them, it was the ex-Ayrton cars and the ex-Mika cars that got my attention the most. Alongside Mario Andretti and Nigel Mansell, those two guys are my two biggest ever racing heroes.'

Brown is now relishing his time at McLaren. He's playing with his train set and having the time of his life. He's busy across McLaren's involvement in F1, IndyCar, Formula E and Extreme E. As leader, he has transformed the team, ensuring he has the right people in the right place to achieve success. But it has not always been easy and his position has come under scrutiny on a number of occasions. Unlike Dennis before him, who was an owner, Brown is an employee of the team and consequently has to deliver. 'I started in tricky times and then got myself into tricky times again', he tells me with disarming honesty. 'I always felt that when you own your business there is nowhere to hide. You either quit or you take it head on. When I started my business, there were many weeks of saying, "FedEx needs to arrive on Thursday or I am not making payroll on Friday."

'So I would like to think I am resilient and tough, and I always felt I had the total support of the board. I walked into McLaren in the worst state it had ever been. The worst results, no sponsorship, a toxic environment. But I always felt like I never created that problem. It gave me comfort knowing that I was here to resolve it. I was very transparent and realistic with the board, and I had time to fix it.'

His straightforward approach has been welcomed by those working at McLaren. He takes the rough with the smooth. His way of working is in complete contrast to the old order under Dennis. The change of culture within the team has been dramatic. A fresh approach to marketing and presentation; to sponsorship and brand identity. McLaren have evolved under Brown's watch and now they are enjoying success after a period of underachievement. He may not currently have the same cult status as Bruce McLaren, the man whose surname is on the car, but they do share similarities in that both were able to combine different skill sets aside from racing cars.

McLaren was an intuitive engineer, an astute businessman and a natural leader – one of Formula One's pioneers. Meanwhile, Brown is an excellent marketeer, a dealmaker and great man-manager with bundles of passion and enthusiasm. Both have shaped the team into what it is today, but not done so single-handedly. They have done it with the respective teams they managed, passing the McLaren DNA through generations. McLaren's story has been a perpetual tale of success and setbacks, a rollercoaster that is now being ridden by its current owners and those charged with driving it forever forward.

CHAPTER 2

BRUCE McLAREN

At the front of the Boulevard in McLaren's factory in Woking, there is a tiny Austin 7 Ulster motorcar that sits decidedly out of place among the race cars that line up across the tiled lobby. There is the latest F1 car painted in the team's current livery, adjacent to the welcome desk that looks out through the huge glass windows and across a lake. There are also some distinctive papaya-coloured McLaren road cars that run along the grey-tiled strip and, if you look further into the distance, you'll see some of the distinctive red and white Marlboro-liveried F1 models made famous during the 1980s and 1990s.

Also next to the unassuming little red Austin is a full-size bronze statue of Bruce McLaren and a brief description telling visitors that the car, which was built in 1929, was not only the very one McLaren had learned to drive in, but also the first car he won a race with – at the age of 15.

We will come on to more details of the impressive McLaren Technology Centre, or MTC as it is more commonly known, but at this point it feels appropriate to contemplate McLaren's statue and his first car, at the very front of the building. Some F1 teams place trophy cabinets at the entrance of their factories, going all-out to impress those who visit. Yet McLaren choose to have their founder at the front of theirs. There is no place for Ron Dennis, the former mechanic turned team boss and then executive chairman who oversaw the team's dominant spell during the 1980s and early 1990s. Nor any of their Formula One world champions such as Lewis Hamilton, Niki Lauda, James Hunt or even the great Ayrton Senna. Instead, it is the diminutive figure of a smiling Bruce McLaren and his Austin 7.

The statue was commissioned by McLaren to commemorate the 50th anniversary of his tragic accident at Goodwood on 2 June 1970. Artist Paul Oz, who has been commissioned to work on a number of F1-related artworks in the past, delivered on the assignment with a poignant memorial of the team's founder. It was unveiled on 2 June 2020 by Bruce McLaren's daughter, Amanda, who lit the 50th candle scattered at the statue's feet. This way, he oversees the comings and goings of the team that still bears his surname.

• • •

Bruce McLaren was born in Auckland, New Zealand, on 30 August 1937. His parents, Les and Ruth McLaren, owned a service station and car workshop in Remuera, a middle-class suburb of Auckland. Les McLaren had previously raced motorbikes but switched to racing cars shortly before Bruce was born. The young Bruce McLaren showed an early passion for cars and spent all his out-of-school hours in the family-owned workshop.

However, when he was nine, he was diagnosed with Perthes disease – a rare condition that affects the hip joints of children, causing the bone to deteriorate. It was devastating for the sport-loving boy, who was confined to home schooling and rehabilitation work. He was not able to walk on his own again until he was 12. Ultimately, it resulted in his left leg being shorter than his right and, despite spending two years in traction, he was left with a permanent limp.

It was during this dark period, though, that he inadvertently started his engineering career. While working with a tutor to further his education, he also spent hours studying engineering textbooks and discussing motor racing with his father. McLaren was obsessed by cars and making them go faster.

McLaren returned to full-time education when he was 11, but did not care much for lessons and homework. He was more interested in stripping down his bicycle, removing any excess weight, so that it would go faster. When he was just 13, he turned his attention to cars, building his first one – the Austin 7, which his father had purchased as a beat-up bucket of bolts. He spent his spare time racing it around a grass track near the family home, and used it to enter his first hill-climb race in 1952, aged 15. McLaren would soon prove that his disability was not going to hold him back and he won his first event, another hill climb, later the same year in his Austin 7, at Muriwai in the 750cc class.

He coupled his prowess behind the wheel with a keen technical mind bent on the pursuit of mechanical perfection. He would always seek to fettle his designs, believing he could extract ever better performance, whether by making the car faster and more responsive or by improving reliability and safety.

After finishing school at Seddon Memorial Technical College, he enrolled at the School of Engineering at Auckland University, but dropped out to concentrate on his racing career after his first year in 1958. According to *The Bruce McLaren Scrapbook: A Pictorial Celebration of a Kiwi Legend* by his sister Jan McLaren and Richard Becht, his student card was rescinded, with 'went motor racing' as the reason given for ceasing his further education.

As he climbed up the motor-racing pyramid, he moved through the classes until he raised enough funding to secure a drive in a Cooper Climax Formula Two car, built by the British Cooper Car Company he would later drive for in Formula One. Having extensively modified the car, he was runner-up in the 1957–8 New Zealand championship series.

However, it was his performance during the New Zealand Grand Prix, at the Ardmore Circuit in Auckland on 11 January 1958, which attracted the most attention. McLaren had already gained plenty of recognition locally, but the NZ GP introduced him to a wider audience. Despite being hampered by a gearbox problem, an issue that had surfaced before the race had begun, an undeterred McLaren still started, albeit some 30 seconds behind the rest of the field. He was forced to retire four laps from the end and unable to finish, but his tenacity and preceding reputation caught the eye of Australian Formula One racing driver Jack Brabham. A future three-time F1 world champion, Brabham became a mentor for McLaren and the two would later become team-mates at Cooper.

He had also impressed the New Zealand Grand Prix organisation, which was pioneering a new scheme to promote local racing talent, and he had done enough to earn himself a spot on its 'Driver to Europe' programme. There are now many such routes to help ferry talent to the top level of motorsport via European competition, where the best racers compete with new talent rising to the top. McLaren, aged 21, was the first inductee on the New Zealand-run programme and secured a place driving for British team, the Cooper Car Company.

Bruce McLaren left New Zealand on 13 March 1958 with his friend and mechanic Colin Beanland, bound for the UK. The Cooper Car Company had been set up in 1947 by Charles Cooper and his son John, and they ran their business from a small garage in Surbiton, Surrey. During the 1950s and 1960s, the Cooper team raced in a number of series across the world, including F1, with plenty of success. Its list of former drivers includes Stirling Moss and John Surtees. The company is perhaps best known for its creation of the Mini Cooper, which dominated rallying in the 1960s and still lives on in the form of the iconic Cooper marque offered on the BMW-made Minis on our roads today.

McLaren's first race for Cooper was in the 1958 German Grand Prix at the Nürburgring, where he would compete in an F2 car. At the race, which was held on 3 August and was a full round on the F1 calendar, organisers boosted the number of cars on the grid to allow F2 cars to compete in the same race as their F1 counterparts, although drivers in the F2 cars would not receive championship points. The race distance was also shortened from 22 laps to 15.

McLaren qualified in fifteenth and was the highest-placed F2 driver. In the race itself, he defied the odds and finished fifth overall, again the highest-placed F2 finisher. It was a remarkable achievement, given he was making his debut in Europe, in an under-strength car, and competing against some of the best drivers in the world – names such as Stirling Moss, Mike Hawthorn and Graham Hill. In his next race, in Morocco, which organisers again opened up to F2 machinery, he was the second-highest F2 finisher in 13th, albeit behind Brabham, who was also driving a F2 Cooper Climax.

McLaren had demonstrated his ability and was consequently promoted to Cooper's F1 team for the 1959 season. There is an insightful extract from his autobiography on McLaren's website, which relates to his first season in F1. The passage refers to the summer when McLaren welcomes his parents to watch him race for the first time in Europe as he competes in both the F1 and F2 races (a scenario that wasn't uncommon for drivers in that era) at the French Grand Prix in Reims.

McLaren recalls how 'the sun was beating down with such intensity that a spanner lying on the ground for ten minutes was almost too hot to handle'. As for the rigours of racing, McLaren adds how the 'first few laps were murder', as it was impossible to keep clear of the battering hail of pebbles from the lead cars: 'My knuckles were being burnt by the hot blast of air coming over the screen. I tried licking them, but it didn't help … I could hardly breathe and was desperately trying to scoop air into the cockpit going down the straight … The mixture of sweat and blood in my goggles was like pink champagne. I raised them and the mess sluiced down over my face.'

McLaren goes on to explain how his goggles had been shattered by no fewer than 35 stones hitting the glass directly and expresses his relief at seeing the chequered flag. He adds that some drivers were collapsed in heaps and revived, in the physical sense, with buckets of water to cool them off.

As if that was not bad enough, after finishing fifth, he also had the F2 race to drive in immediately afterwards, with just a 30-minute break. McLaren recalls trying to overdo it. He says his decision to compete in both classes was ultimately 'dangerous' and he was attempting manoeuvres that he would not normally risk during the opening laps. Suffering from exhaustion, he likens the feeling to being drunk behind the wheel and soon, after seeing Brabham pull over and retire from the F2 race, he did the same a few laps later, deciding it was safer to watch it from the pit lane. Later that afternoon, he vowed to never again compete in an F1 and F2 race on the same day.

Before that race in France, McLaren had also finished fifth in the season-opening Monaco Grand Prix and later took his first ever F1 podium at the British Grand Prix at Aintree. He then won the final race of the season, the United States Grand Prix that was held at Sebring International Raceway in Florida. McLaren was just 22 years 104 days old, becoming the youngest-ever GP winner. This record would stand for more than four decades until Fernando Alonso's victory at the 2003 Hungarian Grand Prix.

McLaren would go on to win the Argentine Grand Prix, the first race of the 1960 F1 season, and finish the season as the runner-up to Brabham with podiums at Monaco, Spa-Francorchamps and the French, Portuguese and United States Grands Prix races. He won the 1962 Monaco Grand Prix on his way to third place in the drivers' championship, cementing his place as one of the best drivers on the grid.

By now, however, he harboured serious ambitions to run his own team and in 1963 founded Bruce McLaren Motor Racing Ltd. While he competed with his fledgling team in non-championship events and in the Canadian-American Challenge Cup (known as the Can-Am), he continued to drive – and win – for Cooper until the end of the 1965 season, when he announced that he would be taking his own team grand prix racing, with fellow New Zealander Chris Amon as his second driver.

The following year McLaren, still alongside Amon, would go on to win the 24 Hours of Le Mans race driving a Ford GT40, cementing what was to be a long-standing partnership between the team and the Detroit-based motor company. The legendary race ended Ferrari's dominance in the competition and was turned into a Hollywood film in 2019 called *Ford v Ferrari*. It was McLaren's seventh attempt at the endurance race, having made his debut at Le Mans in 1959, at the age of only 21, driving a Cooper Monaco. He had just started his first full season as a works Cooper F1 driver, and the endurance race provided him with yet another test. On this debut, he did not finish. In fact, McLaren's victory in 1966 was the first time he had reached the finish line of the 24 Hours of Le Mans race.

Meanwhile, despite his success in France, McLaren remained focused on F1. He had persuaded American racing driver Teddy Mayer to invest in his team in 1964. He had asked Mayer for help with the purchase of the superior Zerex sports car from US racing legend Roger Penske. The two men were aligned in their ambition to reach F1 with their own racing team, which would ultimately be realised with McLaren's F1 debut as a team at the Monaco Grand Prix in 1966.

McLaren needed to decide what colour to paint the team's car. The team's international cast and New Zealand heritage meant that despite being based in Colnbrook, England, from 1965 and racing under an English racing licence, the cars were never painted in the traditional racing-green colours favoured by British-based and owned teams, such as Aston Martin, Cooper, Lotus, Vanwall and BRM. German teams opted for white or silver, Italian teams were red and French teams were painted blue.

Prior to the team's F1 debut in Monaco, McLaren had asked British artist and illustrator Michael Turner, who specialised in motoring and aviation paintings and had previously been commissioned to design the team's kiwi logo, to come up with a livery. Turner had decided upon a green, silver and yellow, but was left disappointed when he arrived in Monaco to discover that McLaren had subsequently agreed a deal with movie director John Frankenheimer to paint his cars white with a green stripe down the middle, to represent the fictional Yamura team in Frankenheimer's 1966 movie, *Grand Prix*.

In an interview on his website, F1 journalist Peter Windsor quotes Turner as saying: 'I had designed the badge for Bruce, featuring the kiwi, and also the maroon livery on the Group 7 sports car. Bruce then asked me to do a scheme for his new F1 car. I did so, but when I arrived in the pit lane, I couldn't see it. The car was simply white with a green stripe down the centre. I asked Bruce what had happened. "Michael," he said, "I'm so sorry. We were going to do the car in your livery but then John Frankenheimer came along and offered us a lot of money to paint it white with a central strip for this film he's making with MGM. It was an offer we couldn't refuse ...'"

The car itself, the M2B, was powered by a heavy V8 Ford 406 engine that was widely used in sports cars and had been adapted to squeeze into the F1 car. It yielded a disappointing debut as reliability proved a problem, with Amon withdrawing from the race and McLaren retiring due to an oil leak. It proved to be a frustrating opening season, with a sixth-place finish in the British GP and fifth in the US as the highlights.

In 1967 McLaren opted to change the livery to red and a new BRM motor looked to have done the trick with a fourth-place finish in Monaco, yet there were further retirements in the Netherlands, Italy, the US and Mexico.

But McLaren's fortunes would significantly improve the following year. Fellow New Zealander Denny Hulme piloted the now papaya-coloured car – picked as it stood out on black-and-white TV broadcasts – to fifth place in the South African GP. He would finish second in Spain and fifth in Monaco, while McLaren would fail to finish both those races.

However, the founder would unlock a significant achievement in the Ford-powered M7A by taking the team's maiden F1 victory at the 1968 Belgian Grand Prix. McLaren won the 28-lap race at Spa-Francorchamps, after winning the Race of Champions, a non-championship event at Brands Hatch, earlier in the year.

Hulme also won the Italian and Canadian Grands Prix later in the year, helping the team to second in the constructors' championship. Using an updated 'C' version of the M7, Bruce McLaren took a further three podiums in 1969, while Hulme won the last race of the season in Mexico.

McLaren's F1 team had gained respect from the rest of the paddock for being a small, slick outfit, with their founder playing a hands-on role as well as serving as their driver. He also inspired fierce loyalty in his workers. In an extract on the team's website, Howden Ganley, a fellow New Zealander who worked for McLaren, said: 'If Bruce had walked into the workshop one morning and told us we were all going to march across the Sahara Desert, we'd have immediately downed our tools and followed him.' Old photographs of McLaren frequently show him smeared with oil and grit from the race track, but with a smile on his face. Not only was he the boss, the designer and the driver, McLaren was also the guy who swept the factory floor and drove the transporter.

McLaren's success was not just in F1 either. From the team's workshops, which moved from Feltham to Colnbrook and then ultimately – and long after McLaren's death – Woking, they produced cars that would race in the aforementioned Le Mans race as well as the Can-Am series. The Can-Am ran from 1966 to 1974 and again from 1977 to 1987 with a very simple premise: to be free of F1's restrictive rulebook so that it could feature radical designs powered by monster motors. McLaren relished the freedom and won the title for five successive seasons between 1967 and 1971, earning some lucrative prize money.

The M1 was the first offering, a small-block engine Oldsmobile that was driven in multiple championships and evolved into the M1A prototype and the M1B. In 1967, things changed when

McLaren produced the M6A and, using a Chevrolet V8 engine, dominated the six-race Can-Am series, with Hulme winning three races and McLaren two to take the title. The following season, the team retained the title but this time it was Hulme who won the drivers' championship with McLaren in second place. In 1969, McLaren Racing dominated and won all 11 races, with Bruce McLaren winning 6 and the drivers' championship.

McLaren Racing's winning streak in the US created a new business opportunity. The aluminium monocoque chassis coupled with Chevy power had proved unstoppable, and it opened the door for McLaren to sell customer cars to fellow race teams, who envied their success. Buying a ready-made entrant is still possible today in some championships, and the sales proved to be lucrative for Bruce McLaren, who was able to redeploy the funds into his F1 operation, which was then notorious for paying poorly when it came to prize money (unlike today, with the lucrative prize fund stretching to around $150 million for the winning team at the end of the season). As his business developed on both sides of the Atlantic, McLaren decided to hang up his helmet and focus on building his cars.

At the start of the 1970 season, he had confided in his close friends that this would be his last as a racing driver. He kicked off the year with a retirement in the South African GP due to an engine problem and in a non-championship race at the Race of Champions at Brands Hatch he was also left with a DNF after suffering an accident on lap 21, while Hulme would finish third behind Jackie Stewart and Jochen Rindt. He would fare better at the Spanish GP, finishing second in Madrid in what would prove to be his final podium. In the BRDC International Trophy at Silverstone he was fourth, while at the 1970 Formula One Monaco GP on 10 May, he would retire with suspension failure. It was what would prove to be his final F1 race; an underwhelming and unfitting end to an astonishing and significant career in motorsport as a racing driver, designer and team owner.

CHAPTER 3

TRAGEDY

Susie Dunbar was working for Bruce McLaren at the team's factory at 5 David Road in Colnbrook, not far from London's Heathrow Airport, on 2 June 1970, when the phone rang. Dunbar recalls the exact moment she learned of McLaren's tragic accident at Goodwood and, as we speak, it is clear she is still gripped by the sadness of his passing. Dunbar was employed as a secretary working for the team and she takes up the story of what happened on that fateful day.

'I was in the office on the phone,' she tells me. 'Teddy Mayer walked in and he told me to put it down. I explained to him that it was a business call, but he insisted, so I did. That was when he told me the tragic news.

'He gave me a list of people to call in America, sponsors and such, and he told me to tell them before news got out. He also told me not to go downstairs to the workshop floor, because the staff didn't know yet.

'In those days you couldn't dial direct to America. You had to go through the operator, and she was amazing. I told her what had happened, and she said, "If you give me the list now, and you don't mind me listening in, as soon as you finish one call, I'll get the next one ready for you." Doing those calls was probably one of the hardest things I'd ever done, because I had to keep it together. I remember driving home that night and I just thought, "Gosh, life will never be the same again." I hadn't closely experienced anything tragic like that before. I was only 21.'

Dunbar was not alone in feeling like her world had changed. As she worked through her list of people to call and break the terrible news to, Mayer had assembled the workforce on the factory workshop floor, urging the staff to put down their equipment. 'Guys, I have the worst possible news,' said Mayer, according to the recollection on McLaren's website. 'Bruce has just bought the farm.' The term was a colloquial euphemism used during the Second World War and meant he had been killed. He told them all to go home and have some time off. The broken workforce sifted out of the building.

For Dunbar, the news was especially painful, as she had formed a close working relationship with McLaren and his family. She had been working for the British Racing and Sports Car Club and was living in Chiswick, west London, when she wrote to all the F1 team managers asking for work. Phil Kerr, who was working for Brabham at the time, replied and offered her a job – but at McLaren, whom he was joining at the start of the 1968 season, along with engineer and racing driver, Denny Hulme. She took the job but, with no other secretary in place, Dunbar found herself working with Bruce McLaren as well as Kerr, and recalls the team's operation during the late 1960s.

'It was a basic workshop but it was kept spotlessly clean and I remember it having pale blue or grey paint on the floor. It was special workshop floor paint that kept the dust down and they could just wash it over each day.

'We had a canteen, which everybody congregated in. And we had an old boy called Fred who made the tea and did the workshop cleaning. There was a sandwich van that came around, which we used to call the roach coach.

'There were only about 25 people working there during those days. We had an engine shop in Detroit, but we made the F1, Can-Am and IndyCars in the factory in Colnbrook. All the engineering was done there. It was amazing how few people were designing and building cars that ran in three different series.

'One of the jobs I had was answering fan letters. I remember when I got the IBM golf-ball typewriter [the IBM Selectric], and I just thought it was the bee's knees! I had to get the drivers to sit down and sign the photographs and then I'd post them back. Sometimes there were up to 500 photographs to sign at a time. Bruce refused to have a stamp made for the signatures. He always wanted them to be individually signed by the drivers. They were all genuine. If there were questions in the letters, then I had to answer them too. I remember when Peter Revson joined us [in 1972], some of the questions were saucy, because he was quite gorgeous!

'Bruce was always incredibly fair, but he was firm. I remember once having a rant and rave about some American sponsor and he said to me, "Be very careful because they pay your wages." He did not raise his voice but he quickly put me in my place. He had a way of doing that – making you feel guilty without even raising his voice.'

Dunbar recalls a lively atmosphere in the workplace: 'I remember there was always music playing. I don't think there was any other team that had the same spirit. There was a sense of humour about the place, but McLaren was a serious business, and if you were asked to work late, you worked late. You were there until about ten o'clock at night sometimes. There was never any question: if they needed you to work, you just did it and you didn't get overtime for it. I didn't get paid an awful lot of money, so I temporarily took a job at a local pub. Then one time Bruce wanted me to work late and I said, 'Well, I'm supposed to be at the pub tonight'. He asked me what I got paid and I think it was a pound for a shift, and he said I will double it if you give it up. So I ended up with a pay rise for giving up the pub job. He was that kind of person.

'We would go to the pub with him on Mondays after the races. About a dozen of us would go down. It was a funny little pub, a sausage-and-chip place, nothing fancy. If Denny was around, he'd come along and they'd both tell us about the race. The TV coverage was sporadic then, and usually only consisted of the British and Monaco GPs anyway, so that was the way we found out what was going on, and Bruce was able to touch base with everybody. It was so nice. He had a great sense of humour, a great mental capacity, but he was never able to finish his stories because halfway through he'd start sketching on a serviette or the corner of his notepad. He would draw car-part designs all the time. At work, I would sit down with him to take notes in shorthand and all of a sudden he'd stop talking and focus on his drawing. I'd say to him, "I'm still here," and he'd apologise.'

News of McLaren's death reverberated through motorsport. Fatalities at the track were tragically common. A total of 14 F1 drivers had perished during the 1960s, and the number was still as high as 12 for the next decade. The details of the accident were initially limited. *Autosport* reported the news under the headline 'Bruce McLaren Killed' with the story beneath saying that he had been 'killed in a testing accident at Goodwood. Early reports said that the engine blew at around 180mph when Bruce was flat out along the Lavant Straight, and the car veered into the bank and disintegrated.' He was driving the team's latest Can-Am car, the M8D, when the rear bodywork came loose, destabilising the car, and he struck a marshal post.

However, there were other contributing factors. Three weeks earlier, on 12 May 1970, McLaren's team-mate Hulme was practising for the Indy 500 at the Indianapolis Motor Speedway when his McLaren M15 caught fire at 200mph. Unable to escape from the burning cockpit due to the speed at which he was travelling, Hulme's hands were burned, which prevented him from taking part in the Goodwood test the following month, in preparation for the Can-Am race at Mosport Park in Canada on 14 June.

In an interview on McLaren's website, Hulme recalls: 'I was out on the track and I saw what I thought was water on the screen. The next lap I saw more, and of course I assumed it was rain. I was waiting for them to throw the yellow [flag]. On my third lap – boof! The thing caught fire. Well, methanol burns with an invisible flame and all I saw was the screen and my helmet visor just folding up. Then it got real hot in there ...'

Hulme had been wearing fireproof Nomex overalls, but only leather shoes and gloves, as was usual for the day. 'My hands had shrivelled to claws, but I finally managed to undo the seatbelt and jump. The fire trucks all went to the car. The only marshal who came near me felt the wall of heat. Luckily, when my visor melted it welded itself all round. The paint on my helmet was blistered to hell. The heat was just enormous.'

McLaren arrived at Goodwood and was due to test the M8D Can-Am car and the M14A F1 car, but, given the upcoming race, the focus was on the M8D, and especially on the car's huge rear wing, designed for maximum downforce. He had his first run in the M14A and put in a handful of laps before jumping into the M8D, after it had been run in by one of the mechanics.

McLaren was not impressed and, after one or two laps, set about refining its design. He sought to correct the oversteer and improve the car's handling by increasing the rear-wing angle. McLaren's lap time dropped significantly as a consequence of the adjustments. He continued fettling the aerodynamics and, unusually, pushed on past midday, putting in some extra laps to further refine the car's performance, when the team would usually have broken for lunch.

Around 22 minutes later, he had his fatal accident, when the rear wing became detached from the car. The immediate loss of downforce meant the car lost contact with the road and eyewitnesses recall seeing it skid off track, with thick black tyre marks veering right as the M8D spun on the grass travelling backwards into a marshal post sitting on top of a concrete mound that was covered in grass. The impact, estimated to be at 150mph, split the car in two and it burst into flames. McLaren had no chance of surviving. At the sight of the devastation, the team jumped into the support van and rushed to the scene, which was a quarter of the way around the track from the pits. They tried in vain to save McLaren, moving him clear of the fire, but he had been killed by the severity of the impact.

The marshal post that McLaren had struck had been abandoned and was scheduled to be demolished and removed to improve safety. It was a tragic combination of circumstances that had led to McLaren's death. Bruce had once written: 'Too often someone pays the penalty just for being in the wrong place at the wrong time when a situation or a set of circumstances is such that no human being can control them.' He'd perfectly summed up his own death.

Denny Hulme had just been to see a specialist about the burns he had sustained to his hands, when he learned of McLaren's passing. 'That day was the worst of my life,' he said, quoted on McLaren's website. 'I heard it on the radio coming back from Harley Street. I'd had no reaction to my hands, no shock, no self-pity. Then suddenly Bruce was gone. It was the worst ever in the week or so after that, because the reactions to both things hit me at the same time.'

Dunbar recalls how Hulme felt responsible for the accident that had killed his friend. 'Denny always blamed himself,' she says. 'He always said, "I should have been in the car, not Bruce." He took it incredibly hard. A short time after the accident, I asked him to take me round the track so I could experience what it was like in a race car, but he told me it was too dangerous and he wouldn't take me.' While he was confident driving himself around the circuit, he did not want the responsibility of taking Dunbar.

As the team digested the news, they defied Mayer's offer to take some downtime to grieve for their boss. While Tyler Alexander, another American who had worked with McLaren and Mayer in the mid-1960s to set up the team, received the news in Indianapolis and immediately boarded a plane back to the UK, Mayer was again addressing the staff who had turned up for work at 8am – just as usual. In Bruce McLaren's absence, Mayer was now the team leader and he stepped up to galvanise the workforce in its darkest hour: 'Well, we don't have a boss, we don't have a driver, and we don't even have a car,' he said, referring to the M8D Can-Am chassis that had been destroyed. 'But we do have a motor race – at Mosport in two weeks' time – and we all owe it to Bruce to race. So we might as well get to it.'

Dunbar adds: 'Everybody had turned up for work the next day. I didn't think I'd be out of a job. I just assumed we would carry on. Very soon afterwards they got Peter Gethin to drive the other car for the next few races.' Gethin was a British driver from nearby Ewell in Surrey and would make his F1 debut at the 1970 Dutch Grand Prix as a replacement for McLaren. Dunbar continues: 'Peter didn't have any proper overalls, so he wore some of Bruce's, but he was much smaller than Bruce, so I used to have to stitch him up the back when he got in the car and then unstitch him when he got back out, and also sew on all new the sponsors' logos.'

In the days that followed McLaren's death, the team would pull together and they all attended a special memorial service at St Paul's Cathedral. 'I remember sitting there and turning around and seeing the whole place was full,' says Dunbar. 'It was on my birthday, 24 June. I came out with tears streaming down my face, and Denny put his arms around me and said that birthday girls shouldn't cry. He was so sweet.

'It was a very difficult time. It was like his memory was in the fabric of the place. It stayed with everybody.'

Responding in a fitting way to the tragic loss of their founder, under the new leadership of Mayer and Alexander the McLaren team not only built a new M8D, but they did so against the clock to make it in time for the opening race of the Can-Am season in Canada, which came just 12 days after Bruce's death. Once the car had been built and shipped, it was down to drivers Denny Hulme and Dan Gurney, a vastly experienced American racer who had driven across multiple championships including F1, to go out and deliver on track. Understandably, tensions were running very high, given the circumstances and the unpredictability of the M8D.

Gurney and Hulme responded decisively by taking pole and qualifying in second place respectively. Gurney would go on to win the race by 16 seconds in what was an emotionally charged victory. Hulme, whose damaged hands had frozen onto the steering wheel in a clawed position, was third. Gurney won again in the second race while Hulme recorded six wins during the 1970 season on his way to the title. Despite the pain and discomfort, he'd defied the odds to take the world crown and had done so in the memory of his friend.

McLaren's success in Can-Am was tempered by a mixed season in F1. After the shock of Bruce McLaren's death, the team's first F1 race came at the Dutch GP in Zandvoort, when Gethin and Gurney, racing together in Hulme's temporary absence, both failed to finish the race, the latter due to engine trouble while the former suffered an accident after 18 laps. The race was remembered for the fatal accident of British driver Piers Courage who, driving for Frank

Williams, the founder of the F1 team that bears his surname today, crashed out due to a suspension failure and flew into a sand-dune embankment, where his car exploded.

The McLaren team suffered mixed results through the rest of the 1970 season, with Gethin finishing just three of the seven races he started. A rare highlight was a sixth-place finish in Canada. Meanwhile, Gurney quit F1 soon after Bruce McLaren's death. He left the team after the British Grand Prix and turned to managing his own team, All American Racers, in the US. Meanwhile, Hulme returned to the track and his four podiums over the season helped take the team to a fifth-place finish in the constructors' championship.

Another tough season followed in 1971. But the following year, in 1972, McLaren took their fifth win in F1 with Hulme's success in South Africa, and McLaren's new driver, Peter Revson, was third in the same race as the team enjoyed a double podium in the Ford-powered McLaren M19A. Hulme scored further podiums in Belgium, Austria, Italy, Canada and the US, while Revson was third at Silverstone and Austria and was second in Canada. It culminated in a third-place finish for McLaren in the constructors' championship.

It is at this point that we start to see a theme emerging that repeats itself throughout McLaren's history in F1: the cycle of steady growth and improved results after a major setback. In this case, Bruce McLaren's death. McLaren, it seems, are in constant evolution, striving to reach the top and, when the team gets there, they are knocked off and, undeterred, they start the rebuilding process to get back up again. It is that abiding spirit to move on and up, forever forward, that keeps the team progressing.

After their third place in 1972, the team repeated the achievement in 1973 with Hulme and Revson taking seven podiums between them. But in 1974, the American Revson was replaced by Brazil's Emerson Fittipaldi. Born in São Paulo in 1946 and the son of a motor racing commentator, he raced motorbikes and also boats with his brother Wilson. It wasn't until Wilson flipped at 70mph during a boat race that both brothers were convinced to focus on racing on land. In 1967, Fittipaldi won the six hours of Interlagos, his home circuit, and won the Brazilian low-cost Formula Vee series when he was 21.

Like Bruce McLaren nearly a decade earlier, Fittipaldi moved to Europe in 1969 to race in Formula Ford, the lower-cost, entry-level single-seater racing category, using his winnings to purchase his Merlyn Formula Ford. Fittipaldi was signed by the Jim Russell Racing Driver School – the same racing school that Zak Brown mentioned in the opening chapter. This offered him the chance to make the step up in class to a quicker F3 car, where he was crowned as the 1969 champion. That was sufficiently impressive, and Fittipaldi was offered a drive in F2 by the Lotus Bardahl team. So, in 1970, he made the next career step up to Formula 2 and finished the eight-race season in third place in the championship thanks to six finishes in the points, including four on the podium.

In the same year, Fittipaldi was promoted to Lotus's F1 team, having turned down a move to Williams as a replacement for Courage after his fatal Dutch GP, and drove for them until 1973. He won his first world championship points in the 1970 German GP at Hockenheim at the wheel of a Lotus 49C. He became the de-facto team leader when his team-mate Jochen Rindt was killed in the warm-up for the Italian GP at Monza. Incredibly, given it was his debut season in F1, he won the penultimate race, the US GP at Watkins Glen.

Fittipaldi's win in the US had increased expectations and the following year he initially struggled under the pressure to regain the same form on his way to a sixth-placed finish in the championship. The standout result was a second place in Austria and a third at Silverstone. However, Fittipaldi came back in fine form in 1972 and won the title after claiming five wins in 11 races. He was 25, and the youngest ever champion at the time.

The following year, he started his title defence with three wins in four, but Lotus's decision to introduce a new car mid-season culminated in a dip in performance that saw rival Jackie Stewart win the title. Unsurprisingly, the Brazilian was not pleased at losing his world crown to Stewart and decided to accept a lucrative offer to join McLaren in 1974.

Driving the first Marlboro-liveried McLaren, the M23, he won back his world title and, with it, McLaren's first constructors' title. Partnering Denny Hulme, McLaren won four races, taking a total of nine podiums in 15 races. Fittipaldi won the title by three points ahead of Swiss racer Clay Regazzoni. It had been an astonishing rise for the team. Out of the figurative ashes of their founder, McLaren had been rebuilt and were now Formula One world champions.

The following season, in true McLaren low-follows-high scenario, Fittipaldi dropped the bombshell that he would be quitting after only two seasons to join his brother's newly formed F1 team, which was backed by Copersucar, Brazil's state-run sugar company, for the 1976 season. Finishing the 1975 championship for McLaren in second place, he had been unable to match the pace of the Ferraris, as Niki Lauda won the title and the Italian team also took the constructors' championship.

Fittipaldi's decision was baffling. He'd made the switch through blind family loyalty, and not on his chances of adding to his world titles. The move to his brother's team ultimately bombed and he was never able to compete at the sharp end of the grid again. However, as McLaren's first world champion, he is still a cherished member of the team's extended family. At 77, he took part in the famous Hill Climb at Goodwood's Festival of Speed in 2024, loving every minute as he had the pleasure of driving one of his old race cars.

As we will see, Fittipaldi going from McLaren's world championship-winning golden boy to F1 mid-table obscurity within a second is synonymous with the team's constantly repeating cycle of unpredictable ups and downs. Within the space of less than five years, McLaren had lost its leader and founder, won multiple titles in Can-Am, won its maiden F1 title and lost its world championship-winning driver to a lower-ranking team. Never straightforward or predictable, but a brilliant rollercoaster that would continue for the next six decades.

CHAPTER 4

THE GOLDEN YEARS

Each Formula One team evolves through the success and low points of its past. That is why we need to look back at McLaren's history to understand the DNA of the team today.

Fittipaldi's shock departure at the end of 1975 to join his brother's Fittipaldi Copersucar team had left McLaren in a hole. The team needed to find a new driver. With all the other leading drivers already under contract elsewhere, Mayer turned his attention to James Hunt. The British driver had been desperately seeking a seat for the 1976 season after his previous team, Hesketh, had run out of funds. Hunt had won the Dutch Grand Prix at Zandvoort in 1975, but was a controversial figure with a reputation for being a playboy, which was out of keeping with the culture of professionalism within McLaren.

Hunt's route to F1 had been unconventional. Born in Belmont, Surrey, and living in Cheam – a London suburb where I also grew up – he started racing Minis, before taking out a hire-purchase agreement to finance a Formula Ford car, which allowed him to take the next step in his career competing in the entry-level open-wheeled racing series in 1968. Hunt progressed through the lower ranks but it was not until he reached Formula Three a year later that he showed real skill, but also a temper, which was on display at the Formula Three *Daily Express* Trophy at Crystal Palace in October 1970. Dave Morgan attempted to pass Hunt for second place on the final corner, and the two collided and ended up out of the race. Hunt responded by climbing from his stricken car, which was in the middle of the track, to shove Morgan to the floor, earning himself a rebuke. Yet his talent behind the wheel was sufficient to convince any sceptics and he reached F1 in 1973, driving for Hesketh.

The unfancied team had purchased a March 731 chassis from March Engineering, rather than building their own, and were immediately written off by their rivals as a bit of a joke, a party team. In more recent history, the Red Bull team had a similar reception when they started life in F1 in 2005. However, as with Red Bull, Hesketh, and in particular Hunt, proved the doubters wrong. Hunt finished his debut season with a second-place finish at the 1973 United States Grand Prix and was subsequently awarded the Campbell Trophy from the RAC, marking his performance in Formula One as the best by a British driver.

In 1974, he won a non-championship race, the British Racing Drivers' Club International Trophy at Silverstone, beating a field made up mostly of F1 drivers. Then the following year he piloted the Hesketh team to glory with a sensational victory at the Dutch Grand Prix, the team's only win in the series. The win at Zandvoort catapulted Hunt to stardom and silenced some of his critics in the F1 paddock. He had qualified third behind Lauda and Regazzoni, who were both in the vastly superior Ferrari. Hunt's victory was by virtue not only of his skill behind the wheel but also of his brave decision to opt for the quicker slick tyres on a treacherous drying track.

In an interview with American journalist Dan Knutson, first published in *Autosport* in December 1992, Hunt said: 'It was very special. Hesketh Racing gave me, and taught me, everything in F1 and it was where my soul was. I have always felt that they deserved more than one GP win.'

He continued: 'It was a significant race for a number of reasons. I had a very patchy path into F1. I had hardly won any races, and had no experience of winning … I had made several mistakes up to that point, when in the lead, without any particular pressure from behind. The 1975 Dutch GP turned that around completely and cured me overnight of that last major weakness in my driving. It was a race under maximum pressure because Niki Lauda was breathing down my neck in the all-conquering Ferrari.'

Hunt had identified the correct set-up to master the wet/dry race. He opted for the undercut, coming in early for slick tyres to benefit from the drying track, and then putting in quicker lap times than the rest of the field, who were still on the slower wet tyres. While the others pitted, Hunt responded by hammering out the laps and increasing his lead until he could no longer be caught. He said the race at Zandvoort 'was the completion of my training as an F1 driver'. It had certainly convinced Mayer, who took a gamble on him for the 1976 season.

The gamble paid off. Hunt won the F1 title in his first season driving for McLaren, giving them an improbable victory in a championship that has since been immortalised in the 2013 Hollywood movie, *Rush*. At the centre of the film is Hunt's titanic battle for the title with Austrian driver Niki Lauda's Ferrari.

Hunt and Lauda's first clash was at the Spanish Grand Prix, where Hunt was disqualified after the post-race scrutineers found that his McLaren was 1.5cm too wide and broke the rules. His disqualification promoted Lauda from second place to first. However, McLaren appealed the decision, and won, and Hunt's victory was reinstated – much to the fury of Lauda's Ferrari team, who refused to enter the Austrian Grand Prix in protest.

Hunt won again in France and looked to have won the British Grand Prix, only to be disqualified from the race for driving down an access road and back to the pits, following an opening-lap multiple car accident. Ferrari contested the taking of an alternative route back to his pit box and, this time, Hunt was stripped of the win, handing victory to Lauda and giving him a 23-point lead over Hunt in the drivers' championship.

Their battle for the title, however, took a devastating turn in the next race. Lauda suffered a crash in the German Grand Prix, and his Ferrari burst into flames. Miraculously, he did not perish in the wreckage and, more unbelievably, made his return to racing under six weeks later at the Italian GP, missing only two races, despite his badly burned face. Lauda's return is one of motorsport's greatest ever comebacks, but his time out of the cockpit had allowed Hunt to close the gap. They went into the final race of the year in Japan with Lauda on just a three-point lead.

The weather for the Japanese Grand Prix was appalling, yet Hunt knew he needed the race to go ahead for him to outscore Lauda to take the title. Lauda, still suffering from the pain and discomfort of his open wounds, with his bandages sticking to his face inside his crash helmet, retired from the race after two laps due to the conditions, saying his 'life was worth more than the title'.

But Hunt was far from assured of victory, knowing that he needed at least fourth place to win the crown. As the track began to dry, he dropped back from the lead. He was forced to pit, which took him down to fifth. But with fresh tyres he made up ground and in the final few laps overtook Alan Jones and Clay Regazzoni, and finished in third place to clinch the title. Incredibly, he'd done it. Hunt was the world champion, while McLaren was second in the constructors' championship, behind Ferrari.

• • •

With Hunt's success, McLaren reached what was to be their 1970s peak, before going into a steady decline for the rest of the decade. In 1977, the team replaced the M23 car with the newly updated version, the M26, as Hunt and German driver Jochen Mass drove for the team. Giles Villeneuve, the highly rated Canadian driver whose racing career would end in tragedy in 1982 following a crash with Mass, would also make his F1 debut driving for McLaren in a one-off appearance at the British Grand Prix. Hunt won on three occasions but Lauda and Ferrari proved too strong, and Hunt and McLaren were eventually placed in fifth and third in the respective championships.

In 1978, Lotus and Mario Andretti took the titles. They had benefitted from their revolutionary car, which was designed by a number of talented designers, including Colin Chapman, who was the founder of Lotus Cars; it was the first ground-effect car in Formula One. In a design departure from aerodynamics, ground effect used the underside of the car to create suction, pull it closer to the floor and improve grip around the corners. The basic principle was to reverse the lift created by an aeroplane wing.

McLaren could not compete and, by the end of 1978, they had also decided to drop Hunt in favour of Lotus's number-two driver Ronnie Peterson. However, tragedy struck in the 1978 Italian Grand Prix at Monza, before Peterson had even competed in his first race for McLaren. The Swedish driver had a shunt in practice and bruised his legs, damaging his Lotus 79 race car. He was therefore required to take the spare car for the race, which had been set up for his smaller team-mate, Mario Andretti.

In the race, Peterson was caught in a bunched pack of cars that had been caused by a bungled start. The race had been given the green flag too early by a starter in haste, as the cars arriving at the back of the grid had not yet come to a complete stop. That meant the cars at the back benefitted from a rolling start and were quickly able to catch those in the midfield. Peterson, who had also made a slow start himself driving in the spare car, was caught up in the melee and sent crashing into the barriers.

Peterson's Lotus caught fire and rebounded back onto the track from the barriers. He was trapped. A number of drivers, including Hunt, tried to help and they managed to pull him clear of the wreckage and lay him on the track. He was alive, but in considerable pain. Once he was at the hospital, they discovered the full extent of his injuries. Burns aside, he had suffered close to 30 fractures in his legs and feet. He underwent surgery to realign the bones but overnight his condition deteriorated rapidly. He suffered a kidney failure and died at 9.55am on 11 September 1978.

McLaren turned to John Watson, the British driver who had raced for a number of the back-markers with limited success. He was partnered with Frenchman Patrick Tambay, who had driven as Hunt's team-mate the previous season. The 1979 campaign saw Watson score one podium finish in the season opener in Argentina, on McLaren's way to a lowly seventh place in the championship. From the highs of Hunt's title win in 1976, the team was now again at a low ebb as it headed into the 1980s.

McLaren reshuffled its driver line-up for 1980, replacing Tambay with fellow-countryman Alain Prost, who drove alongside Watson. Prost had previously won both the French and European F3 championships and had been courted by a number of F1 teams, but opted for McLaren. He finished in the points four times, but his debut season was also full of technical failures and mistakes. He broke his wrist and suffered concussion in separate accidents. In the other car, Watson finished the season five places better off in 11th place.

McLaren's failure to challenge for a title was now of grave concern for their sponsors, tobacco firm Philip Morris, who owned the Marlboro brand, and their executive John Hogan. They started putting pressure on Mayer to merge McLaren with Ron Dennis's Project Four Formula Two team, which was also sponsored by Philip Morris, and showing signs of progress. It would prove to be the most important partnership in the team's history, as Dennis would go on to develop the DNA first laid down by Bruce McLaren, and also impart his own stamp on the culture of McLaren Racing, a legacy which endures to this day.

Ron Dennis was born in Woking, England, and studied motor vehicle engineering at Guildford Technical College, before getting a job with the Cooper Formula One team in 1966 as a mechanic. Dennis was 18 and struck up a working relationship with German racer Jochen Rindt. He followed Rindt to Brabham before forming his own racing team, Rondel Racing, in 1971 with Brabham's Neil Trundle. They achieved some success competing in Formula 2.

Meanwhile, Dennis harboured aspirations to take a team into F1, but lacked the funding. His prospects began to change in 1976 when he secured sponsorship from Philip Morris, who used his newly formed team Project Four Racing to promote their Marlboro brand, initially in Formula Two and Three. The investment from Philip Morris allowed Dennis to be competitive with drivers' salaries and equipment. His reputation had been growing and now he had the resources behind him, he was able to show what he could do as a team owner. Project Four won the F2 and F3 championships in 1979 and 1980.

Dennis was an obvious fit for McLaren. He was talented, hungry and ambitious with a clear work ethic. In many ways, he was similar to the team's founder, Bruce McLaren. Dennis's Project Four team was assimilated into McLaren in 1980 where he quickly hired the English designer John Barnard, who had worked at McLaren in the early 1970s and gone on to establish a strong reputation in the United States, where he had been designing Indy cars. Barnard returned to England to start work on McLaren's revolutionary new F1 car, the MP4/1.

The design name originally stood for Marlboro Project Four, and subsequently all McLaren's F1 cars from 1981 until Dennis left the team in 2017 ran the 'MP4' prefix. Featuring a new carbon-fibre composite chassis, the MP4/1 was incredibly strong but lighter than the team's rivals.

While Dennis was unable to stop Alain Prost from leaving McLaren and joining Renault, as the Frenchman had been frustrated by the McLaren's reliability in the 1980 season, he was otherwise building the team and recruiting staff, one of whom was mechanic Indy Lall, who still works with McLaren today as one of the longest-serving members of staff. As we chat in the MTC midway through the 2024 season, we discuss Dennis's management style.

'I started with Ron at Project Four,' he says, 'and then I moved on with him. I was there at the start of the amalgamation between McLaren and Project Four. Ron's vision, right from then onwards, was we could be better than anyone, by applying a little bit of thought to how we make and do things.

'He'd make us tidy up because, as he said, there's nothing great about finishing work going home smelling of grease and oil. This is absolutely true. The muckier you are doesn't mean the harder you're working. So from the offset, it was very much a case of everything needs to have a place. Not necessarily minimalistic, but if it can be, then it looks better to an outsider looking in.'

Dennis's way was at odds with many of the mechanics and engineers of the day. His stipulation that all things must be in order initially earned him a reputation from others in the pit lane for being eccentric and a taskmaster, which Lall says was incorrect.

'I think lots of people got the wrong impression of Ron,' he continues, 'that he was very stark and led with a stick. Actually, he was just shy. He's a very reserved individual. When [Spanish F1 driver] Pedro de la Rosa joined us on the test team, he told me how everyone would look into the McLaren garage and think, "You lot are cold with no sense of humour," but it's just so not true. Obviously, once you are in here, and you're part of the family, it's completely different.

'It's important to have a sense of seriousness in the job. It's not just about us [mechanics and engineers], it is about the partners, sponsors and, not least of all, somebody sat in that car. It's a hell of a responsibility, so it should be taken seriously. But equally, you've got to find the humour in it as well.'

Another long-serving McLaren employee is mechanic Gary Wheeler. Rather fittingly we speak at the MTC on 15 July 2024 on what was his 40th anniversary of joining the company. He'd signed from small German F1 team ATS, which was struggling for finances, and he speaks passionately about Dennis, whom he calls 'Ronnie D', which made me chuckle.

'When I got the opportunity to join McLaren I jumped at it,' he says. 'The difference between the two teams was night and day. Ronnie D was the guy who set the standards. In the other teams you'd have to beg and borrow to get the car on the grid. But here, it seemed money was no object. That was the first thing I noticed. "Whatever you want, we'll get it," was the attitude.'

Wheeler also draws upon Dennis's penchant for attention to detail and his disdain for mess and items being out of place. 'I think a lot of people ended up working for Ron because secretly they like things done properly and correctly. They were tidy people by nature and Ron put that extra little bit of emphasis on it. When we came in, if something was on the bench, we put it away. If you were a Joe Bloggs mechanic who liked being covered in grease, then this was never going to be the team for you. He set the benchmark at McLaren when it comes to presentation, and it remains to this day. Whether the car's at the front or at the back of the grid, we are always going to look good, regardless, in everything.'

During Dennis's reign as McLaren's team principal he transformed their fortunes, installing a work ethic, foundations and approach that set the standard for others to follow. In 1982 he persuaded Niki Lauda to come out of retirement and the French Saudi Arabian-born tycoon Mansour Ojjeh to invest and become majority shareholder. By the end of 1983, he had secured the return of Alain Prost, who had finished second in that year's drivers' championship, but had grown disillusioned with Renault.

Driving Barnard's MP4/2 car, McLaren won 12 races of 16 and both drivers' and constructors' titles in 1984. Lauda took the drivers' crown by a half-point from his McLaren team-mate Prost, with both drivers scoring more than double the tally of the third-placed Elio de Angelis. It had been a staggering turnaround. In just four years since taking over, Dennis had turned McLaren into a front-running team.

In 1985, it was Prost who took his first world title with McLaren, and he repeated the achievement in 1986. McLaren also held off Ferrari to win the constructors' title in 1985. They were second in 1986 when Finnish driver Keke Rosberg replaced Lauda, with Rosberg ending the season in sixth place. Rosberg suffered

8 retirements in 16 races and would leave F1 at the end of the season, as McLaren's form started to drop.

A disappointing campaign in 1987 saw Dennis reach out to Japanese engine makers Honda, who had been supplying rivals Williams and Lotus, and convincing them to supply engines to McLaren instead. It proved to be one of the most potent technical relationships in F1.

The other significant change midway through 1987 was the recruitment of Ayrton Senna for the 1988 season. The highly rated Brazilian had worked closely with Honda at Lotus and he joined McLaren to partner Prost in what proved to be a fiery partnership.

Senna's spectacular achievements behind the wheel are well documented in many excellent books and documentaries detailing his life and career, so, although he was a childhood hero of mine, I'm not going to revisit those stories here. My focus is on the key moments in the team's history, which is why it is important to analyse the relationship Senna had with Prost, and how it turned into a rivalry. It's crucial to look at how McLaren handled the situation to understand how they approach racing today.

The team's objective is to obtain the maximum points available from both drivers in the team and win the constructors' championship, which is where all the prize money is. Team orders within F1, however, have always been a divisive subject. In some teams, the structure is clear and there is a defined number-one and number-two driver. Perhaps the best example is Michael Schumacher at Ferrari and his understudy Rubens Barrichello. The German benefitted from being the number one and having the support of the Brazilian.

But sometimes teams opt to have no differentiation between their drivers. One such team is McLaren, who have always maintained they have two number ones. The philosophy should be applauded but it also means that it is difficult to manage, especially when you create a competitive car for them both to race, for you can only have one winner.

That is what proved to be the case at McLaren during the explosive, combustible and, on paper at least, dream pairing of Senna and Prost. With Prost's support, Dennis signed Senna for the 1988 season, maybe expecting the Frenchman to power the McLaren Honda to glory and eclipse his new team-mate.

Yet Senna won his first drivers' world title, beating Prost by three points. The two had traded wins on McLaren's way to winning 15 of the total 16 races that season, and both the drivers' and constructors' championships, the latter 134 points clear of second-placed Ferrari.

Senna, who had made a bad start to the season with a gearbox failure in his home race, recovered to win 8 races with 13 pole positions, while Prost had 7 victories with just 2 pole positions.

The statistics proved that Senna had the edge on single-lap qualifying pace. The Brazilian's dominance had led Prost to question whether he was indeed getting equal treatment from Honda, with the Japanese engine maker preferring Senna's aggressive driving style verses his own more measured approach.

At the Portuguese Grand Prix, their relationship had also been tested when the two came close to making contact in the pit straight, with Prost declaring afterwards: 'It was dangerous. If he wants the world championship that badly he can have it.'

The following season, the two fell out at the San Marino GP, when Senna broke a gentleman's agreement with Prost that the car behind would not challenge the other going into turn one. Prost had decided that he would no longer partner Senna and agreed to sign for Ferrari. Prost won the Italian GP and dropped the trophy to the Ferrari fans, the ever-devout *tifosi*, below, much to Dennis's frustration.

The final flashpoint in their turbulent relationship came at the penultimate race in Japan. Prost went into the race with a 16-point lead in the drivers' championship, ahead of the Brazilian 76 points to 60. Senna took pole position, with Prost in second. However, the Frenchman got the better start. Then, on lap 47, Senna, desperate to pass Prost, tried to overtake him at the last chicane, but the two collided. The coming together of the championship rivals remains one of the sport's most contentious moments. Senna, with the help of the marshals, was pushed back into the race.

Dramatically, he recovered to win. However, he was soon disqualified for re-entering the track illegally, with the assistance of marshals and by driving down an escape road. He was expunged from the classified results, which was enough to hand Prost the title.

Senna was furious and took his case to the Fédération Internationale de l'Automobile (the FIA, the sport's governing body), only for it to be promptly dismissed. McLaren had won the constructors' and drivers' championship titles in back-to-back years, but they had become embroiled in controversy and disharmony.

• • •

After a turbulent end to his time at McLaren, Prost left for Ferrari at the end of 1989. But that did not stop his rivalry with Senna.

Despite now being in different teams, the 1990 season once again came to a head at the Japanese Grand Prix. Senna, still driving for McLaren, headed into the penultimate race of the season at Suzuka, knowing that he needed to finish ahead of Prost. Or, if the pair were both to crash and not finish the race, then there would not be enough points left for Prost to catch him. He would be crowned world champion.

Senna had taken pole but was left frustrated by being placed on the dirty side of the grid, meaning that Prost, starting in second place and on the clean side, got the better grip at the start. The two inevitably made contact, sending both out of the race. The controversial moment split F1, with many believing the manoeuvre was predetermined by the Brazilian, taking revenge on his former team-mate. Senna and McLaren were both crowned world champions. Prost was left seething and contemplated retirement from the sport.

Senna and his new team-mate Gerhard Berger would help McLaren retain the constructors' title in 1991, while Senna added his third and final world title. But, as we are seeing, the McLaren story is not without pitfalls after notable success.

In what was to prove to be an extremely costly departure for McLaren on many levels, Honda decided to cease their F1 engine supply. The Japanese company had worked closely with Senna and responded positively to the Brazilian's demands for improved reliability and performance. However, in a knee-jerk response to the economic situation in Japan where the 'bubble economy', which had greatly inflated stock market prices, burst in 1992, sending prices crashing, Honda decided to withdraw from the expensive F1 programme. That left McLaren with no option but to search for a new engine partner, a move that also unsettled Senna, who had seen Williams's rapid rise and the progress they had made with their Renault engine partner. A deal for McLaren to secure Renault engines fell through and they again turned to Ford.

The move had not impressed Senna, and he agreed to compete on a race-by-race contract for the 1993 season, as he felt McLaren could no longer be competitive without the Honda engine. Nonetheless, he won five races, including a record-breaking sixth victory at Monaco, while at the European Grand Prix he went from fifth to first on the opening lap. His team-mate Michael Andretti was not so successful and he was replaced by test driver Mika Häkkinen for the final three races of the season. The constructors' championship was won by Williams with Prost taking the drivers' title. Senna's mind was made up: he had lost faith in McLaren and would join Williams for the 1994 season.

'It was a low point for everyone in the team,' Wheeler recalls when we discuss Senna's departure and the impact it had on the team. 'Our main focus was getting a decent engine,' he says. 'That MP4/8 [chassis for 1993] should have had a Honda engine in it. It was designed to have a Honda V10 engine in it. And then, in typical Honda fashion, they said, "That's it!" So we had to go back to having a customer Ford engine. The car was amazing, but it just lacked a bit of grunt, compared to the Williams Renault. Ayrton, although he did not win the championship that year, was driving his absolute best. And in his last ever race for us at the Australian GP in Adelaide, he went out and won it. You can't top that. He was wringing the next level [of performance] out of that car. He left because we didn't have a good engine any more and F1 drivers all want to be in the fastest car with the best engineer, the best crew, the best of everything.'

Senna's decision to leave McLaren was a bitter blow for Dennis, both personally and professionally, but he did not have time to wallow in his losses as he searched desperately for a competitive engine partner. The team tested a Lamborghini V12 engine ahead of the 1994 season before eventually deciding to use Peugeot engines. However, poor reliability meant Häkkinen and Martin Brundle, who was at the tail end of his F1 career and had been chosen by McLaren at the 11th hour after they had failed to tempt Prost out of retirement, finished the season without a single win.

McLaren's form tumbled and they finished the season with a staggering 17 retirements across both cars during the campaign. Eight podium finishes spared some blushes and the team finished fourth in the championship, but the reality was they were no longer championship contenders. The decline from the top of the podium had stung Dennis, but he was resolutely focused on the rebuilding process and managed to secure two vital signings. Firstly, engine manufacturers Mercedes were brought in as a supplier, and secondly, Dennis had persuaded designer Adrian Newey to join from Williams. The arrival of the two lifted team morale and set them up to get back to where they belonged.

Newey became a technical director at McLaren in 1997. For Wheeler, Newey's design approach, accompanied with Mercedes's reliability and power, was an obvious, potent mix. 'You could see how good he was, even with the Leyton House cars [Newey's first F1 team], how neat and efficient they were, aerodynamic-wise. But you didn't realise just how good this guy was until you start building the car he's pencilled out on paper. There was a reason behind everything he did. If you use a thin washer instead of a thick washer, it would save weight. If you do little bits like that all over the car, you end up saving quite a margin.'

Indeed, under Newey's pen, McLaren produced the Mercedes-powered MP4/13 that would win the constructors' championship in 1998 while, behind the wheel, Mika Häkkinen was victorious in the drivers' championship. Back from the brink, McLaren had done it again. Having been faced with the departure of Senna and his subsequent tragic death, plus losing a major technical partner in Honda, under Dennis's stewardship, they had returned to the top step of the podium.

• • •

Dennis, who owned 25 per cent of McLaren at the time, stepped down as CEO of McLaren in 2009 and handed control to Martin Whitmarsh. He was to return to the position in 2014 on the mandate that he would find extra investment for the McLaren Group. However, amid deteriorating relationships with Mumtalakat Holding Company, the sovereign wealth fund of the Kingdom of Bahrain, and the other shareholders, in November 2016, he was suspended from his position as chairman. His contract with McLaren expired in January 2017 and, by the summer, it was announced that he had agreed to sell his remaining shares in both the McLaren Technology Group and McLaren Automotive.

I was not working in F1 for the majority of Dennis's time at McLaren and indeed had not got to know him well. Our first meeting was in 2012 when I visited the MTC. There was a strict dress code that indicated suits were required, and I had decided to wear one I'd had made by Brighton tailors Gresham Blake, which was purple. On seeing the colour of my suit, Dennis interrupted my introductions as the *Sun*'s then F1 correspondent, countering that he 'thought I was the half-time cabaret'. But his departure and the circumstances surrounding it made me feel quite sad. Dennis was not afforded the dignity he deserved and, in the same way as Bruce McLaren before him, did not receive the plaudits for what he had achieved, albeit in different circumstances. Dennis is a fundamental part of McLaren's DNA, extending beyond the team's drivers. He installed a work ethic and a best practice and encouraged the team to become a better version of itself. For those who worked with him, he left a lasting impression.

'When it was all done and dusted and the championships were in the bag,' says Wheeler, 'it was party time. And he did the best parties. Really awesome. He would fly us and our wives and other halves and girlfriends, take us to Paris for the weekend and back. When it was time to work, we worked, and then it was time to play. They were good times, but he set standards that are still upheld today.'

Those standards, of course, were not the only legacy Dennis had left behind. There is also the MTC.

CHAPTER 5
THE MTC

> It is a challenge to achieve perfection, but that does not mean we should not try … I have gained notoriety for my attention to detail and urge to identify and correct imperfections wherever I see them. I mention this because there are moments when I look around and think, 'This is a fantastic place to work. It is a privilege to be here.' It is times like these I recognise what an achievement the McLaren Technology Centre truly is.

I can hear Ron Dennis's voice in my head as I read these words at the start of a McLaren-produced book to celebrate the opening of the MTC. During my time working in F1, I had grown accustomed to what people would call 'Ronspeak', an affectionate term used to describe Dennis's verbose, frequently grandiloquent, language.

Here's another example:

> Focus is thought to be good, obsession is thought to be bad. But basically they're the same thing. And then there's ego. Ego is a core ingredient of ambition. Ambition and ego are close bed-fellows. And, like everybody I suppose, I seek happiness.

> It's an uncomplicated objective. I don't see happiness as laughing or clapping your hands. I see it as the opposite of unhappiness, the opposite of anger, of depression. If you can get into that state of mind, you're going to be far more productive.

Translate to: Dennis was only happy when the team was winning.

Neil Oatley, a race engineer who became chief designer at McLaren, is a self-confessed Bruce McLaren fan. He tells me he grew up following McLaren's racing career and, as an engineer, had great admiration for the way the New Zealander transitioned from the cockpit to the design desk. The current McLaren factory is the third one he has worked in. 'When I joined, we were in the very old factory – it was actually two factories ago,' he says. 'The design office was in the old building, and manufacturing had already moved into Woking Business Park, so there was a period of three or four months where some six or seven of us were working in one place, away from everyone else. Of course, it was before email, so you had to drive over to the other factory to discuss things and to see them for yourself, but it all worked rather well.'

Our discussions move on to working for Dennis and, as we sit together in a fittingly immaculate meeting room at the MTC, he shares a story I haven't heard before, though many similar tales do the rounds about the iconic team leader: 'Ron used to live in West Byfleet near a girls' school. The parents used to pull into the little cul-de-sac where he lived to drop the kids off. They'd scuff the kerbs with their tyres, and there are stories of him going out there with a scrubbing brush and soap, and scrubbing the black rubber off the kerb stones.'

The opening of the MTC was without doubt a revolution in F1. The space-age structure had been designed by leading architect Norman Foster and opened in 2003. It boasted the very best in everything. Dennis led the project with the same money-no-object approach that he applied to racing, and as a result nobody is certain as to the total cost, except perhaps him.

'The MTC was almost solely driven by Ron,' says Oatley. 'I think the rest of the board would have been happy with a standard industrial shack with perhaps a bling front to it. But I think Ron pushed it. It was one of the few projects the architects and builders did not make a profit on because they had to redo things all the time.'

The building is impressive. Situated in Woking on the site of an old ostrich farm, the first thing that you notice is the vast lake in front of the glass structure. The lake is not only aesthetically pleasing, but also functional. It contains over 30 million litres of water, which is pumped through heat exchangers, which in turn help to cool the building and dissipate the heat produced by the wind tunnel. When viewed from above, the lake and the MTC form a perfect circle. Inside, the supporting beams for the building's facade have been designed to look like suspension wishbones on an F1 car. The building took 2 million hours of labour to build and contains approximately 43,000 square metres of glass – all of which Dennis ensured would remain spotlessly clean.

Inside, the fastidious attention to detail is impressive. Dennis required that the dimensions of the building were adapted to ensure no tiles needed to be cut to fit, including around the heavy machining equipment. I learned on my first visit to the MTC that it was imperative that none of the old race cars on the Boulevard leaked oil, as a stained tile would necessitate the removal and replacement of all the other floor tiles. It seemed improbably extreme, but then became more believable the more I learned about Dennis and his way of operating.

Inside the MTC, the Boulevard contains a mix of old and new McLaren cars, including Bruce McLaren's Austin 7, and a somewhat morbidly fascinating Can-Am car that was the evolution of the one in which he perished. As your eye sweeps across the other racing cars, you notice the absence of tobacco sponsorship, which has been outlawed in F1 since 2006. Purists would argue the lack of the Marlboro logo on some of the otherwise familiarly liveried cars of the late 1980s detracts from their authenticity, but the cars are still special in their own right. It is a privilege to get so close to them, peer into the cockpits and marvel.

Once at the end of the Boulevard, you are struck by the vast cabinet that houses the majority, but not all, of the team's silverware won in F1 and other categories over the years. Some of the trophies are easily identifiable, such as the one for the Japanese GP, which traditionally was a bowl shape, while the Australian GP's trophy is a large silver dish inside a steering wheel. And the most intriguing is the one Daniel Ricciardo won at the Italian GP during the COVID pandemic. The blue trophy has lost some of its colour due to all the alcohol in the hand sanitiser that was widely being used at the time, so the ceramic trophy is white in parts, rather than blue.

The location of the silverware is pertinent. It is not displayed at the front of the building, as is the case with other teams. Red Bull, for instance, have a huge trophy cabinet in the main reception for all to see upon their arrival. In the MTC, however, it is strategically placed at the one-way entrance to the canteen, where the fruits of the team's success empower the staff and serve as motivation every time they walk past. There's something else about the canteen that, upon hearing, made me laugh. The atmospheric pressure in the McLaren restaurant is set slightly lower than elsewhere in order to contain the smell of food and prevent it from wafting down the Boulevard. Dennis, it seems, had thought of everything.

Dennis's attention to detail also goes below the surface, as Oatley points out. He tells me: 'If you look underneath and go two floors down from where we are sat on the first floor, the piping and cabling is exactly how you'd expect to see it on a racing car. It runs in parallel lines and when it is required to turn around a corner, it is all meticulously fitted as close to the wall as possible, so it looks neat and tidy. 'Ron was always doing a personal check on the place. I used to work on a Sunday, and sometimes he would come in during the afternoon and walk around by himself, drawing up a list of jobs to do.'

Indy Lall tells me that Dennis's approach to design also applied to his recruitment policy. He says: 'Dennis's eye for detail was immense, not just in how things looked, but also the calibre of people in the team. Ron set a benchmark for F1 in general, and for us as a team, which we enjoy even now. There aren't many businesses you can go into where you are more or less given free rein to make it the best that it can be. If it's tooling that we needed, or if we needed to manufacture something, if that's the way forward, and he agreed with it, that's what we did. His approach was, "If I haven't got the money, I'll find the money." Then when it is done you can genuinely say that it's yours, and you feel like it's yours.'

Lall, who still occasionally speaks to Dennis, continues: 'He is super proud. When he bought this site, he asked me to come and have a look. I came one Saturday morning, and there was nothing here, just an ostrich farm. There were these bloody great big diggers that had been flown in from the United States and, because the water table was so high, they needed to build this trench all the way around, fill it with slurry, then drain it and build on it. Ron was beaming with excitement. He pointed out what was going to be what.

'It was fantastic to see it evolve over five years. Nobody knows how much money it cost to build, but Ron wanted to get it right, and you cannot deny someone that.'

Queen Elizabeth II inaugurated the McLaren Technology Centre in May 2004. From conception to completion the MTC was a 10-year project, and the official opening is recalled on McLaren's website by Michael Edgecombe, acting in his role as the company's director of brand experience. 'It's not every day you meet your monarch,' he says in the reflective piece, which was published in 2022. The team's entire stable of living drivers, past and present, was involved, with Mika Häkkinen, Emerson Fittipaldi and Alain Prost joining the 2004 pairing David Coulthard and Kimi Räikkönen at the opening.

Edgecombe said: 'Everything had to be absolutely immaculate. Ron Dennis had left the building that evening, saying: "This needs to be exactly as I've left it now. It's perfect and ready for tomorrow." But on the evening prior to the event, a helicopter arrived, spraying the windows with water from the lake, and they had to be completely re-cleaned.

'The Queen and the Duke of Edinburgh, plus some 350 guests, were greeted by our three main shareholders at the time, Dennis, DaimlerChrysler chairman Jürgen Schrempp, and Mansour Ojjeh, president of TAG Group.

'The Queen was really interested in the entire business and was completely informed on us as a company and the work that we had been doing. She had a wonderful sense of humour. It was surreal – a massive day for McLaren and for Woking. Inside the hall, it was floor-to-ceiling lavender, even the tablecloths and plates were lavender. Once lunch was finished, the royal party walked back through the building and met everybody who helped put the day together – the employees had lined the VIP walkway. I was lucky enough to present the gifts. The Duke was fond of horse-drawn carriages, while The Queen rode horses herself, so we presented them with horsewhips made of carbon fibre.'

• • •

While McLaren ushered in new life in the MTC, the 2004 season would prove to be a largely fruitless one. The MP4-19 car had been designed by Adrian Newey, Paddy Lowe, Pat Fry, Mike Coughlan and Peter Prodromou – sizeable names in the world of Formula One aerodynamics. The project was headed by Oatley, who was the executive engineer. The accomplished design team had hoped to take the MP4-18, which was used in 2003, and make some necessary refinements. However, the cars were plagued by reliability problems, suffering eight retirements in the opening seven races. They then hurried through a new car, the MP4-19B, which came with an upgraded aerodynamic package and did deliver an uptick in performance. Coulthard qualified in third place for the French Grand Prix on its first outing, while Räikkönen's solitary victory of the season at the Belgian Grand Prix also came in the MP4-19B. However, ultimately, the new era of the MTC had seen the team finish fifth in the constructors' championship – McLaren's worst ranking since 1983.

Coulthard departed for Red Bull Racing at the end of the 2004 season with McLaren having opted to sign Colombian racing driver Juan Pablo Montoya in his place for 2005. It was an exciting driver line-up, pairing Montoya with Räikkönen.

The technical staff had all remained in place. They had come up with yet another new design, with the revised aerodynamics and suspension set-up that the 2005 regulations required. It proved quick, as the Mercedes engine was the most powerful on the grid. But it also proved to be somewhat unreliable and ultimately cost Räikkönen the world championship. He came second to Fernando Alonso and McLaren lost the constructors' championship to Renault, while Montoya finished fourth in the drivers' standings.

One month after the final race of the season at the Chinese Grand Prix, F1 was rocked by the news that Adrian Newey would be leaving McLaren. His future in the team had been the subject of much speculation over the previous four years. In the spring of 2001 he had signed a contract with Jaguar F1 team to work with his close friend Bobby Rahal, only for Dennis to persuade his star designer to remain with McLaren, citing that the Jaguar team itself was not on a stable footing, with Rahal's position under threat from Niki Lauda. The Austrian had co-run the Jaguar F1 team with Rahal in a confusing managerial set-up, but the two had many disagreements, the most notable when Rahal tried to sell Eddie Irvine's contract to the Jordan team – a move that Lauda vetoed in order to keep the driver. The tension between the two resulted in parent company Ford intervening and they sided with Lauda, which ultimately saw Rahal sacked.

Newey agreed to stay but the rumours would not go away and he was also linked to a return to his former team, Williams. But Dennis continued to deny Newey was departing and it was largely expected that he would see out the 2006 campaign with McLaren.

However, on 8 November 2005, Red Bull Racing confirmed that he was in fact joining them for 2006. The wording within McLaren's press release was pointed:

> The pressures of working for a front-running Formula One team are intense and we have been aware for quite some time that Adrian was looking for a new challenge with a smaller team. The decision to leave McLaren was both amicable and mutual and we wish him all the best in the future.

Evidently, his defection had not gone down too well at McLaren and was a setback for the team.

The story was resurrected when, in September 2024, Newey announced he was leaving Red Bull for Aston Martin, saying one of the deciding factors had been the new facility Aston Martin had built – a lavish new factory at Silverstone of which he had been given a private tour before agreeing to join. At his press conference to confirm his arrival at the team, Newey referenced the new campus, saying it made for a 'positive environment' before adding:

'I have seen some new buildings that have not fulfilled that.' He stopped short of mentioning McLaren's name, but it was obvious this was a barbed reference to the MTC, which he once called a 'heavily oppressive grey building'. For Newey, spending time at the MTC was simply not conducive to his best working practices.

By way of a parting gift, he left the MP4-21, which he had designed before joining Red Bull. Around 90 per cent of the 11,500 components had been changed from the previous year's car, while there was a new Mercedes-Benz V8 engine. It was covered in a striking chrome livery and made a solid start to the 2006 campaign with Räikkönen taking a podium in Bahrain.

However, there were five retirements in the first seven races for the MP4-21, as McLaren lacked the grunt to compete with Ferrari and Renault. But the ongoing absence of competitiveness would not be a deterrent for Fernando Alonso, who would go on to win his second successive title for Renault at the end of the 2006 season: he had already decided to switch to McLaren for 2007.

Responding to the news of the imminent arrival of the world champion, Montoya quit McLaren mid-season to join the Chip Ganassi Racing NASCAR team, following a substantial compensation payment in McLaren's direction.

Despite a number of podiums for Räikkönen, Montoya, plus his replacement Pedro de la Rosa, McLaren finished the season without a victory – the first time since 1996 the team failed to win a race. Räikkönen finished in fifth place in the drivers' championship while McLaren finished third in the constructors' championship.

The debrief had begun, and it was easy to point to Newey and Montoya's departures as contributing factors in the team's winless campaign, with the lack of stability leading to underwhelming results. Other elements, too, were blamed, including the team's move to the MTC and the logistical challenges that posed. Dennis had brought his dream design to life, building the most technologically advanced factory in F1. In the meantime, though, that would not necessarily equal success. The site of the grand MTC had also served to put some noses out of joint in the F1 paddock. The MTC was a vision for Dennis, a statement of intent from the McLaren Group, but it had also made them a target.

CHAPTER 6

THE RISE OF HAMILTON AND SPYGATE

No F1 season has ever been like the one experienced by McLaren in 2007.

What had promised to be one of the most exciting in the team's history turned into a devastating mess that left the team teetering on the brink of its existence. This was the season where Fernando Alonso had joined McLaren from Renault as the two-time and defending world champion. He was partnered by Lewis Hamilton, the most exciting rookie to reach F1 in years. But the year would culminate in a $100 million fine from the FIA, after one of F1's biggest scandals shrouded McLaren in controversy.

Alonso's signing had been confirmed in December 2005, twelve months before his arrival and before he had won his second title with Renault in 2006. The news that the Spanish driver was joining the team came just days after Vodafone was announced as the team's new title partner. These were two significant moments for McLaren. Alonso was a fantastic talent and a blockbuster signing who had been expected to remain as part of Renault, for there was no need for him to change teams while he was winning races and titles. And the lucrative title sponsorship from Vodafone, one of the biggest telephone network suppliers in the world, was a sign that the team had to be in good health, on and off the track, to be attracting such a brand. Dennis gushed at the time: 'It's great that our strong belief in the strength and competitiveness of the Vodafone McLaren Mercedes package has been further endorsed by the world champion. We always make it clear that we want to be the best and the only way of achieving this objective is by attracting the best people, the best drivers and the best sponsors.'

At the time of Alonso's signature, McLaren had not yet made a decision on who to partner him with. But all that changed during the 2006 GP2 season, now known as Formula Two and, as effectively the undercard to F1, the route through which the majority of those on the grid progress. During the 2006 season, McLaren lost both of their drivers as Juan Pablo Montoya switched codes halfway through the year to race in NASCAR, while midway through the 2006 season McLaren announced at the Italian GP that Kimi Räikkönen had opted to join Ferrari at the end of the season. It meant that for the following year, Alonso was taking one seat – having agreed it in December 2005 – but the other position was up for grabs. There were three likely contenders to take the vacant seat in the garage opposite Alonso. Former F1 driver Pedro de la Rosa and the team's test driver Gary Paffett were the obvious candidates, while Hamilton was an outsider for the seat.

Sir Lewis Carl Davidson Hamilton was born on 7 January 1985 in Stevenage, Hertfordshire, to parents Anthony Hamilton and Carmen Larbalestier. His parents separated when he was two, after which he lived with his mother and older half-sisters, Samantha and Nicola, until he was twelve. He then moved in with his father, stepmother Linda and his half-brother Nicolas.

Hamilton's early racing career started by virtue of racing radio-controlled (RC) cars, when his father purchased one when he was just five. The following year, he finished second in the national BRCA championship, competing against adults. That Christmas, his dad bought him a go-kart. Hamilton, still only six, turning seven in January, brokered a deal with his dad, who agreed that in return for his son focusing at school, he would support his fledgling career.

I have been fortunate enough to get to know Hamilton relatively well over his career, and whenever he speaks about his early karting days, his eyes light up with the memories. He recalls how his stepmum would be cooking in the back of a cramped van to cater for the family at the race track and looking after his younger brother, while his father engineered his kart. Anthony Hamilton took multiple jobs to pay for the kart's tyres, engines, fuel and entrance fee to each competition.

Meanwhile at school, Hamilton's education was marred by bullying. In a social media post on 17 June 2020, he posted a photo of himself as a boy, wearing a karate outfit and the words: 'This was me learning to defend myself. As a kid, I wanted to be able to stay safe but also be able to defend those who didn't feel they could fight for themselves. Helping out a kid from being bullied was probably the only highlight of my school life, but one I'm grateful for.'

Hamilton's struggles against racism from an early age came to light later in his career, when he revealed the shocking abuse he had suffered. In an interview with the Press Association published in January 2023, he said: 'School was the most traumatising and most difficult part of my life. I was already being bullied at the age of six. At that particular school, I was one of three kids of colour and bigger, stronger, bullying kids were throwing me around a lot of the time. And the constant jabs, the things that are either thrown at you, like bananas, or people that would use the N-word. People calling you half-caste and not knowing where you fit in. That was difficult.

'In my [secondary] school there were six or seven black kids out of 1,200 kids and three of us were put outside the headmasters' office all the time. The headmaster just had it in for us – and particularly me. I felt the system was up against me and I was swimming against the tide. There were a lot of things I suppressed. I didn't feel I could go home and tell my parents that these kids kept calling me the N-word or I got bullied or beaten up at school today, I didn't want my dad to think I was not strong.'

Incredibly, Hamilton's turmoil at school did not impact his performances at the karting track and he rattled through the categories. He started racing in 1993 at Rye House kart track in Hertfordshire, in a second-hand kart. His dad's decision to take multiple jobs to cover the costs paid off, for within two years, at the age of ten, Lewis became the youngest driver to win the British cadet karting championship. That was the year, 1995, he famously met Ron Dennis at the *Autosport* Awards, asked for an autograph and said: 'Hi. I'm Lewis Hamilton. I won the British Championship and one day I want to be racing your cars.' Dennis wrote in Hamilton's autograph book: 'Phone me in nine years, we'll sort something out then.'

Amazingly, within only three years, Dennis called Hamilton after he had won his second Super One series and British championship in 1998, to offer him a place on the McLaren driver development programme. Martin Whitmarsh, who would later run the F1 team in place of Dennis, was put in charge of overseeing Hamilton's career. He told the BBC: '[Lewis] had this youthful, naive, warm personality about him. You wanted him to make it. I don't know whether I could have said back then that he was going to be a multiple world champion. You just saw that he was a really likeable kid who came from a modest background, and had a pretty pushy father.

'He wasn't arrogant or cocky. There are a few things he's done in his life where from afar you think, "Oh, God, Lewis …" but actually he's not bad. He's got a sincere humility about him. That lad came up and you thought, "There's something here. It's got to be worth a punt."'

Now supervised by Whitmarsh, Hamilton continued his progress in the Intercontinental A (1999), Formula A (2000) and Formula Super A (2001) series. This resulted in him stepping up to the full Formula Renault UK season in 2002, driving for Manor Motorsport, in which he finished third overall. He stayed with Manor to compete in the same series the following year, winning the title with two races to spare. Instead of competing in those dead-rubber events, Hamilton skipped them to compete in the British Formula Three Championship, making his debut in the final race of the campaign.

Hamilton continued to race with Manor in the 2004 Formula Three Euro Series, a step up from British F3, finishing the year in fifth place in the championship, while also winning the Bahrain F3 Superprix. Hamilton and his father then expressed their intention to move straight into GP2 and bypass the F3 2005 championship. However, Whitmarsh disagreed and felt his racing career would be better suited to staying in F3 and dominating the season. The McLaren man's decision angered the Hamiltons, who felt Whitmarsh was holding back the racing driver's career.

Tempers were raised, and Whitmarsh ripped up Hamilton's contract. In what could have been a defining moment in his career, it looked like Hamilton's F1 prospects had vanished when Whitmarsh refused to play ball. Around six weeks later, Hamilton called Whitmarsh back to agree to his plan and the two parties signed a new contract. It had been a bold play by Whitmarsh and could so easily have backfired.

Hamilton dominated the Formula Three season in 2005 and Whitmarsh's plan was ultimately seen as the best decision for the driver's career. He won 15 of the 20 rounds driving for ASM, which would later become known as ART Grand Prix and was run by Frenchman Fred Vasseur, who would go on to become Ferrari team principal and welcome Lewis to the Italian F1 team in 2025.

Hamilton progressed to Formula Two in 2006, driving for ART Grand Prix, where he won 5 times in 21 races on his way to the title. Two of those victories came on the Silverstone Grand Prix weekend, when he won both the feature race on the Saturday and the sprint on the Sunday. Hamilton's growing reputation as a star of the future had spread around the F1 paddock to such an extent that many mechanics, engineers and journalists downed tools to watch the support series in which he was competing. The

Silverstone crowd, known for their astute knowledge of motorsport, had also been keen to witness Hamilton's performance. His reputation had now spread to many within the grandstands who, rather than head for the food trucks, watched on in excitement. His races were perhaps the most intently watched in the history of the feeder series.

Hamilton's talents were too good to ignore and by now, with a seat available, Dennis started to warm to putting him in the F1 car, despite some reservations from the incoming Alonso, who felt taking a gamble on a rookie would cost the team – and in turn himself – a shot at the championship. Those at McLaren, however, were confident in Hamilton's ability.

When Hamilton was starting out, there weren't the same number of young driver development programmes that F1 teams have today. These programmes now help to identify racing drivers with potential and nurture their careers in the form of specialist coaching, simulator work and assisting with budgets, allowing them effectively to pay for a seat. Seeing that Hamilton was too good to ignore, McLaren had asked engine suppliers Mercedes, who already had a fledgling programme running – plus connections in the junior categories – for assistance. Mercedes had contributed the funding and helped Hamilton secure his place in F3, winning the series before dominating F2.

Indy Lall was one of the McLaren staff who had got to witness Hamilton's progression. He told me: 'Over a winter period, when we were testing with him, I used to speak with Ron every day. I'd tell him what had happened and what progress we'd made. Lewis was on the agenda, and I said, "You should offer him a drive, simple as that. I think he is that good." I knew that he was ready for it. Ron was obviously worried, coming up against Alonso, but I told him that, genuinely, this guy is that good that, if he doesn't get overwhelmed mentally by Alonso, then I think it'll be great.'

Gary Wheeler also recalls Hamilton's promotion to the pinnacle of motorsport, adding: 'We couldn't wait for him to get in our cars. He was absolutely dynamite.'

Hamilton wasted no time in impressing. Alonso, who arrived with back-to-back world titles having put a stop to Michael Schumacher's dominance at Ferrari, presumed that he would become McLaren's de facto number-one driver. But Hamilton had other ideas. In the opening grand prix in Australia, he passed Alonso and ran ahead of his experienced team-mate for the majority of the race, though Alonso did eventually pass him on his way to second place, behind Räikkönen, while Hamilton was third on his debut. He was second in Malaysia, Bahrain and Spain and by the end of the fourth race of the year in Barcelona was already leading the championship. It was unprecedented. The best-ever start to any rookie campaign.

The Brit's astonishing rise had rattled Alonso, who responded in true world-champion fashion by winning the Monaco Grand Prix, but not without pressure from Hamilton, who ignored team orders not to press his team-mate. It is worth noting that, at this point in F1 history, team orders were banned from interfering in the outcome of the race and McLaren's instructions to Hamilton warranted an FIA investigation after the race. F1's radio rules have a complicated past. At the time, it was forbidden for teams to radio their drivers with information relating to the performance of the car. Naturally, relaying information about a mechanical failure was permitted but the FIA wanted to rule out the notion of coaching a driver through a lap, telling them what to do at each corner. Since 2023, F1 has eased radio restrictions between drivers and the pit wall; conversations are now much freer and can take place during the formation lap, which was otherwise banned.

During the investigation, Dennis was able to argue that the race had been wrapped up and that telling a driver to slow down did not interfere with the outcome. Responding to the FIA's report, which came three days after the race once the regulators had listened to the audio exchanges between the pit wall and the drivers, Dennis said: 'The entire team was understandably disappointed that outstanding drives from both Fernando and Lewis, resulting in a great one–two victory and McLaren's 150th win, was temporarily tarnished. The efficient intervention and subsequent inquiry into the allegations has removed any doubt about the manner in which the team ran its cars during the 2007 Monaco Grand Prix. The team, Fernando and Lewis, who were leading both world championships, can now concentrate on the Canadian Grand Prix.'

Hamilton had been motivated by his desire to secure his maiden GP win, and he did not have long to wait, clinching it at the Canadian Grand Prix on 10 June 2007. The victory in Montreal was a landmark moment in Hamilton's career. The sheer fact it had come in only his sixth F1 race had taken everyone by surprise. He followed it up with a second win, taking victory in the US GP and leaving the Indianapolis Motor Speedway with a ten-point cushion over Fernando Alonso.

However, Hamilton's heroics at the US GP – and his deteriorating relationship with Alonso – would take a backseat to one of the biggest scandals to rock F1.

Spygate, as it became known, gripped the sport as it plunged McLaren into uncertainty and embroiled the team in accusations of espionage.

It had started when Ferrari filed a formal complaint against one of its most senior members of staff, Nigel Stepney. The British mechanic was part of the Ferrari team during its peak with driver Michael Schumacher, team principal Jean Todt and technical director Ross Brawn.

Early in 2007, Stepney, who was a chief mechanic, had voiced his concerns about Ferrari's restructuring and had publicly stated he was seeking other opportunities but, during the weekend of the 2007 United States Grand Prix, which fell in mid-June, the team launched an investigation. On 3 July, Italian newspaper *Gazzetta dello Sport* revealed that Stepney had been sacked by Ferrari. The team also announced they had taken legal action against an engineer at McLaren – later identified to be British engineer Mike Coughlan, who had previously worked for Lotus – with a search conducted at his home.

Coughlan was caught with 780 pages of confidential Ferrari information that basically pertained to the designs of the 2007 Ferrari F1 car, which had been passed to him by Stepney. This was damning evidence. Formula One teams are notoriously secretive about their intellectual property and protect it at all costs. It is why gardening leave is such a huge factor in departures from teams. Wanting his own copy of the near 800 pages of highly sensitive, top-secret information from Stepney, Coughlan, McLaren's chief designer, asked his wife Trudy to get them copied at a photocopy shop in Woking. As luck would have it, the staff member at the photocopying shop was a Ferrari fan and, sensing something was not right about the documents he was being asked to copy, emailed Ferrari out of curiosity. That email triggered a chain of events, with the Italian team already suspicious of Stepney's unhappiness with the team.

Coughlan attended a High Court hearing on 10 July 2007. He did not submit an affidavit but instead both he and his wife agreed a contra deal with Ferrari who, in exchange for dropping the case against them, would receive full cooperation into how the documents came to be in his possession.

A few days later, on 16 July, McLaren revealed the conclusion from its internal investigation that neither the factory nor any employee from the wider team (other than Coughlan) was in possession of any Ferrari material. This initial explanation pacified Formula One's governing body, the FIA, who had been invited to inspect the McLaren team's cars to prove they were not using any of Ferrari's designs.

At the extraordinary meeting of the FIA World Motor Sport Council on 26 July the FIA found McLaren to be in breach of the International Sporting Code – effectively the F1 rulebook – in light of Coughlan being in possession of the documents but found no evidence that they had used the information, so no punishment was issued. The decision had left Ferrari angry, with Dennis also furious with how the incident had been instigated and handled by the Italian team.

With turbulence off track, things were poised to take a turn for the worse on it as Hamilton and Alonso's simmering relationship was about to boil over. The two drivers had been at odds since Hamilton defied team orders not to push Alonso so hard during the Monaco Grand Prix. And at the Hungarian GP, it was the Brit who again initiated the disharmony.

Alonso was due to take to the track first during qualifying. In this era of confusing F1 rules relating to fuel loads and when teams could and could not replenish the tanks, McLaren had opted to alternate which driver went out first during the season in a balanced and fair approach. However, Hamilton defied team orders and went out first, then refused to allow Alonso through on his flying laps, meaning the world champion would struggle for pole.

Alonso pitted for new tyres before Hamilton, and in order to pay back the Brit's insubordination, he sat in his pit box, taking longer than required, serving to block Hamilton from entering the pits. Alonso calculated just how much time he needed to get from his pit box to cross the line and start his qualifying lap, and waited just long enough so that Hamilton didn't have enough time to do the same. Hamilton was left seething, knowing that his team-mate had prevented him from setting a flying lap on fresh tyres, as the session was over before he could change tyres and get back on track.

Dennis was furious that Alonso had deliberately blocked his team-mate and Alonso was later issued with a five-place grid penalty for his action. The following day, Dennis remonstrated with him and, in an act of defiance, Alonso threatened to go to the FIA with emails from an exchange he'd had with McLaren's test driver Pedro de la Rosa. He claimed these contained sensitive and damning information pertaining to the Spygate case and he'd share them unless the team favoured his race strategy over Hamilton's, meaning he would be given the best chance of victory. Alonso's bombshell, given Dennis had explicitly trusted that his driver was in no way implicated in Spygate, had knocked him for six. It's been said he wanted to sack him on the spot. Instead, he was retained for the rest of the season, but the relationship between Alonso, McLaren and Dennis had become untenable, and the driver's three-year contract with the team was cancelled after only one season.

While Alonso did withdraw his threat, it was too late. Unbeknown to Dennis at the time, FIA president Max Mosley – who had a long-running fractious relationship with the McLaren boss – had his suspicions, despite having initially cleared the team in the hearing at the World Motor Sport Council on 26 July. On 5 September 2007, the FIA announced that it would reopen the case based on new evidence. Incredibly, that new evidence was indeed an email exchange between Alonso and Pedro de la Rosa.

Writing in the *Guardian*, F1 correspondent Alan Henry reported:

> The FIA president, Max Mosley, has confirmed that Bernie Ecclestone, the Formula One commercial rights holder, originally alerted him to the significance of the email exchange between the McLaren drivers Fernando Alonso and Pedro de la Rosa, 'Yes, he spoke to me about them and told me they were compromising,' Mosley was quoted in *La Gazzetta dello Sport*. 'I don't know who gave them to him, but I have a suspicion.'

Writing on the BBC website, Andrew Benson said: '[Mosley] already knew about the emails. [Flavio] Briatore, Alonso's manager, had told Bernie Ecclestone, who had told Mosley – and the hearing was already inevitable, even if Dennis did not know it.'

At the second hearing, Alonso, de la Rosa and Hamilton, who was summoned as part of the process despite appearing to have no direct involvement in the case, were asked to provide evidence and, in return, the FIA offered assurance that any information made available would not result in any proceeding against the drivers personally, under the International Sporting Code or the Formula One Regulations. On 13 September, the FIA hearing issued McLaren with a whopping $100 million fine and expunged the team from the 2007 constructors' championship on the charge of possessing information on Ferrari. No information about the contents of the emails was ever made public.

Dennis was furious and argued that the punishment exceeded the crime. The rumour in F1 is that Mosley once leaned across to Dennis and said $5 million of the fine was for the crime and the other $95 million was 'for being a c***'.

The chaos created by Spygate had no doubt impacted the two drivers. Hamilton had come agonisingly close to the championship in his debut season. At the Chinese GP, he had led from pole on a drying track but he was left out too long and, on his worn tyres, he slid off in the pit lane and ended up beached in a gravel trap, allowing Räikkönen to win the race from Alonso. Hamilton headed into the final race of the season in Brazil with a four-point lead, but the Brit qualified second behind Massa, suffered a poor first lap and then went off track trying to pass Alonso. To add to his misery, he suffered a hydraulic problem and finished seventh. Räikkönen took the victory, which meant he won the world title by one point from Hamilton and Alonso, who were tied on 109 points.

The Spygate saga had left a devastating impact on McLaren and those involved. Stepney was found guilty by an Italian court of 'sabotage, industrial espionage, sporting fraud and attempted serious injury'. Despite being handed a prison sentence, he did not serve time. He was dismissed by the F1 fraternity but continued to work within motorsport.

Tragically, in May 2014, Stepney was killed in a road-traffic accident on the M20 motorway in Kent in mysterious circumstances. Reporting on the KentOnline website on 10 October 2014, Suz Elvey wrote:

> An ex-Formula 1 engineer dived in front of a lorry on the M20 days after changing his life insurance policies, an inquest heard. But despite chilling evidence from the lorry driver and police that suggested former Ferrari chief mechanic Nigel Stepney committed suicide, a coroner said she could not be certain he had intended to take his own life. Dutch lorry driver Jan Byl was travelling along the same stretch of motorway at about 1.30am, en route to Detling Aerodrome Estate near Maidstone, when he saw Mr Stepney's van on the hard shoulder. In a statement Mr Byl, who had been driving HGVs for 30 years, described how he started to move into the next lane to 'give the van some room' and suddenly spotted Mr Stepney. He said: 'All of a sudden I saw the figure of a person dive out from the left. His arm was stretched out above his head. It was

> almost as if he'd been crouching down in front of the van and thrown himself into the path of my vehicle.'

The punishment from the FIA left McLaren's staff broken. Unsure if the team would ever be able to recover financially, having spent millions on the recently opened MTC, they were left fearing the worst.

The fine had left McLaren on the brink and opened inevitable questions as to who was at fault: the disgruntled Stepney and Coughlan, undoubtedly, but had Dennis been overly naive? Would the incident have passed had it not been for Alonso's involvement? Whatever would happen next?

CHAPTER 7

THE RENAISSANCE

With Dennis left reeling and McLaren on the brink of extinction following the substantial fine dished out by the FIA, going into the 2008 season would prove to be an uncertain time for the team's workforce. Alonso had departed amid all the turmoil, going back to Renault, and Hamilton would be partnered by Heikki Kovalainen, who was coming from Renault. The Finn had previously served as their test driver before completing his first full F1 season in 2007, where he finished in seventh place in the drivers' championship.

Another new arrival was Matt Bishop, who had been appointed as the team's new director of communications and was charged with leading McLaren's media output as they navigated their way back from such a devastating setback. I start with asking him about Spygate when we sit down to talk about his time at McLaren.

'Ron had first approached me about working for McLaren on the Thursday of the 2007 Turkish Grand Prix. I'd got to know him well and I had interviewed him many times in my role as *F1 Racing* editor.

'During 2007, when Spygate was happening, McLaren had some very good press officers but they were up against Richard Woods [the FIA's director of communications, who worked alongside the body's former president Max Mosley], who was a consummate spin doctor, and Luca Colajanni, who was the director of communications at Ferrari, who was also a very capable man. They used to ring me, because I was a journalist and an editor at the time, so I used to receive their spin, which I'm not knocking them for – that's the job.

'Then I'd ring McLaren and say, "This is what I'm hearing, and we're going to have to report this. What would you like to say?" And they'd say, "Oh, we're not commenting." I would explain that if McLaren's opinions were not included, it would mean the story was going to be FIA and Ferrari-centric when it appeared. That happened a few times and then Ron rang me and said, "Why is all the reporting FIA and Ferrari biased?" I said, "Because you're not engaging. You need a strategic communications director."

'That's when he rang me, when I was in Turkey for the Turkish Grand Prix. He invited me into the McLaren hospitality, called the Brand Centre, the big, curved, black, reflective glass building, and I went in there and he just offered me a job.'

Bishop creates a picture of how the landscape was forming, with the tide being turned against the Woking-based team because they had failed to respond to the agenda being set by Ferrari and the FIA. I ask him about the rebuilding process following his arrival and he continues to explain in great detail.

'When I got to McLaren and I started work, I knew all about it and everything that had happened,' he says. 'Ron was in the shit, and it hadn't been handled particularly well. I have great respect for Ron and gratitude. He had this unimpeachable integrity, which he used to talk about. He had been very trusting. He had assumed certain things were not happening, that actually were happening, like the emails between Fernando Alonso and Pedro de la Rosa.

'Max already knew there were emails. Alonso had told his manager, Flavio Briatore. Briatore, as he always did, told Bernie [Ecclestone] everything. And Bernie told Max. So Max listened patiently to Ron, saying "no, no, no", but knew it was untrue all along.

'Ron handled it wrongly. What he should have done is gone on bended knee and beg forgiveness, because Max was a sadist and if you want to sway a sadist, you have to humiliate yourself. And Ron didn't work that out. So this is probably why the penalty was such an inconceivable amount of money …

'So when I got there, McLaren was reeling from having had to pay the $100 million fine and an atmosphere of defensive pessimism hung over everything. At the same time, Mosley had taken the *News of the World* to the High Court. He had been the subject of a front-page splash which claimed he was involved in a sado-masochistic sex act with several prostitutes, incorrectly labelled as "Nazi-themed" by the newspaper. The accusation was particularly pertinent given Mosley was the son of Oswald Mosley, the leader of the British Union of Fascists in the 1930s. Max Mosley was awarded £60,000 in damages but the harm to his reputation in F1 was colossal and he developed a deep distrust of journalists. I remember the emails. "Should we invite the journalists to dinner in Bahrain?" and instead of saying yes, it was, "Will that upset Max? How many people are you going to have? And, OK, no music." It was like trying to make sure that we weren't antagonising Max, who had wanted to punish the team so badly that it would fold. No more McLaren. End of story. End of McLaren.'

Bishop continues to say, 'Max's original plan was to exclude the team and prevent it from competing at all in 2008. Now, if that had happened, that would have been the end of McLaren, because the sponsors would have gone as the team would have been in breach of their legally binding contracts. Also, all the good people would have been poached. So, there would have been nothing left, and the expensive McLaren Technology Centre would not have been able to be run. It would have been a disaster. It was actually Bernie who then said, and I don't know if he used these exact words, "OK, Max, but you've had your fun. It doesn't actually suit me or anyone that we destroy one of the most successful teams in the history of Formula One."

'My first race for McLaren was Australia 2008,' continues Bishop. 'The atmosphere of defensive pessimism pervaded and there were people in the team who thought their jobs were going to disappear. And then Lewis won the race. I don't think I've ever seen so many grown men cry at a sporting event. It was an extraordinary feeling of relief. Senior people in the team just choking, out of control. "Fuck me. We're back. We're OK. It's OK." Ferrari would win the next four races between Felipe Massa and Kimi Räikkönen. And then we went to Monaco, and we won again. Lewis was on it. He won in Monaco and we started to think, "Is it possible? Can we actually do it and win the title?"'

Hamilton won again at the British Grand Prix and the German Grand Prix, while Kovalainen won in Hungary, giving McLaren a three-race winning run. Massa won Round 12, the European GP held in Valencia in Spain, before the season was plunged into controversy at the Belgian GP at Spa.

Hamilton crossed the line in first place but was sensationally denied the win at the hands of the FIA stewards. In the second half of the race, after the second pitstops, Räikkönen was five seconds ahead of Hamilton, but the Brit was closing in on the Ferrari. It started to rain and, in his haste to pass Räikkönen at the Bus Stop chicane, he went wide and cut across the chicane to avoid a collision. In doing so, Hamilton had passed Räikkönen and was now leading the race. However, fearing a penalty, he did allow Räikkönen to re-pass him.

The two battled for the lead when a spin for Nico Rosberg forced Hamilton onto the grass, and Räikkönen then succumbed to the conditions and crashed out, allowing Hamilton to win the race ahead of Massa. He then appeared on the podium and in the post-race press conference explaining his move on Räikkönen to get ahead of the narrative, protesting his innocence in fear of a penalty. He said: '[Räikkönen] pushed me to the point where I would either have been on the kerb and crashed into him or have to go on the escape route, so I went on the escape route. I understood I had to let him past, so I did. I got in his tow and he was ducking and diving left and right and I did the same and managed to get back to the inside of him. But then he hit me at the apex of the corner but I think I was pretty much gone from there.'

But two hours after the race, the FIA released a statement saying Hamilton would be penalised for cutting the chicane and gaining an advantage, and he was consequently issued with a

25-second time penalty. As a result of this, Massa was now crowned the race winner and, once the penalty was applied to his total lap time, Hamilton dropped to third place.

McLaren were left flabbergasted, as Hamilton had given the place back to Räikkönen, and the team launched a complaint with the FIA. At the hearing, McLaren claimed they were told twice by the race director Charlie Whiting that Hamilton had given the place back to Räikkönen, yet the FIA responded by ruling that the appeal was inadmissible. The decision drew criticism from former world champion Niki Lauda, who hailed it as 'completely wrong'. My friend and former colleague, Byron Young, wrote in the *Daily Mirror* that the ruling 'mars sport and turns fans away. That ruins the efforts of even the best competitors, taints the day and leaves fans wondering what exactly they are fans of.'

The season culminated at the Brazilian Grand Prix in São Paulo. Hamilton arrived with a seven-point lead over Massa, who was in second place in the championship. It meant that Massa could still win the title if Hamilton finished in sixth place or lower – otherwise Hamilton would be crowned champion. In the constructors' championship, Ferrari had an 11-point lead over McLaren going into the race, which had a maximum of 18 available, so if McLaren's drivers were to significantly outscore those of Ferrari, it meant that both titles were on the table – astonishing given the predicament they had faced after the FIA fine.

Massa took pole position while Hamilton was on the second row having qualified in fourth place, one spot behind Massa's teammate Räikkönen, with Toyota's Jarno Trulli starting in second. In the race, Massa made a great start and stayed out in front, while

Hamilton was stuck in sixth place for the majority of the race. By lap 54, Massa had extended his lead over Alonso, who had started in sixth place, to almost 10 seconds, while Hamilton, who was in fourth, was under pressure from Sebastian Vettel, who was just 2.2 seconds behind the McLaren in his Toro Rosso. Then it started to rain and the front-running drivers stopped for intermediate tyres that were better suited to deal with wet conditions – all except Timo Glock, the German driver who climbed to fourth place as a consequence of those stopping ahead of him. Hamilton's title prospects looked to be over when he skidded off track in the wet on lap 69, allowing Vettel to pass him. Hamilton was now sixth and, if he were to finish there, would surrender the title. As the rain intensified, Massa crossed the line to win the race, sending the Ferrari garage into delirium, but their joy was short-lived.

Unbeknown to the Ferrari garage, on the final lap, Glock had begun to slow in his Toyota as he struggled for grip on the wet track. That had allowed Vettel to pass, and Hamilton, on the final lap in the final corners, was also able to pass Glock and finish in fifth place, enough to win the title by a single point.

Massa, whose dream of being F1 world champion had lasted for around 30 seconds, stood on the podium in his home race, overcome with emotion, but gave credit to Hamilton. He later said in the press conference: 'We need to congratulate Lewis because he did a great championship and he scored more points than us, so he deserves to be champion. I know how to lose and I know how to win, and as I said before it is another day of my life from which I am going to learn a lot.' It seems that the news was not as well received by Ferrari president Luca di Montezemolo. According to F1 folklore, he destroyed his TV in anger at the result, despite Ferrari having earned enough points to win the constructors' championship.

Bishop recalls those final moments in Brazil with understandable affection: 'Brazil was the most fairy-tale finish. You never would believe it, last corner of the last lap of the last race, which I can't really talk about even now without the little hairs on the back of my neck standing up, and I can't watch it without weeping, all these years later. It's one of those sporting moments, isn't it? Sport does that! You know, whether it's football or somebody needs to hit a boundary off the last ball of the last over, and they do it. The absolute euphoria.

'What a story that was. For the team that Bruce built to have gone so close to being bankrupt and ceasing to exist, to actually win the world drivers' championship – and to beat the old enemy, Ferrari …

'It wouldn't have been done without Lewis Hamilton. We would have had a good season and we might have had a few race wins, but Massa would have been the world champion.'

• • •

The following year would prove to be difficult for McLaren and Hamilton, with the Brit winning just twice, in Hungary and Singapore. The 2009 season was remembered for Jenson Button's title success while driving for Brawn. It came after Honda had decided to withdraw from F1, announcing their departure in December 2008, with immediate effect. A management buyout by team boss Ross Brawn safeguarded the team's future, with Honda committing financial support to the tune of $100 million, which had allowed Brawn GP to acquire the Honda-developed car, the equipment and staff, while also retaining Button and experienced Brazilian driver Rubens Barrichello.

Brawn knew how good the car was that Honda had developed. He had been desperate not to see the potential – plus all the jobs – go to the wall and brokered a deal to purchase the team for £1, while he also negotiated with Mercedes to supply the engines. Brawn would then sell the team to the German car manufacturer at the end of 2009. Meanwhile, the team's success on track attracted sponsorship from Virgin, and ESPN reported that in its one season in F1, the Brawn GP team made a £98.5 million profit. Website pitpass.com reported that Brawn eventually made £100 million through the sale of the team to Mercedes, with Nick Fry, his co-owner at Brawn, earning around £56 million from the sale.

Despite Button's success and the subsequent takeover by Mercedes, rumours that he would not remain with the team for 2010 refused to dissipate, and, as Bishop takes up the story, Button's future would take a turn towards McLaren, where he would form an all-British partnership alongside Hamilton in what was a marketeer's dream.

'In 2009, we had a shit car at the beginning of the year,' says Bishop, 'but then the engineers worked really hard to improve it. And then, in Hungary, Lewis famously won brilliantly, and at the end of the race, everyone from Ron Dennis down was just feeling relief and thankful that we did not have a winless season.

'I went to collect Lewis afterwards, and was walking him to the TV pen where he did his post-race interviews and I said, "Well done, mate. Fantastic." And he went, "Never mind about that. Have you done the sums? If I win every single race from now to the end of the season, can I still be champion?" Nothing to do with relief. Just sheer, naked ambition. He won only once more, in Singapore, that season.'

Button was confirmed at McLaren on Wednesday, 18 November 2009. Button, who was 29 at the time, had said that leaving Brawn had been a 'difficult decision', and despite being the world champion, acknowledged the size of the task ahead of him going up against Hamilton.

In an article on the BBC website, Button is quoted in the press release penned by Bishop, saying: 'I've followed the McLaren team ever since I was a small boy, and it feels unbelievable to finally be a part of it. When I visited the McLaren Technology Centre earlier this month, it wasn't simply the technical resources and the incredible standards of excellence that impressed me. I was equally struck by the ambition, the motivation and the winning spirit that flows through everybody there ... From a personal point of view, it's also a great pleasure to be joining a fellow British world champion. Lewis has achieved an incredible level of success in a very short period of time, and he's a wonderfully gifted driver who has earned the respect of every Formula 1 driver.'

Button was believed to be earning £6 million a year for three years, and, significantly, Martin Whitmarsh, who was running the McLaren team following Dennis's decision to step back, only to remain as chairman, alluded to the finances of the deal in a statement at the time: 'It has always been our policy to employ the two very best possible drivers. In Jenson and Lewis, we feel we not only have the fastest pairing on the 2010 grid but also the two most complete, professional and dedicated drivers in Formula One. I want to make clear that Jenson's decision to join us was in no way motivated by money. We'll be paying him no more than he could be getting elsewhere.'

Interestingly, the move was criticised by former British racing drivers Sir Jackie Stewart and John Watson, who both believed Button was making a mistake. In a separate interview on the BBC, Stewart told them: 'It's a mistake and will be like walking into the lion's den for Jenson,' while Watson added: 'It's hard to understand what it is about McLaren which Jenson Button wants to engage in.'

Button's arrival at McLaren was the first all-British F1 pairing since Graham Hill joined Jim Clark at Lotus in 1968 but, had it not been for Bishop, the move might not have happened at all.

'Jenson wasn't Whitmarsh's first choice,' says Bishop frankly. 'He wanted Kimi, but his managers wanted a lot of money for him. Then Whitmarsh was going for Nick Heidfeld.

'I actually had a big hand in this – I was friendly with Richard Goddard, Jenson's manager. I said to Richard, "Mate, why don't you come to us?" And Richard said, "Well, we might be able to stay with Merc." I said, "You're not going to. They're going to have this German dream team. They're going to have Michael Schumacher and Nico Rosberg." And he said, "But you're going for Kimi, aren't you?"

'I then said to Whitmarsh, "Why don't we go for Jenson?" And he went, "Well, no, Jenson's going to stay with the new Merc team, isn't he?" I said, "I don't think so. And I've spoken to Richard Goddard, and Jenson is quite young, and the reigning world champion."

'In the end, it was just pure luck. I was sitting waiting outside Ron's office about three days later, waiting to see Ron, and Whitmarsh walked up to Ron's PA, and he said to her, "Do you have John Byfield's phone number?" So I thought, I'm going to have to say it. And I said, "Excuse me, sorry, Martin, but why would you want John Byfield's number?" And he said, "Well, I'm surprised you're asking me that, you've already told me I should be hiring Jenson and I want to speak to his manager." I said, "Byfield hasn't been Jenson's manager for many years, but I can give you Richard Goddard's mobile number right now."

'So anyway, Whitmarsh then rang Goddard, and Goddard and Button came at about seven o'clock one Friday evening, when it was quiet, to have a look around the McLaren Technology Centre, and Jenson said, "This place is amazing. How come you don't win every race anyway?"

'We did the deal, and it was very exciting. We had this British dream team, which Vodafone were completely over the moon about. And also Santander, because they were taking over some of the UK's banks.'

Button and Hamilton kicked off their partnership in 2010, with Button winning the second race of the season in Australia and then again in China, while Hamilton won three times. Hamilton ended the season in fourth place in the drivers' championship and Button in fifth, while McLaren were second in the constructors' championship to Red Bull Racing.

In 2011, McLaren were second again behind a dominant Red Bull driven by Sebastian Vettel, while in 2012 the team were placed third in the constructors' championship, which belied the fact that the car was the most competitive on the grid. However, following retirement in the Singapore Grand Prix with a gearbox problem, having taken pole, Hamilton had made up his mind – encouraged by a conversation with Niki Lauda, who was the Mercedes F1 team chairman at the time – to join the Silver Arrows upon the conclusion of the season.

Hamilton cutting ties with McLaren was a seismic shift and one that, on paper, did not make sense. For while McLaren were capable of producing a car that was able to win races, Mercedes, which had evolved from the ashes of the Brawn team, had looked off the pace with Michael Schumacher and Nico Rosberg.

I was at the final race of 2012 in São Paulo, and I remember that when Button won the Brazilian Grand Prix, he expressed great enthusiasm for McLaren's prospects in 2013, for the car had won seven races that season – Hamilton with four wins and Button with three.

Hamilton's time alongside Button is remembered fondly by Bishop as the two drivers contested 58 races together. The statistics from their partnership are interesting, with Hamilton taking nine pole positions to Button's one, while Hamilton won ten times and Button eight. That said, Button had three more podiums than Hamilton and finished in the points in 47 races compared to Hamilton's 45. In summing up, Button had scored 672 points in total, eclipsing Hamilton's tally of 657 – not quite the 'lion's den' that Jackie Stewart had predicted. The Button/Hamilton pairing 'was a lot of fun', says Bishop. 'They were never really mates but they never really had any real friction. They were a wonderful pair, because in terms of out-and-out pace, very few people have ever been quicker than Lewis – and Jenson wasn't – but he still scored more points than him over their three years together in the team.'

Hamilton's defection to Mercedes was undoubtedly a blow to McLaren, as he had turned his back on the team that had given him his opportunity in F1. His departure was seen as a huge loss, as was the exit of technical director Paddy Lowe, who followed him to Mercedes. Lowe had been instrumental in designing the McLaren car for 2013, but was now working for their rivals, leaving McLaren hamstrung with an underperforming car they did not understand how to improve. It was a miserable, winless campaign as the team laboured to a fifth-place finish in the constructors' championships, with Button's fourth-place at the final race of the season in Brazil the highest finish. Hamilton's replacement, Mexican driver Sergio Pérez, who was signed from Sauber, also failed to deliver consistent points. Button finished the campaign in ninth in the drivers' championship and Pérez in eleventh. Meanwhile, Hamilton, who had joined a team that had been struggling for points let alone podiums, took five podiums, including a victory in Hungary, on his way to fourth place in the championship.

Halfway through the 2013 season, in May, McLaren announced that they had struck an engine deal with Honda as a supplier, which would come into effect for the 2015 season. The message from within the team was clear. It was driven by Dennis, who saw that the only way the team would be able to compete with the engine manufacturers was to have their own bespoke supplier. Dennis felt that Mercedes, who were their current supplier, would not provide equal parity when they had their own works team. McLaren were simply a Mercedes customer, and any updated components or software would be given to the works team first.

The deal came at a crucial time. The 2014 season saw McLaren struggling once more, ending the campaign again in fifth in the constructors' championship, with no wins for either Button or promoted reserve driver Kevin Magnussen, who had replaced Pérez. But now we would see the introduction of hybrid turbo engines in what was the biggest ever change in F1 technology.

The 2.4-litre V8 engines were being dumped for a complicated 1.6-litre V6 turbo-charged power unit that would be assisted by a battery technology, rather like a modern hybrid road car. The Honda announcement came when McLaren were struggling for points and they were at the end of their lucrative partnership with Vodafone. It was a rare bright spot and gave some much-needed optimism. Whitmarsh was quoted by the *Guardian* saying: 'It is a partnership synonymous with success. Together, in 1988, we created the most successful Formula One car of all time which was driven to victory 15 times out of 16 (grands prix) by Ayrton Senna and Alain Prost. For everyone who works for both companies, the weight of our past achievements lies heavily on our shoulders. But like McLaren, Honda is a company with motor racing in its blood and it's the mark of ambition we both share that we want to recreate past glories and take McLaren-Honda back to the top.'

It was optimistic, and Whitmarsh could not have been more wrong.

CHAPTER 8

THE HONDA DEMISE

Having watched McLaren struggle to finish on the podium on a regular basis since 2012, the 2015 season offered a welcome degree of optimism with the return of Honda engines. But things started going wrong almost immediately – along with one of the most bewildering appointments in F1 history.

Seeing the team struggle to such a degree prompted Dennis to come back and take charge again, at the expense of Whitmarsh, who formally parted ways with McLaren midway through 2014. Dennis's return was driven by his desire to see his team back on top and he saw having their own engine partnership, rather than being a paying customer of Mercedes, as the only viable option. Dennis also felt that in order to facilitate the return of Honda, he needed a driver line-up that would complement the technical deal. Button was an obvious choice to retain for the project, for he had experience working with the Japanese car giant and engine maker from his previous spell with BAR Honda. Button embraced the Japanese culture and had married his long-term Japanese girlfriend Jessica Michibata, although the couple separated in December 2015. The second driver, however, was a staggering choice.

Fernando Alonso, the man who had threatened Dennis with going to the FIA over the details of Spygate, ultimately leading to McLaren's record fine, was re-signed. Having left Ferrari to make way for Sebastian Vettel, Alonso's arrival at the team was confirmed on 11 December 2014, marking an astonishing, and bewildering, appointment by Dennis. While there was no question about Alonso's abilities, his arrival was greeted with mixed feelings by those working in McLaren, as Matt Bishop goes on to explain. 'I had not worked with Fernando because he left the team in 2007 and I'd not joined until 2008,' he says. 'But I had been used to hearing the old McLaren stalwarts saying over the years, "Oh, my God, he was a nightmare. You weren't in the team. You don't realise what it was really like." Personally, I don't think he was the right hire, but not because I don't have the highest respect for him, because I do. And when I did work with him for two and a half difficult years, he was perfect to work with.

'The reason he wasn't the right hire is that we had Kevin Magnussen and Button in 2014 and it was the simplest, easiest driver line-up any of us had ever had. Two nice guys who got on with each other, perfectly capable. Jenson had all the qualities of experience, while Kevin was a young gun who we thought might be shit hot. Jenson was earning about $15 million a year and Kevin was on $2 million, so that's $17 million in total.

'I remember Ron saying, "We're going to have to hire Fernando." And I said, "Look, Fernando is brilliant, but I don't see that this is the right decision now, because next year is going to be a building year." I had been to Honda in Japan with [former sporting director] Sam Michael, who obviously knew more about engineering than I did by a long chalk. He told me that if they think they are going to be ready to produce race-winning engines in 2015, they're wrong. It was going to take longer than that, and he had confided in me that he feared that it would not be until 2017, at the earliest, that Honda would be up to speed.

'While we were walking around the factory, one of the engines was being tested on the dyno [a machine that can be programmed to simulate racing stresses on the engine], there was a big boom, and a lot of embarrassed Japanese faces because the engine had blown up in front of us, when we'd flown all the way from England to Japan to see it!

'Despite what Sam had said, Ron was adamant that Honda would be brilliant. But then we spoke about Alonso and he said that McLaren were looking to pay him $40 million a year – $38 million more than the person we were going to flick to make room for him. I tried to explain that I was not denying that Fernando was a greater driver than Kevin Magnussen, but let's say he was a couple of tenths quicker on every lap. If that delta is enough to deliver the difference between third and first, then, yes, it's worth $38 million a year. But if it's enough only to make the difference between 14th and 12th, then it's not worth $38 million, it's a waste of $38 million.

'I remember Ron saying that Alonso is quicker than Räikkönen in the same Ferrari car. And I said, "Ron, have you heard what I said? I'm not denying that he's quicker than Kimi in the same car but it is a three-year deal and you are spending $120 million and we're probably not even going to have the benefit of where that extra pace is." In the end Alonso was there for four years, so $160 million was spent on Fernando Alonso, and was there even a podium? No, there wasn't.'

Alonso's return to McLaren got off to the worst possible start. At the first preseason test in Jerez in Spain, the media had assembled and we were excited to see the new cars and, in particular, the new McLaren Honda. The previous year had seen the introduction of the V6 hybrid turbo engines that had replaced the traditional V8s and there had been understandable teething problems, but while all those other engine makers were now on top of the mechanical problems, newcomer Honda's vulnerabilities were exposed. It was embarrassing to witness the repeated problems.

After the four-day test, the team tried to put a brave face on things, insisting they were not worried about the lack of pace of their new car, because the engine had not been at full power. Engineering director Matt Morris told the media: 'We are not running at maximum performance at the moment. It would be nice to be further up but we have great simulation tools. We know where we are in terms of performance.'

The reality was that over the four days, Alonso and Button had driven just 79 laps when it was common for some teams to drive over 120 laps a day. Asked how McLaren's new driver Alonso had responded to the test, Morris said: 'Fernando has been absolutely itching to get in the car for the last few months and it has been a frustrating few days for him, but he's happy. I think he's going to push us on as a team. His motivation levels when he is in the garage, in the simulator, are massively high and that knocks on to everyone else and pushes everyone else on.'

At the second test in Barcelona, things would go even worse, as Alonso suffered a mysterious accident. The second test, another four-day stint but this time at the Circuit de Barcelona-Catalunya, which was home to the Spanish Grand Prix, would normally allow teams more time to practise and refine their cars ahead of the final four-day test, also in Barcelona. As such, fewer journalists attended the event for it was often not as newsworthy as the other two tests, but we all missed out on a big story, which remains unexplained.

It happened on 22 February 2015, during the final session of the day, and Alonso was driving the McLaren MP4-30 when suddenly he veered off and crashed into a wall at Turn 3. It was an unusual place for an accident to happen and Sebastian Vettel, who was driving for Ferrari in the car behind, commented that he felt it was a strange accident, especially given the car was only travelling at around 90mph, and it appeared that Alonso had turned into the wall, with the impact on the side of the McLaren, so damage was at a minimum, not like when a car goes into a barrier nose or tail first.

Despite the relatively slow nature of the crash, medical crews were dispatched to Alonso's stricken car because he did not extract himself from the cockpit, as is the norm in this situation. What was more alarming was that it appeared that Alonso was being treated by the medics immediately at the scene, and then he was airlifted to hospital.

McLaren later issued a statement saying that the accident had been caused by unpredictable gusty winds and that Alonso was now recovering in hospital. The Spanish driver would go on to spend three nights in hospital and, as a result of the accident, was unable to compete in the season-opening Australian Grand Prix on 15 March and would – ironically – be replaced by Kevin Magnussen, who had been demoted to reserve driver. The whole incident has aroused suspicion.

After the crash, Alonso claimed that the steering had locked, and appeared to contradict the team's initial explanation of wind, saying that 'even a hurricane would not move the car at that speed'. Wild theories surfaced, including that Alonso had been electrocuted or had grown drowsy and lost consciousness due to inhaling toxic battery fumes. Others included Alonso suffering memory loss and had him waking up speaking Italian, as he believed he was still driving for Ferrari. Yet the most staggering was a report that Alonso had come round thinking he was a 13-year-old boy who was racing go-karts!

Alonso made his season debut in the second round in Malaysia. The race was dominated in the run-up by questions about his return to action, but ultimately remembered for McLaren's double retirement, with both Alonso and Button suffering engine failures during the race. Two races later, the Bahrain Grand Prix, Button did not even start – his weekend, qualifying and race ruined by a defective engine. Honda's return had been marked by poor performance, and was widely lampooned.

Dennis tried to put on a brave face, offering assurances that the mechanical struggles were temporary. Ahead of the British GP in July (by which time Alonso had only completed two out of eight races), he spoke about improvements in lap times and how McLaren were now making up ground on their opponents, while

Honda's head of F1 operations Yasuhisa Arai also declared himself happy with his company's progress. However, Éric Boullier, who was McLaren's racing director having joined from Lotus in 2014, elected to criticise the performance of the Honda engine, much to the rest of McLaren's dismay and confusion.

Bizarrely, Honda had started naming each engine that would be in either Alonso or Button's car, given them a unique avatar and identity – but that quickly stopped due to the rate of engines they went through, making it impossible to keep up.

By the Italian GP on 6 September, it was believed the Honda engine was a whopping 120bhp down on the Mercedes equivalent, which was widely considered to be the best power unit on the grid. The nature of the Monza track with its long straights means that this is a power-dependent circuit and those teams with the best engine, as in the most powerful, coupled with a low downforce set-up to reduce drag, would perform best. It was painful viewing for McLaren fans, as Alonso was classed in 18th and Button in 14th. It proved too much for Alonso, who blamed the engine, saying it was costing him three seconds of lap time compared to the Mercedes. It was damning criticism and the first real sign that cracks were again forming in his relationship with McLaren.

McLaren and Honda were soon at loggerheads. Discussions were often misunderstood between the two teams as there was a clear breakdown of communication not helped by the language barrier. Meanwhile Honda had underestimated the time and resources they had needed to commit to their F1 operation, also pointing out that McLaren's car design had compromised their engine design in that the tight aerodynamic shape that McLaren had constructed had left little or no room for engine cooling, which had resulted in poor reliability and performance. The fragile relationship was now being tested to breaking point by its frustrated drivers. At the 2015 Japanese Grand Prix, Alonso famously shouted over the team radio 'GP2 engine'. It was cryptic but a damning moment. Alonso had not only compared Honda's F1 offering to the power produced by the engine used in the racing class below, he had chosen to do so in Honda's home race at a circuit they owned – causing maximum embarrassment to Honda and their executives.

The misery continued. At the Mexican GP in November 2015, Button set a new record for grid penalties triggered automatically when a driver breaches the set allocation for changing engine parts, designed to encourage teams to be more sustainable. Button had taken so many components over the season, it was enough to warrant a 70-place penalty, so ultimately he was guaranteed to start at the back.

In the penultimate race, in Brazil, Alonso was forced out of qualifying in São Paulo with a mechanical failure and, instead of heading back to the paddock immediately, found a fold-up chair and sat with his eyes closed, facing the sun. It was high-jinks, a bit of fun, as the hashtag PlacesAlonsoWouldRatherBe trended on social media, with the image cropped into different backgrounds. The moment summed up the terrible season that Alonso, Button and McLaren had endured, and he perhaps wished he'd been elsewhere.

McLaren finished the season in ninth place in the constructors' championship – nine points behind back-markers Sauber. The MP4-30 had only scored points in 5 of its 19 races, with the best result Alonso's fifth place in Hungary – and it was his worst season since joining F1 with minnows Minardi in 2001. Arai left his role within Honda at the end of the miserable campaign.

• • •

For the 2016 season, McLaren in fairness enjoyed a stronger pre-season with improved reliability. However, a hefty crash for Alonso during the season-opening Australian Grand Prix was another setback. The high-speed accident meant he was sent to hospital, with many claiming it was a miracle that he survived. Alonso was then ruled out of the Bahrain Grand Prix as a result and he was replaced by Belgian Stoffel Vandoorne. McLaren suffered a further eight retirements that season as improvements were still urgently needed. The team finished sixth in the constructors' championship and not in position to challenge for podiums. The pressure caused irreparable cracks in the relationship with Honda and rumours started to emerge that McLaren sought an engine deal to return to Mercedes, who were also supplying Force India and Williams.

The 2016 campaign would also prove to be Button's last full season, before taking a step back from F1. In his final interview session held for the British press, Button spoke about his excitement at taking a break from racing – he had grown tired of the repeated problems. He would, however, return for one race in 2017 – the Monaco GP when Alonso competed in the Indy 500 Race, which ran on the same weekend. At the 2016 season finale, Button was given a guard of honour as he walked to the garage for what was supposed to be his final F1 race. Sadly, a suspension failure cut short his finale and he was already back in the team's hospitality before the race had even reached the halfway point. Incidentally, the drivers' championship was won by Nico Rosberg, who himself retired just a few days afterwards.

In 2017, Vandoorne was promoted to replace Button in what became another terrible season for the team. Any hopes of the McLaren/Honda partnership building on the positives in 2016 were quickly dissolved. Incredibly, McLaren (including Button in his single-race return) suffered 13 retirements and two 'did not starts' during the course of the season, finishing the campaign in second to last in the championship. It proved to be too much and on 15 September 2017, the news was confirmed that McLaren would split from Honda. The partnership that Dennis had believed was the only way to make the team F1 world champions again had ended in an embarrassing failure for both parties.

In the accompanying press release to break the news, McLaren confirmed that they would be switching to Renault engines while Honda would now move their supply to Toro Rosso, Red Bull's sister team. One of the principal factors behind McLaren's decision to dump Honda hung on whether Alonso would commit to a new contract. He was coming to the end of his initial three-year deal and McLaren wanted him to stay – only the Spaniard did not want the team to use Honda engines. It was a tough call for McLaren. Honda contributed around $100 million in terms of a free engine supply, sponsorship and paying half of the drivers' wages. But, ultimately, McLaren felt that the engines were doing more harm than good and were jeopardising the team's future to be competitive and run as a sustainable business.

McLaren Group executive chairman Shaikh Mohammed bin Essa Al Khalifa said in a statement: 'Honda is a great company which, like McLaren, is in Formula One to win. Although our partnership has not produced the desired success, that does not diminish the great history our two companies have enjoyed together, nor our continued efforts to achieve success in Formula One.

'At this point in time, it is in the best interests of both companies that we pursue our racing ambitions separately.'

The Honda failure was a blow to the staff at McLaren, especially for those who had worked with the Japanese company during the successful years between 1988 and 1992.

It was Bishop's job to steer the narrative during some difficult times and poor results. 'Putting a brave face on yet another failure was tough for McLaren, but also my colleagues working for Honda, who were feeling as though they were getting a drubbing from Alonso and Button in the media. The problem we had was making the whole marriage work,' says Bishop. 'Actually, Fernando didn't cause any problems [for McLaren], other than costing a lot of money. But it was a real pity. I remember there were people at McLaren saying get rid of Honda. Jonathan Neale [chief operating officer of the McLaren Group] was the prime mover behind getting rid of Honda. Him, Éric [Boullier] and Zak Brown, who arrived in November 2016.

'I remember saying to them in early 2017, "Look, we've had Honda for three horrible seasons but they're finally about to go and get it right. Don't get rid of them now. You could have maybe got rid of them two years ago, but don't go for a customer Renault [engine] now."

'I'm sorry to say I was right, because Honda went from Toro Rosso to Red Bull and ended up winning the world championship.

It was very difficult at McLaren in 2015, 2016 and 2017, and it was very difficult for me personally because that was a period in which I lost control of the comms narrative, because Jonathan and Éric kept saying Honda are a disaster. Zak too, when he arrived, was very negative about Honda.

'And yes, Honda weren't great, but basically the combination of senior management figures at McLaren simply weren't up to it at that point. I'm not blaming Zak because he only arrived at the very beginning of 2017, and he has gone on to lead McLaren to great success since then. But I don't think Ron had a huge amount of respect for either Jonathan or Éric. I got on well with Éric personally, but he was in a very difficult position because, although he was ostensibly the team principal, actually his boss was Jonathan. Then when Zak came in, he wanted to make changes – quite rightly because everything had been going wrong.

'It was a difficult time when he took over. It was the third year of Honda. Everybody was under stress. Éric was having a difficult time. Jonathan was having a difficult time. A lot of people lost their jobs, there was a lot of churn. And with that, the shareholders, the Bahrainis [the Bahrain Mumtalakat Holding Company] and Mansour Ojjeh said this is not good enough, we need to improve and we need to win.'

Switching to Renault in 2018 immediately brought an uptick in results. Alonso finished inside the points in the opening five races, while Vandoorne also scored well, comparatively to how the team had started the previous three seasons. However, they were still down on power compared to their rivals and now with Honda being omitted from blame, there was no hiding place –

especially for the team's management structure, which became the focus for the media. It came to a head at the French Grand Prix on 24 June 2018 and the story which is now fondly remembered as 'Freddogate'. The story was run as an exclusive in the *Daily Mail* by Jonathan McEvoy two days before the race, in which he claimed staff were being rewarded for their hard work – with miniature Freddo Cadbury chocolate bars.

McEvoy wrote that McLaren's Formula One staff were considering going on strike in response to McLaren bosses offering them 25p chocolate bars as a thank you for their hard work. The article explained there was a 'toxic' atmosphere, with the source labelling their bosses as 'clueless'. The anonymous source is quoted saying: 'We have been working all hours of the day, sweating blood, and they give us 25p Freddo bars. The management hand them to the supervisors to divide them out to employees in their team. Strictly one each.'

Boullier attempted to defend the situation, suggesting that most staff had enjoyed it as a joke, and that it was just a matter of a couple of people who were angry. On 4 July, he resigned from his post at McLaren, just days before the British GP, leaving Brown in place to reshape the team's future. Brown had worked on the periphery of the team in 2017 but was quick to address the problems under Boullier's stewardship, while Neale was now working for the wider McLaren Technology Group and not directly in F1. 'This is not the fault of the hundreds of committed and hard-working men and women at McLaren,' said Brown in a statement. 'The causes are systemic and structural, and require major change from within. With [the Boullier] announcement, we start to address those issues head on and take the first step on our road to recovery.'

He probably did not realise at the time, but he was about to start shaping a new era of McLaren that we can associate with today's team. Brown acted swiftly to make some crucial decisions, bringing in Indianapolis 500 winner Gil de Ferran as sporting director. Simon Roberts joined as chief operating officer and was charged with overseeing production, engineering and logistics. Perhaps the most crucial appointment was promoting Italian Andrea Stella to performance director, responsible for trackside operations. And in another major signing, Brown had already recruited Lando Norris into the team's young driver programme in 2017.

CHAPTER 9

ANOTHER LEASE OF LIFE

It is not normal for F1 teams to make their reserve drivers available to the media, mainly because there is often little to speak to them about. It is even rarer when the driver has not yet driven an F1 car. But in November 2017, McLaren invited the journalists working for British newspapers to come and meet 18-year-old Lando Norris at the Abu Dhabi Grand Prix. McLaren had burned through drivers who had promised to be the next best thing, be it Pérez, Magnussen or even with their current driver at the time, Vandoorne, and we were curious to see how this latest cab off the rank, so to speak, would compare.

Norris had been briefed by the McLaren communications team, with my good friend Charlotte Sefton leading the session alongside her excellent and experienced colleague Silvia Frangipane, who would later work as head of communications at Scuderia Ferrari.

Norris was nervous as he faced around eight or nine of us journalists, trying to get a line out of him, as he sat in the team's hospitality unit in the Yas Marina paddock. Quickly, comparisons were drawn between him and Hamilton, given that both had come through the McLaren junior programme. There was an awkward moment when one reporter asked if Norris has received any messages from Hamilton, now he had made it into the team. Norris was confused by the question and could not understand why Hamilton would do so given he was racing for rival team Mercedes. Still pursuing the Hamilton angle, the group asked Norris if he had a photo of the fellow Brit on his bedroom wall when he was growing up. He didn't. Instead, he had an image of Italian MotoGP legend Valentino Rossi.

The question of where he would be living while working as McLaren's reserve driver came up. The family home was in Glastonbury, Somerset, home to the famous music festival, whereas McLaren were based over 100 miles away in Woking. Norris confirmed he was leaving home and would be moving in with a driver called Sacha Fenestraz, a French–Argentine racer who was the same age. It was the first time he had lived away from his family, and as a result needed to learn how to cook and fend for himself, though he'd already established that Fenestraz would do his ironing!

And finally, we heard about his unusual Christian name and its origins. He laughed, and explained with a smile it was his mum Cisca who had the idea, and that it was definitely not based on Lando Calrissian, the character in the *Star Wars* movies, played by actor Billy Dee Williams, who was the original owner of the *Millennium Falcon* until he lost it in a bet to Han Solo. There were many memorable moments in that 20-minute interview, and it's fair to say that he had an immediate impact on us journalists.

Bruce McLaren sits on a tyre in the pit lane at the Nürburgring 1,000km race in May 1965, dressed in rudimentary safety equipment.

The McLaren Racing team makes its Formula 1 debut in Monaco, May 1966. The car was painted white with a green stripe as part of a deal with John Frankenheimer's movie, *Grand Prix*, which was filmed throughout the summer of that year.

Bruce McLaren wins the team's first grand prix in 1968, beating Mexico's Pedro Rodríguez at Spa-Francorchamps in Belgium.

The McLaren M8Bs of Bruce McLaren and Denny Hulme, who finished first and second respectively at the 1969 Can-Am race at Watkins Glen, New York. The car featured a new high rear wing and a 630bhp engine.

Hulme and Emerson Fittipaldi ahead of the 1974 season. Fittipaldi would go on to win McLaren's first F1 drivers' championship title, taking three wins over the season. Hulme came seventh in the championship, with a victory in the Argentine Grand Prix.

The Marlboro and Texaco livery on the McLaren M23 at the Anderstorp Raceway in Sweden, as Fittipaldi and Hulme wait in the pits during the 1974 Swedish GP.

Fittipaldi celebrates his second F1 world championship title on the podium after he held his nerve to finish fourth at the US Grand Prix in October 1974.

The McLaren team celebrate on the track at Watkins Glen after Fittipaldi's fourth place in the season finale clinched them their maiden world championship title.

James Hunt is watched by King Carlos of Spain as he celebrates his victory in the 1976 Spanish Grand Prix at Jarama. Ferrari would contest the legality of his McLaren; this race was the first clash between Hunt and Niki Lauda.

Hunt wins the 1976 F1 drivers' championship title in Japan after overcoming treacherous driving conditions. You can see Teddy Mayer, McLaren's team manager, holding up three fingers to signal to Hunt that he'd finished the race in third place, scoring enough points to beat Lauda.

Ron Dennis (right) was encouraged to merge his company, Project Four, with McLaren and work with Mayer to form McLaren International in 1981.

Lauda shows off three fingers after winning his third drivers' title. He is joined on the podium at the 1984 Portuguese GP by Alain Prost and Ayrton Senna, who was then racing for Toleman. Ron Dennis can be seen behind Prost, who actually won the race.

At the 1985 European GP at Brands Hatch, Prost wins the title and celebrates with Keke Rosberg, with a cigarette in his mouth, Nigel Mansell and Senna. Rosberg would join McLaren in 1986 to replace Lauda.

Senna and McLaren pose after winning both the drivers' and constructors' championships in 1988. Together, Senna and his team-mate Prost won 15 of the 16 races that season in an impressive display of dominance. McLaren team principal Ron Dennis is standing behind Senna.

Senna and Prost famously clash at the Japanese Grand Prix at Suzuka in October 1989. The fallout between the two McLaren drivers was seismic and reflected a widening rift.

Mika Häkkinen (right) stands with his technical director Adrian Newey on the pit wall during practice for the Italian GP in 1998, while Michael Schumacher is interviewed on screen. Häkkinen would go on to beat the Ferrari driver and win the drivers' championship title.

Norris was born on 13 November 1999 in Bristol to parents Adam and Cisca. He has an older brother, Oliver, who would also kart competitively between 2008 and 2014, and who now runs his own racing-simulator business. He also has two sisters. Norris's father is a wealthy businessman. An early highflier, he was made managing director of UK firm Pensions Direct at the age of 33. Now Adam Norris is the CEO of Horatio Investments and also the founder of Pure Electric Ltd, producers of electric scooters that zip through cities across the world and are frequently spotted in the F1 paddock. It is perhaps fitting that he now produces scooters, as two wheels were a childhood passion of his son's.

Norris started riding horses with his mum when he was just four, before his father bought him a quadbike. At the age of six, his father upgraded him to a motorbike, around the time the family started enjoying watching MotoGP on the TV, and Rossi became a hero to the young Norris. A year later, Norris was to get his first taste of competitive karting when he went to watch the Super One National Kart Championship, the breeding ground for British talent, including Hamilton, Button and Coulthard. After pleading with his parents, he joined the series the following year in 2008, aged just eight.

Norris made an immediate impact, taking pole position on his debut. He made his way through the karting pyramid, finishing 35th out of 41 on his debut season – incidentally he was one place above his brother. George Russell finished that season in 20th place. He placed 14th in his second season and in his third year, in 2010, he finished in 3rd place.

Norris's father was overseeing both his sons' fledgling racing careers and decided to get some extra help from Mark Berryman and Fraser Sheader.

Both former kart racers, Berryman and Sheader established ADD Management in 2010 as a partnership to nurture and develop young racing drivers, helping them progress through the lower categories with a view to reaching F1. It quickly became apparent to Berryman that it was the younger of the two sons who had the most ability and he agreed to take Lando Norris under his wing.

I got to speak to Berryman in depth about his relationship with the F1 star, for my 2023 book *Lando Norris: A Biography*. He told me how the young Norris would not initially take his advice on board, and that his father Adam would urge his son to focus, making it clear that he would not simply be purchasing the latest equipment. He instilled a work ethic in his son, mirroring the ethos shared by Berryman and Sheader. They focused on ensuring their young driver grew into a stronger, more rounded racer, and as a result more adaptable to different circuits and track conditions.

With advice particularly from Berryman, who would remain at his side up to F1, Norris rattled through the ranks. Part of Berryman's approach was to get him into different cars and races so that he would gain more experience. This was not usual practice, for some drivers only focus on the series they are competing in rather than being exposed to other classes. In 2012, Norris raced in seven different competitions, finishing second in the Super One National Championship in the Rotax Mini Max class and winning the Formula Kart Stars, also in the Mini Max class. In the same year, now old enough to compete (aged 12), he raced in the WSK

Final Cup, driving for Ricky Flynn Motorsport in the junior division. Norris flourished while racing for Ricky Flynn, who are based in Waltham Abbey in the UK, and in 2013 he won the CIK-FIA European Championship and the International Super Cup as well as the WSK Euro Series. In a busy schedule, he was also second in the WSK Super Master Series and was fourth in the flagship event, the CIK-FIA World Championship in the junior series. He won that flagship event in 2014, making history as the youngest world champion at just 14 years old.

Norris attended the fee-paying, prestigious, Millfield School near his home in Glastonbury. However, it was soon apparent that he was not keen on education and, with the school's blessing, he and his brother Oliver were granted special dispensation to skip lessons on the proviso that they both had a tutor, who would travel with them during race weekends to ensure they were on track with their studies. Only the tutoring quickly dried up, and the brothers switched to online lessons. Those too did not last long and Norris's education ceased altogether, quitting school a year before his GCSE exams, which afforded him the opportunity to race in the Ginetta Junior Championship, also in 2014. Ginetta G40s sports cars were bigger, heavier and required a different skillset to the light, nimble go-karts he had been used to. The series was the support event to the British Touring Car Championship, and saw him race at Brands Hatch, Donington and Silverstone. In his debut season, he finished third, having taken four wins and eleven podiums to clinch the Rookie Cup.

In 2014, a pivotal year for Norris, his management team recruited the help of Jon Malvern, a fitness and conditioning coach who still works with him in F1. Norris would also meet Trevor Carlin, founder of the former Carlin Motorsport team, which had considerable success in the lower formulae, before he left in 2023. Carlin boasts an impressive roster of alumni, with 28 of its former drivers reaching F1, including Vettel, Russell, Ricciardo, Magnussen and Rosberg. Carlin had watched Norris's career blossom and offered him a seat in 2015 to compete in the MSA Formula Championship, now called the F4 British Championship. Norris benefitted from the experience he gained behind the wheel in the Ginetta Junior Championship the year before, and won eight times, took ten pole positions and fifteen podiums to win the championship, clinching the title at Brands Hatch.

As he had done the previous year, in 2015, he was enrolled into the class above, the ADAC Formula 4 Championship, for three of the eight rounds that made up the championship, again to get some experience racing at F1 venues – Spa-Francorchamps, Nürburgring and Hockenheim – winning once in Spa with second places at the other two circuits. On top of that, he also drove in the Italian Formula 4 Championship, racing in Monza, Mugello and Imola, gaining more experience of F1 tracks. It was an effective way for ADD Management to stretch their young driver, opening him up to superior racing cars on circuits that would become significant in the career they had mapped out for him. Adam Norris's money was being spent wisely as his younger son was progressing through the ranks, while Oliver had now stopped competing.

By the end of 2016, Norris had laid out credentials worthy of a driver with considerable potential. It was a staggeringly successful – and extremely busy – season, winning the Eurocup Formula

Renault 2.0 by a whopping 53 points with 5 wins and 12 podiums in 15 races. He also was victorious in the Formula Renault 2.0 Northern European Cup, winning at Silverstone, and had two wins at Spa. Earlier in the season, he won the Toyota Racing Series in New Zealand. Norris also competed in four rounds of the BRDC British F3 Championship, winning 4 times and taking a total of 8 podiums in 11 races. Finally, he also squeezed in three races in the FIA Formula 3 European Championship.

The management trio of Berryman, Sheader and Malvern were certainly getting results and nurturing their talent, but it was becoming obvious that, as they neared F3, Adam Norris's funds would only stretch so far and additional help would be required to open the necessary doors, not only in terms of negotiations with teams, but also from a commercial point of view. It is estimated that the cost of progressing through the lower ranks in order to reach F1 (factoring in logistics, buying a place in the team, insurance, racing licence and equipment) is in excess of £6 million. Extra investment from either sponsors or a manufacturer would facilitate the necessary financial backing to secure a seat on the grid.

A fortuitous meeting between Sheader and Zak Brown midway through 2016 would change the trajectory of Norris's progress. Sheader explained to me, when we spoke at the Abu Dhabi GP in 2021, that he had gone to see Brown and Richard Dean, the two co-owners of United Autosports. The meeting took place at the Circuit Paul Ricard in France, when Norris was competing in the Eurocup, while Brown had a team running in the four-hour Le Castellet race in the European Le Mans Series on the same weekend.

They were all there to discuss ADD Management working with another driver, who had been identified as a potential star by United Autosports. However, the conversation turned to Norris and they explored a separate deal. Brown would offer some high-profile status to the business and act as a representative, or advisor if you will, on behalf of ADD Management. As someone who could open the doors to racing teams at the top and could start negotiations with both leading F1 teams and sportswear companies, Brown would legitimise ADD Management in the eyes of the major players. Brown had the commercial nous and a growing reputation, and he would be able to tout Norris to potential suitors.

Now, ADD Management had the tools to help mould Norris into an all-round modern athlete. He was more than capable on track, as the results proved. However, they felt they needed help to manage his profile in the media and sought to recruit Martyn Pass, an experienced journalist and publicist who had previously worked with Lance Stroll during the Canadian's time in F3. Pass, who would eventually form part of McLaren's media team at races, was adept at helping Norris's fledgling career from a media perspective.

When we spoke back in 2021, he talked with a fondness for Norris, explaining how he was impressed by the racer's attitude and desire to be successful. He also recalls how he was incredibly tough on himself, a trait we would come to see frequently in F1, which would often be painful to watch. Norris only wanted to win. Second place was no consolation. It was all about winning.

Pass travelled with Norris during his F3 and F2 campaigns, writing previews and reports, and he says Norris was obliging for the best part. But there was one occasion where he wasn't. It came at an F3 race in Pau in France on 21 May 2017. Pass recalls how Norris was leading comfortably until he suffered a suspension failure, sending him out of the race. The British racer was so angry with himself at not winning, he refused to give Pass a quote for the press release. Norris would go on to win the Formula 3 European Championship title that season, taking 9 victories and a total of 20 podiums in 30 races.

In fact, 2017 would prove to be another major step in Norris's career. Early in the season he was confirmed as a junior driver for McLaren and now part of their young driver programme. Little attention was given to the announcement, coming so close to the start of the F1 campaign and subsequent car launches. Norris, who was 17, was hailed by Brown as a 'fabulous prospect'. He added that Norris had blown 'the doors off his rivals in not one but three highly competitive race series' in 2016 and 'capped that by establishing himself as the clear winner of the McLaren Autosport BRDC Award', a prestigious award that recognises young talent. He added: 'It was an impressively mature performance, and we'll be developing him this year as part of our simulator team, whereby he'll be contributing directly and importantly to our Formula One campaign at the same time as honing and improving his technical feedback capabilities.'

Norris did not disappoint, winning the opening race of the 2017 Formula 3 European season at Silverstone. He also took pole position and set the fastest lap in a clean sweep. Norris added another win in Monza, and McLaren were now sufficiently impressed to offer him an important and potentially career-defining opportunity. Norris was given the chance to drive their current F1 car in the mid-season test at the Hungaroring, immediately after the 2017 F1 Hungarian GP.

It is always a crucial time for teams to refine their race cars ahead of the second half of the F1 season, but it also offered McLaren the chance to see just how good Norris was. He'd impressed on the team's simulator, but could he do it in real life? He did so with gusto. Replacing Vandoorne in the cockpit, Norris set a best time that split the two Ferrari drivers, and finished just 0.2 seconds behind Sebastian Vettel, who was leading the F1 championship. Norris's astonishing first run was reflected in comments from Éric Boullier, who was still McLaren's racing director at the time. Impressed by the teenager's maturity, he said, 'His feedback with the engineers has been valuable and accurate, and he's certainly an asset to our test driver line-up – not to mention a potential star of the future.'

Norris would add to his two Formula Three victories and impressive first test with more wins at the Norisring in Nuremberg, Spa, Zandvoort and the Nürburgring, and swept his way to the title with two races of the F3 season still to go. To put his success into context, it was his fifth racing championship title in four years.

Before the end of the year, Norris was promoted to the position as McLaren's test and reserve driver for the 2018 season, acting as understudy to Alonso and Vandoorne. The team also confirmed that in order to prepare him for his new role, he would participate in a special Pirelli tyres test that would follow the conclusion of the Brazilian F1 GP towards the end of the 2017 season. Norris flew all the way to São Paulo's Guarulhos airport before checking in at the Hilton São Paulo Morumbi Hotel. He was having a relaxing bath after the 14-hour journey when he received news that the test was being cancelled amid security concerns. It came after eight members of the Mercedes team were robbed at gunpoint after leaving the circuit on the Friday night of the GP weekend and teams did not fancy hanging around for some extra days following the race.

The apprehension was justified, for the Brazilian GP was a notorious target for such hold-ups. In 2010, Jenson Button's vehicle was chased by armed robbers, and he was fortunate to escape thanks to his quick-thinking driver.

Norris's second crack at driving an F1 car had been scuppered. It had been a long and wasted journey, travelling all the way to Brazil for a bath, on what was his 18th-birthday weekend.

His final duties for the year included his F2 debut at the Abu Dhabi GP – where he so memorably spoke to the assembled press for the first time. Norris replaced Ralph Boschung, the 20-year-old Swiss driver who had cut his ties with the Campos team, and he retired in the feature race and finished thirteenth in the sprint race – it proved to be an unspectacular end to what was a particularly spectacular year.

The 2018 season saw Norris move to the FIA Formula 2 Championship, the final rung on the motorsport ladder before reaching the pinnacle, F1. At this stage of the motorsport pyramid, competition for a spot on the grid is incredibly tough and requires substantial financial backing or the support of an F1 team, who pay for the seat in F2 for their driver to compete (the cost of which is estimated to be around £2 million a year). Norris had the latter, and a place in the Carlin team, but this F2 campaign would be the ultimate testing ground. He was going up against George Russell, who was driving for ART along with fellow Brit Jack Aitken. The London-born Thai racer Alexander Albon and Canadian Nicholas Latifi were at DAMS, and the Dutchman Nyck de Vries was picked by Prema. Brazilian racer, Sérgio Sette Câmara was in the other Carlin car alongside Norris for his second season in F2, and had previously been on Red Bull's junior programme. The 2018 season would be a steep learning curve and Norris knew it.

He made the perfect start to his first full season in the championship, following his Abu Dhabi taster, winning in the opening race in Bahrain. Norris rounded out the two-race weekend by finishing fourth in the sprint race. At the next race, in Azerbaijan, Norris continued to impress with a sixth in the feature race and fourth in the sprint, while in Barcelona he was third in both races and left Spain leading the championship, 13 points ahead of Albon, on 80 points. Russell, thanks to wins in Baku and Barcelona, had climbed to third on 62 points.

Norris capitalised on a double retirement for Russell and Albon in Monaco and took a third place in the Monte Carlo sprint for a memorable podium. It was around this time, at the end of May, when I reported in the *Sun* that I had received information he was now being eyed up by Red Bull Racing as a potential candidate for the Toro Rosso seat, replacing New Zealand driver Brendon Hartley. Fearing they could lose their highly rated driver to a rival, McLaren were quick to shut down the move.

Norris scored further podiums in Austria at the Red Bull Ring and at Silverstone in his home Grand Prix. The British Grand Prix was a special moment to witness. Work stopped in the paddock and mechanics downed tools to watch the race as Norris went head-to-head with Russell. But it was Albon who took the chequered flag in the feature race and Russell was second. Norris was a disappointing tenth. In the Sunday sprint race, Norris improved to finish third, but Russell had finished ahead of him in second, scoring some valuable points across the weekend.

At the Belgian Grand Prix, Norris was handed another opportunity to impress in McLaren's F1 car, only this time it was on the biggest stage. He would take part in a free-practice session as part of the team's preparation for the Belgian Grand Prix at Spa-Francorchamps. Norris deputised for Alonso for the Free Practice 1 (FP1) session on the Friday, ahead of qualifying. The time is allocated for system checks and set-up changes, in preparation for qualifying and the race on Sunday. As such, it was crucial that Norris stuck to the programme and did not cause any damage. Despite being a more experienced driver than Vandoorne, Alonso was selected to make way, as the Spaniard had confirmed he was leaving the team at the end of the season, to be replaced by Carlos Sainz, arriving from Renault. However, there were also questions over Vandoorne's future at McLaren. Despite his excellent reputation in the lower formula, he had struggled to show much evidence of that ability in F1, though he was, admittedly, hamstrung by poor Honda and Renault engines.

Norris's FP1 outing for McLaren was limited to running through the testing programme and he did not get the opportunity to set any flying laps, but he'd showed maturity by understanding the team's brief and not trying to overdo it and make a mistake.

Norris had to switch back to his F2 car 25 minutes later and recalibrate his senses to cope with the reduced engine power and braking. He did so and finished fourth in the feature race, unable to find a way past Russell, who was placed third. The following day, after making some changes, Norris finished second in the sprint race behind winner De Vries.

McLaren gave Norris another FP1 outing a week later, this time at Monza, home of the Italian GP. However, the run was limited to nine laps due to thunderstorms. Nonetheless, McLaren had seen enough before the F2 season had even concluded and on 3 September 2018, the team released a statement confirming that he would be promoted to the F1 seat in place of Vandoorne for 2019.

In the final two rounds of the F2 championship, Norris suffered a double retirement in Sochi and could only muster a fifth- and second-place in Abu Dhabi. By contrast, Russell, who had been gaining momentum, won in Sochi, home of the Russian GP, and in Abu Dhabi as he clinched the Formula 2 title ahead of Norris. The latter was disappointed not to win but he already knew he had an even bigger prize waiting in 2019 – a full seat on the F1 grid driving for McLaren. It had been a remarkable rise.

CHAPTER 10

NORRIS'S RISE IN F1

There was an entirely different feel about McLaren coming into the 2019 season. With Alonso and Vandoorne gone, Norris was promoted from his role as reserve driver and paired with 24-year-old Spaniard Carlos Sainz.

It marked another fresh start for the team but one that was youthful and exciting. McLaren had been linked with a move for Ricciardo, but the Aussie decided to join Renault from Red Bull, forcing Sainz out of the team, and McLaren snapped up the opportunity. Sainz was highly rated. He had spent two years on loan at Renault from Red Bull where he had matured and delivered some strong performances, even if the results on paper did not always back that up.

Meanwhile, Norris was still over the moon at having made it to F1. When the team had confirmed the news in September 2018, he wrote on Twitter, 'dream come true', accompanied by a childhood video of himself spinning around in a mini kart. At the press conference called a day after he was confirmed as McLaren's driver for 2019, he was asked if he had celebrated his promotion by buying anything nice. 'I've not bought anything. I am just focusing on the job itself,' he said. 'And if McLaren give me a car, that's fine,' he added cheekily. 'I don't tend to buy fancy stuff anyway. The most expensive thing I have ever bought is airbrush equipment for my painting. I like to paint my own helmets. I take them apart, sand them down and repaint. I think that's my favourite hobby after racing.' He also confessed to once lying about stealing a sweet from a shop, earning a telling-off from his mum, and admitted that his trainer had been trying to change his diet, but that he was still enjoying his Weetabix with full-fat milk each morning. He had a youthful innocence about him.

In an in-depth conversation for my biography on Norris with Charlotte Sefton, she revealed that from the very beginning, the team was instructed not to indulge Norris's boyishness. This directive had come from within his close network, including Berryman and his trainer Jon Malvern, who had specifically told Sefton not to 'mollycoddle' him. She was instructed to correct Norris immediately if he stepped out of line.

Although it was Norris's debut season in F1, he was by now fully integrated into the team. Since moving to Woking, he had easy access to the MTC. He was frequently in the factory on the simulator and he was well versed in all the team's procedures. So, when he noticed Sainz arriving for team meetings dressed in non-team attire, Norris objected, only to be told to stop complaining and reminded that Sainz was now in his fifth season in F1.

After the politics and negativity that had enveloped the team following the fallout with Honda, life with Renault engines showed slight improvement, but McLaren remained stuck in the middle of the standings. The team needed a lift and eyes turned to Sainz, who had already experienced stints with Toro Rosso and Renault in the four years since his F1 debut in 2015. With the youngest line-up on the grid, expectations were tempered. While victories were not anticipated, the internal message was clear: this was a crucial phase in the team's rebuilding process.

The assumption was that Sainz would simply blow his young team-mate away. Norris had told us journalists at the car launch, 'I'm sure there's going to be times when I do things wrong, and everyone's going to think I'm terrible and rubbish. I've spent a lot of time over the winter to try and prepare myself in every way for this moment and for the races, but there's some things you can't learn until you're on the track.'

Norris and Sainz were the main focus for the media, while behind the scenes Zak Brown was restructuring the team. Tim Goss had left his role as technical director and was replaced by James Key from Toro Rosso, and Matt Morris had resigned from his position as chief engineer. Pat Fry returned as engineering director, having previously worked for McLaren between 1993 and 2010, before moving to Ferrari. Andreas Seidl, who had run Porsche's successful World Endurance Championship team, would also be joining in May as managing director. It was clear McLaren were evolving, but the question remained, would Norris and Sainz be quick enough?

Just as we had seen in Norris's F2 debut, he wasted no time in making a strong impression. At the first preseason test, and on his first day as a Formula One driver on 19 February 2019, Norris neared the top of the timesheets. The previous day, Sainz, who had been given the first test drive, notched up nearly 120 laps, but he was outclassed by his rookie team-mate, who finished second quickest to Ferrari's Charles Leclerc. McLaren and Norris were making progress.

At the season-opening Australian Grand Prix, Norris revealed that he had driven the track over 600 times on the team's simulator and on his own computer set-up at home. He had been determined to do as much homework as he could but he was nonetheless still incredibly nervous, and understandably so. Sefton tells me how Norris arrived for Sunday's race without having slept the previous night. She recalls how he would 'go quiet', and that he had messaged her expressing his fear that he was going to muck up his first grand prix. She provided some words of encouragement, telling him he had nothing to lose and reassuring him that there was no weight of expectation on him.

As he took to the track for the first practice session, he notched up 31 full laps – more than any other driver – while adhering to McLaren's pre-race instructions to help optimise the car's set-up. Norris's feedback would be pivotal in getting the car dialled in for qualifying. He was not especially quick, finishing all three practice sessions in 18th place on the timesheets.

The following day he came alive and qualified in eighth place – a result that stunned the paddock. He had out-qualified Räikkönen, Pérez and Sainz, who was only good enough for 18th. Sadly, Norris was unable to convert his grid standing into points, crossing the finish line in 12th place. In the post-race media interviews he was rather hard on himself, saying how the team 'gave me a good car, with enough pace for me to be in the top ten, but I made a couple of mistakes which cost me any chance of scoring points, so I'm a little disappointed'. It was his first ever competitive run in an F1 car and he was downbeat with the result, feeling he could have done more.

Two weeks later, at the Bahrain Grand Prix, Norris would get his first points on the board, scoring a sixth place, sandwiched between Vettel's Ferrari and Räikkönen's Alfa Romeo, while Sainz was forced to retire with a gearbox problem. There would, however, be no celebration drinks for Norris: 'I want to stay away from that stuff this year. This is my chance to do well. Things can happen when you drink too much!'

Norris and Sainz's combined results meant that by the end of the fourth race, McLaren were up to fourth in the constructors' championship. Norris's form especially had caught the eye of team bosses and, ahead of the Spanish GP, he was rewarded with a new company car, a £150,000 McLaren 570S in papaya orange, replacing his VW Polo for runs to the supermarket. 'I don't drive it that much and I don't drive it fast,' he told us at the pre-race press conference, having only just driven a handful of miles in the car. 'I've got a job I need to keep, so I can't be that stupid!'

At the British Grand Prix in July, McLaren held a media day at Dunsfold Aerodrome, better known as the *Top Gear* test track. It was fun to spend time with Norris and Sainz, who took us out for a spin in some McLaren 600LTs. Normally at these days, F1 drivers seem to love the opportunity to put us journalists out of our comfort zone by driving us around a track at high speed. On this occasion, however, it was fun and good-humoured. We all went to dinner afterwards and at the end of evening, while Norris waved and said goodbye to us as a group, Sainz went around and shook everyone's hand individually. What a class act.

The following day, McLaren revealed that Norris had been offered a new contract. It was widely reported that his salary, estimated to be £380,000 a year, rose to around £2.5 million. The contract ran until 2020 and, while clearly rewarding Norris for his achievements in his debut season, it also served to fend off interest from Red Bull, who were seeking a replacement either for Pierre Gasly or Alex Albon, and had been making enquiries about his availability.

In the penultimate race of the 2019 season in Brazil, McLaren enjoyed their best result of the year, with Sainz crossing the line in fourth and Norris in eighth. However, a five-second post-race penalty for Hamilton for clattering into Albon dropped him from second to seventh, meaning Sainz was promoted to third. It was McLaren's first podium since the 2014 Australian GP. When the decision finally came through long after the fans had left the Interlagos circuit, staff recreated their own podium celebrations and the partying continued into the night, with many hungover faces among the team, but not the alcohol-free driver, on the flight back to London the following day.

Sefton believes that podium for Sainz was a key moment for Norris, who had been desperate to deliver the first piece of silverware for the team in years. While Norris was consistently in the points, Sainz, after a slow start, had got the edge and finished sixth in the championship. Norris was down in 11th. It was nonetheless an impressive start to his F1 career, particularly given the rapidity of his rise, and he was also facing other challenges that many of us were unaware of at that time.

Two years after his debut season, Norris opened up about how he was struggling with his mental health. Speaking on *This Morning* on ITV in 2021, he admitted to being 'depressed a lot of the time'. He said: 'I guess people, when you just watch TV, don't realise many things that a driver goes through. It's a bit of a shame, but there's more programmes now where you get to see what the driver is like behind the scenes, and the amount of pressure and stress that they have to cope with. Especially at my age, coming into Formula One at 19, there's a lot of eyes on you. Dealing with all these pressures took its toll on me. I often felt uncertain, wondering what would happen if things went wrong, if I didn't perform well in the next session. Would I still be in F1 next year? If not, what would I do? I'm not really good at many other things in life. All of that, combined with feeling depressed when I had a bad weekend, made me think I'm not good enough. When those feelings add up over a season, along with the pressure from social media, it really starts to hurt you.'

• • •

The 2020 F1 season was placed on hold after the Australian Grand Prix was cancelled at the last minute due to the COVID pandemic. As the world was put into lockdown, for the first half of the year Norris was confined to online sim racing. During this time, his social media profile continued to grow. At the end of March, he took part in a Twitch stream event that raised more than $2.2 million for the World Health Organization's COVID-19 Solidarity Response Fund. Norris had promised to shave his head if he reached his target of $10,000. An anonymous donation of

$700 took him over the goal, and after buying some hair clippers on Amazon, he shaved off his hair.

The fundraising was a noble thing to do but, closer to home, financial matters were becoming a concern for McLaren and others on the grid. The lack of racing meant that income streams from sponsors were drying up, and some F1 teams were facing bankruptcy. McLaren confirmed they had furloughed members of staff – placing them on government-funded temporary leave of absence with a reduced salary.

Even though there was no racing during the pandemic, the world of F1 continued with its business, and in May 2020, McLaren revealed that Ricciardo would be joining the team for 2021. Brown had finally got his man at the second attempt, having missed out when Ricciardo opted to join Renault from Red Bull in 2019. The signing freed Sainz to go to Ferrari. Brown said at the time: 'Signing Daniel is another step forward in our long-term plan and will bring an exciting new dimension to the team, alongside Lando.'

McLaren believed that by signing Daniel Ricciardo, they could help him regain the impressive form he demonstrated during his time at Red Bull, where he won seven grands prix. However, Ricciardo had been struggling since 2016 and needed to get back to his best. While he was a high-profile addition to the team, his signing also meant the end of the successful partnership between Carlos Sainz and Lando Norris, which was working incredibly well, as the 2020 season would prove.

The delayed season eventually kicked off in Austria on 5 July 2020, and it brought Norris's first podium in F1. It came after Hamilton was issued a five-second penalty for colliding with Albon (a repeat of Brazil in the previous season) as the two made contact on a number of occasions, subsequently dropping the Mercedes driver from second to fourth, promoting Norris to third when he had crossed the line in fourth.

Norris had become the third-youngest podium finisher in F1 history at 20 years and 235 days old. He celebrated on the podium dousing himself in champagne, saturating his COVID facemask and finding himself unable to breathe. He said after the race: 'I am speechless. There were a few points in the race where I thought I had fudged it up. But I did not give up. I kept on going and I ended up on the podium ... I'm so happy and so proud of the team, considering where we were a couple of years ago. I'm proud to be part of it.' The COVID protocols required social distancing during the celebrations, but Norris did get a big squeeze from Brown, which inadvertently crushed his ribs, something Norris would complain about for weeks!

Norris and Sainz continued to deliver excellent performance and results. Reliability, too, had improved, but it was really about each driver gathering points, rather than being in contention for podium places. That said, Sainz did take second at the Italian GP in Monza, while in the same race Norris was fourth in the team's best result of the season. Norris joked with Sainz that he would be better off staying put, rather than joining Ferrari, who were having their own technical problems. 'There have been a few jokes. I'm not going to lie,' said Norris.

The banter continued and it was clear the partnership was probably the friendliest in modern F1. 'They got on really well,' recalls Sefton when we spoke for *Lando Norris: A Biography*. 'We were at the Eifel Grand Prix at the Nürburgring and it was really cold and wet. We were working in the marketing office and we could hear this giggling from the drivers' room next door ... I went in to speak to them and they were both lying on the massage bed watching YouTube or Instagram videos together. We all started pissing ourselves laughing at first, but I then said to them, "What the fuck are you doing? Why aren't you in the garage? Everyone is looking for you!" I was like an ogre telling them off all the time. But I realised then that they actually enjoyed spending time together.'

At the 17th and final round of the curtailed season in Abu Dhabi, Norris finished fifth and Sainz was placed in sixth, which was enough for McLaren to secure third place in the championship, ahead of Ferrari, incidentally, and earning Brown and Seidl the plaudits for their leadership. The prize money was a welcome boost for the team after furloughing staff a few months earlier. At the end of the year, the team also received investment from US firm MSP Sports Capital, worth £185 million according to some estimates.

With Ricciardo joining in 2021 – and a new engine deal with Mercedes coming into play in the new year – the future for McLaren was looking good.

• • •

At the season launch, Ricciardo attracted most of the attention, but it was a chat with Norris that piqued my interest. He spoke about how he had changed his lifestyle to get in shape. He had ditched the Weetabix and pizzas, and had made substantial improvements to his diet. Norris meant business. Brown had sensed it too and at the car launch said: 'Everyone is expecting them to be a goofy odd couple but I am expecting more seriousness. They are both out to prove something. Daniel is at the stage of his career where he wants to fight for a world championship and Lando is no longer the "younger brother" of his team-mate. Carlos and Lando gave each other a lot of room when they raced, but I think Daniel and Lando will be closer wheel-to-wheel. We might need to make sure that everyone races hard, but also races clean.'

Norris knew he needed to up his game against a seven-time race winner. At the 2021 season opener in Bahrain, I spoke to former McLaren driver David Coulthard for the *Sun*, who agreed with Norris and said: 'This is a great test for Lando. In Carlos he had a quick team-mate but also one that was pretty easy-going, and part of knowing your competitors is knowing your team-mate. And with Daniel, he's easy-going off track, but he is pretty ruthless on track and has that racer's heart and edge. It will be a difficult time for Lando. But it's also a great opportunity for him to step up and show he can get his elbows out.'

Norris made a solid start to the campaign, scoring a fourth in Bahrain and taking a podium at Imola, while Ricciardo was seventh and sixth. Norris again finished ahead of his more experienced team-mate in Portimão for the Portuguese Grand Prix, where he left the circuit in third place in the drivers' championship. By mid-May, he had been rewarded with a new contract, estimated to be worth around £6 million a year. A week later, at the Monaco Grand Prix, he secured the third podium of his career. He finished behind Max Verstappen and his former team-mate, Sainz – his two closest friends in F1. It was an emotional moment for him. 'I'm super happy,' he said in his post-race interview, '[a podium] is more special here in Monaco. We thought it would be one of the toughest [weekends] all season but it's almost turned into one of the opposite. It's pretty insane, pretty incredible. It feels amazing!'

Ahead of the British Grand Prix on 18 July, I met Norris at the MTC and we chatted about the upcoming race at Silverstone. We'd casually discussed England's defeat to Italy in the Euro 2020 final, which Norris had attended. He did not mention it at the time, but I later discovered that upon leaving the stadium he had been targeted by thieves, who bundled him to the ground and stole his bespoke Richard Mille watch, said to be worth £40,000. A week after this experience, which must have shaken him, he still managed to finish fourth at the British Grand Prix, narrowly missing out on what would have been a special podium in his home race.

Norris was clearly edging the intra-team battle with Ricciardo, but it was the Aussie who took McLaren back to the top step of the podium for the first time since the 2012 Brazilian Grand Prix. Ricciardo's victory came at the Italian Grand Prix – an explosive race that will be remembered for the dramatic crash between Verstappen and Hamilton during their title duel. Ricciardo was in position to take full advantage, not only winning the race, but also a bet with Brown, which would see the McLaren boss get the Monza circuit tattooed on to his arm.

Incredibly, Norris was second in a one–two finish for the team for the first time since the 2010 Canadian Grand Prix. Norris felt that was his to win, had he managed to squeeze past his team-mate in the early stages of the race. He had radioed his team to urge them to tell Ricciardo to pick up the pace; Norris was hoping that in putting the pressure on McLaren, they would in turn spot that he was the quicker car and instruct Ricciardo to allow him to pass. When he crossed the line, Norris congratulated Ricciardo but, deep down, he had desperately wanted that victory.

He had another shot at the following race, the Russian Grand Prix in Sochi at the end of September. Using slick tyres on a drying track, Norris had powered his way to his first pole position, and McLaren's first since the 2012 Brazilian Grand Prix. Norris made a slow start to the race and dropped behind Sainz, but on lap 13 managed to regain the lead. However, Hamilton had started to cut his way through the field and, come the final few laps, the reigning world champion started putting pressure on the McLaren driver, especially when it started to rain around lap 47.

Norris ignored pleas from his team to pit for intermediate or wet tyres to get better grip in the conditions, instead trying to tiptoe his way around the track in the slippery conditions in the vain hope he could hold on to the lead. While Hamilton did indeed stop for a change of tyres, Norris was determined to stay out. If he pitted, he would surrender the lead. When Hamilton came back into the race, he was 25 seconds adrift of Norris, but on the correct tyres, the gap closed to two seconds. With three laps to go, Norris's luck finally ran out. He aquaplaned off the track and Hamilton passed by. It was agony for Norris, who would eventually finish the race in seventh place. He had missed his opportunity to secure his first win.

The result in Sochi had taken the wind out of Norris's sails, but he still finished the season sixth in the drivers' championship, two places ahead of Ricciardo. It had proven to be Norris's most impressive performance to date and, contrary to many predictions, he had beaten his more experienced team-mate.

On 9 February 2022, just two days before McLaren launched their car for the new season, Norris signed a new and improved deal to stay with the team for a further four years. This was unprecedented, especially given he had only agreed new terms nine months earlier. As with his initial contract, the belief was that McLaren had been keen to fend off interest from the competition. Norris had proven himself to be a valuable asset and Seidl confirmed that his contract did not contain any 'get outs for both sides', which is unusual. Contracts in F1 normally contain a number of exit and performance-related clauses. Norris's signing came as Brown also agreed new terms to stay on at McLaren, as the team continued to refine its plans for the future. However, there was no such move for Ricciardo.

Norris again dominated the intra-team battle, taking another podium in Imola. After the opening seven races, Ricciardo's only points finish had come in his home race in Australia – sixth place and behind Norris, who was in fifth. Questions about his future intensified, with American driver Colton Herta and Spanish IndyCar champion Álex Palou both linked with replacing him. By the halfway point of the 2022 season, Norris had out-qualified Ricciardo in 9 of the 11 races and scored 47 points more. Ricciardo took to Instagram in an attempt to stop the speculation. He wrote:

> There have been a lot of rumours around my future in Formula One, but I want you to hear it from me. I am committed to McLaren until the end of next year and am not walking away from the sport. Appreciate it hasn't always been easy, but who wants easy? I'm working my arse off with the team to make

> improvements and get the car right and back to the front where it belongs. I still want this more than ever. See you [at the next race] in Le Castellet.

At the French Grand Prix, however, Ricciardo was again beaten by Norris. He was also beaten in Hungary. Ahead of the Belgian Grand Prix in August 2022, McLaren confirmed he would be leaving the team. The announcement came one month after Ricciardo's Instagram post.

The Australian described the decision as 'bittersweet' as he had wanted to fight for his place in the team, but he was not matching McLaren's aspirations. Norris, who would finish the season in seventh place in the drivers' championship, delivered a blunt assessment of Ricciardo's pending exit. Asked at the Belgian GP if he had any sympathy for Ricciardo, Norris said: 'I hate to say it, but I would say no. I've just got to focus on my driving and my job.'

Ruthless or simply honest, Norris had asserted himself and McLaren were clearly making progress on and off the track. The next piece in the jigsaw was to recruit a driver who would not only be quick but offer a perfect foil to Norris. The team had identified who they had believed to be the perfect candidate to take them forward: Australian Oscar Piastri.

CHAPTER 11

OSCAR PIASTRI'S STORY

When Oscar Piastri's name was first linked with a move to McLaren, it came as a surprise to the paddock. He was, after all, part of the Alpine young driver programme. The Australian had shown astonishing ability coming through the junior ranks and had looked an obvious choice for Alpine. They thought so, too.

Piastri was thrust into a media storm before getting a car for his first F1 race. Even Mercedes boss Toto Wolff weighed in about his move to McLaren, talking about 'integrity' and 'karma' in relation to what could be seen as the team's poaching of the driver.

The signing followed a tussle between Alpine and McLaren, which was brought before F1's Contract Recognition Board (CRB) – the legal department associated with driver contracts and the super-licences they need to compete in F1. Piastri had been part of Alpine's academy since 2020, when he won the F3 championship. A year later, he won the F2 championship, too. The F1 system is designed to encourage driver promotion to the top, so any driver who wins the F2 title cannot remain in the championship to defend it. However, with Alonso and Esteban Ocon signed to Alpine for 2022, Piastri found himself in the unusual situation of being without a drive, and was subsequently offered a role as Alpine's reserve driver.

His manager, former F1 driver and fellow Australian Mark Webber, had received an agreement from the team that set out plans for Piastri's career progression at Alpine, as required by the CRB for a reserve-driver role. The details would include information such as salary, whether the team would cover the driver's travel costs, paddock passes for guests and even whether he was entitled to take part in the practice sessions. Webber had asked for additional terms guaranteeing a seat in the Alpine F1 car from 2023 onwards. However, despite assurances that the paperwork was being completed, it took some time to arrive. Then, after a frustrating delay, Webber initially received only the usual agreement for the reserve-driver position. When the F1 full-seat contract from 2023 onwards did eventually arrive, it included a terms sheet with the words 'Subject to Contract' written across the top and detailed a career map that was not received well by the Piastri camp, with a loan to Williams in 2023, extended to 2024 if Alonso remained with the team.

It meant that Piastri potentially would not race for the Alpine team until 2025. As a result, the contract was not signed and Webber and Piastri started to look at other options.

For McLaren, signing Piastri was a no-brainer. His racing record was exemplary, while Ricciardo was struggling to find form. The teams started negotiating, in strict confidence, though it was later reported that Ricciardo was at this point made aware of conversations, potentially about his seat. A preliminary deal arrangement between McLaren and Piastri was then signed on 4 June 2022. Unbeknown to Alpine, exactly a month later, the two parties signed a final contract, giving him a spot on the grid for 2023.

Much to Alpine's surprise, Alonso then announced that he would leave the team at the end of the season to join Aston Martin. In response, Alpine issued a press release saying Piastri would be driving for the team in 2023 as his replacement.

However, at 7pm on 2 August 2022, Piastri wrote on Twitter: 'I understand that, without my agreement, Alpine F1 have put out a press release late this afternoon that I am driving for them next year. This is wrong and I have not signed a contract with Alpine for 2023. I will not be driving for Alpine next year.'

It was a massive bombshell that left Alpine reeling. They had lost Alonso, and now their reserve driver, who had been earmarked as his replacement, was not interested in driving for them.

Alpine believed that they had a contract in place with Piastri and escalated the matter to the CRB, who unanimously agreed that the terms sheet labelled 'Subject to Contract' meant it was not valid and that the only legitimate contract was with McLaren. Whether the terms sheet had, or had not, been signed, it was still invalid without the contract attached, which was not signed. The verdict was announced on 2 September 2022, just ahead of second practice for the Dutch Grand Prix. The FIA announced that the tribunal had 'issued a unanimous decision', adding that 'Mr Piastri is entitled to drive for McLaren Racing Limited for the 2023 and 2024 seasons.'

• • •

Piastri's route to F1 was not dissimilar to that of the team's founder. Although born in 2001 in Melbourne, Australia, rather than New Zealand, like Bruce McLaren, Piastri came though the local ranks before making a move to Europe to further his career. Again like McLaren, Piastri's father worked in the automotive industry and was the inspiration for his son's passion for motorsport.

I spoke to Piastri midway through the 2024 season and asked him about his earliest memories of motorsport. 'My first direct involvement was remote-control race cars. My dad is in the car industry and one day he came back from a business trip with an RC car and I started driving that around the backyard. I was about six at the time.'

Piastri raced go-karts against adults in much the same way Lewis Hamilton had done as a kid. Once he had shown that he had impressive hand–eye coordination, a few people suggested that he try his hand at racing a go-kart. He made his karting debut when he was nine.

He continued: 'On my first time in a proper go-kart, I spun at the first corner! Apart from that, I got up to speed reasonably quickly during that first run. I think I got within, let's say, a second off the pace of the quickest driver, like, very quickly, but getting that last second or the last three- or four-tenths, really that took quite a bit longer. But yeah, it came reasonably natural for me.'

One of the first people to have a hand in setting Piastri on the path to F1 was fellow Australian and two-time national karting champion, James Sera. He told me that it was a mutual friend who encouraged Piastri's father, Chris, to get in touch with him. 'At the time Oscar was around nine years old and was racing RC cars. I was running a business in karting, selling, servicing and coaching drivers all round the country, and after a very short conversation with me, Chris bought Oscar his first go-kart.

'I worked with Oscar between the ages of 9 and 14 – before he left for Europe. We went away karting most weekends of the year together. He had an outstanding attitude and he was just so likeable. To be honest, I was blown away by his calm professionalism and how extremely intelligent he was. I knew early on that Oscar had something different to the other kids I had coached and mentored over the years.

'As he came up through the ranks here in Australia he got an opportunity to go race the IAME World Finals [held on 19 October 2014 at Le Mans] where he grabbed third place [and also set the fastest lap]. Although there were no F1 talks that early, I encouraged his family to send him to Europe. No easy feat for a 14-year-old.'

Sera's encouragement did the trick.

I asked Piastri about how he found moving from Melbourne to the UK to further his racing career at such a young age. He said: 'I was with my dad for the first six months. I was 14 when we moved, almost 15, and we were living in Hoddesdon, 20 miles north of London.'

It was during that initial six-month period in 2016 that Piastri was spotted by talent scout Rob McIntyre. I met McIntyre to discuss his involvement with the young racer's early career.

'My background is professional go-kart racing,' he began. 'I have worked in motorsport my whole life in various guises but my real passion is karting, because it's more about the driver, and you can see what's going on. Typically, I go to two or three big international races a year and, back in 2016, I went to a European championship race, which is where all the current F1 drivers have come through. It is the professional top level of karting. I saw this little Aussie kid batting round and I thought, "OK, yeah, you're quite good." He was driving for Ricky Flynn Motor Sport. I had a word with Ricky, who was best man at my wedding: "So, OK, the little Aussie kid's pretty fast. What do you know?"

'Rick basically said, "Yeah, really fast, very technical, super smart."'

McIntyre revealed that karting in the UK initially presented a challenge to the 15-year-old because of the increased intensity and physical demands. 'However, when I examined his data, I noticed his exceptional dexterity with the steering wheel and pedals. Modern go-karts are equipped with data-acquisition systems that record every detail, and his data revealed an incredible feel for the vehicle. I realised then that this kid was destined to excel in a car, beyond just karting.'

At the time, McIntyre was working with Arden International, owned by Garry Horner and his son Christian, and helped to bring a few drivers into their young driver academy.

'So I got Oscar's father's telephone number and rang him and said, "Hey, you don't know me … I work with Arden International. When you want to go in a car, give me a shout." Simple as that.'

I asked him how the relationship with Chris Piastri developed. 'We met up,' he tells me. 'We had a sandwich, we talked about intelligent electronics. I'm not an engineer, but I'd done my due diligence and made an effort to understand Oscar's father's business.

I also had my passion for racing and straightaway there was a bit of rapport. Oscar sat there as a typical 15-year-old, eating his fries and not saying a word. Then a couple of weeks later, Chris and I went and had dinner and I started to build a relationship mainly about trust. When you start karting these days, the investment and complexity are incredibly high. When you get into cars, everyone claims to be the next champion, eager to help but also to take your money. Chris was looking for some guidance, so we began to talk and started to set things up. I got Oscar into Arden, where he tried out the simulator.' Arden were impressed.

'We then organised a session at Anglesey, despite Oscar never having driven a racing car before. We used an old BRDC F4 car on a damp track. Oscar took to it immediately. At one point, he clipped a seagull with his wing mirror, breaking it off. When he came in, we looked at the data and he hadn't even lifted off the accelerator. The Arden engineers kept saying to me, "He's definitely been in a car before," but I assured them he hadn't.'

Arden set a benchmark time that had been established by Jack Aitken, who had raced in F1 for Williams in 2020. 'They told Oscar that if he could get within three seconds of that time, then happy days! By the end of the day, Oscar had exceeded the benchmark.'

Six months in, Oscar was enjoying racing in Europe when his dad presented him with a choice: 'It got to July or August and my dad said, "I'm going back home to live with the rest of your family. Either you can come back with me and try and make a career in Australia, or, if you want to keep going down this pathway, you can stay here, but it will mean that you go to boarding school." I obviously wanted to try and pursue my dream of being an F1 driver, so I knew that I had to stay, and I went to boarding school.'

With Piastri's mind made up, McIntyre offered himself to the family in a supporting role.

'Oscar started at Haileybury College in September 2016 and I was actually living nearby. Although I was just down the road, he was incredibly independent and rarely needed my help. Occasionally, he would call if a flight was cancelled and ask for assistance with rebooking. As we moved into 2017, I attended all the races. The British F4 season went exceptionally well for him. He won numerous races, and the championship came down to the final weekend, where Oscar finished second.'

I asked Piastri if he ever got lonely, living on the other side of the world from his family as a teenager: 'No, not really,' he said. 'To be honest, I think in some ways going to boarding school was actually a very helpful thing for me.' The six months living with his dad had been enjoyable, but they didn't know many people. 'I spent pretty much all my time in a small apartment, doing remote school learning online with everyone I knew in a different time zone. So that part of it was quite lonely. Then when I started boarding school, especially with many of the people in my year also boarding throughout the week, including some international students who stayed over the weekends, it helped me integrate into a community and make friends. Going to school and having a daily routine was a really positive thing for me. It kept me from constantly thinking about how I could have done turn 6 on lap 12 differently. It gave me something different to focus on other than racing.'

Like Norris, Piastri was juggling schoolwork with travel across the UK and Europe to fulfil racing commitments. But unlike his McLaren team-mate, who left school before his GCSEs, Piastri completed them and passed his A levels.

'A lot of the time, testing started on a Wednesday or Thursday,' he told me as we talked about his time at Haileybury. 'So basically I would miss half a week at a time. The school were very, very supportive of it, but I knew that I was expected to make up the work at some stage. And you know, I would say I was fortunately semi-gifted academically, so I didn't find it such a burden to do that. When I got to my A levels it became much harder, and I actually needed someone to kind of guide me through it much more. I took maths, physics and computer science A levels. I got two Bs and a C, which, considering my attendance in my last year of school was 35 per cent, I thought was solid.'

McIntyre recalled one moment in 2018 when Piastri was competing in the Eurocup and was potentially going to miss two races because of his GCSEs. He tried to get him to sit an exam in Monaco but the papers proved not to be exactly the same, so he deferred the exam. He also remembers Piastri skipping a practice session at Silverstone to do an exam before heading back to the track the following day.

At the start of 2019, Piastri, his father and McIntyre recognised the need for additional support to advance his career. Given the high costs associated with competing in F3 and F2, it was crucial to allocate finances wisely and enlist the right people to ensure a smooth progression. They decided to approach former F1 driver and fellow Australian Mark Webber through a mutual contact,

Simon Sostaric, who had been working with Piastri and knew Mark. Chris Piastri and McIntyre met with Webber and his wife Ann. Oscar took up the story:

'Towards the end of my Formula Renault championship season in 2019, I was preparing to move to F3 the following year to join the F1 weekends. Things were starting to get more serious, so we reached out to [Webber], and he was keen to work with me. He definitely understands the decisions involved in moving from Australia. At that point in my career, homesickness wasn't really an issue for me, although I know it can be for others. By then, I had moved past those doubts. However, having someone who had followed a similar path as an Australian was incredibly valuable. Mark had a very convoluted journey to F1, to say the least. But as I got closer to F1, having his insight on what lies at the end of that path, and understanding what it takes to stay in F1, has been a key part of our relationship.'

Piastri would close out the year winning the Eurocup, taking 7 wins in 19 races. He was now highly sought after, with the leading F3 teams all vying for his signature.

In 2020, Piastri began racing in Formula Three, where he could showcase his talent to the world as part of the F1 bill – winning the title at the first attempt. He had chosen to drive for Prema Racing, whom he selected over the many teams competing for his services. During that season, which was curtailed due to the COVID pandemic, McIntyre travelled with him to all the races, as Chris was unable to attend due to travel restrictions and protocols in Australia.

McIntyre said: 'Oscar was a typical teenager. After he won the F3 championship, I asked if he had spoken to his parents, as he hadn't yet given them a call. When he did, after my question, I captured a wonderful photo of him making the call. I was keeping an eye on his wellbeing, what was going on within the team, making sure he was being looked after, and also being the communication piece with home, with family, with friends.'

Piastri progressed to F2 in 2021, sticking with Prema, and won 6 of the 23 races, beating Robert Shwartzman, his team-mate, by over 60 points. He had now completed his apprenticeship and was primed for F1.

McIntyre, who got to know him better than most during this stage of his racing career, pinpointed what sets Piastri apart. 'It's his feel, his dexterity,' he said, 'the supercomputer. The brain. Also, the Oscar you see is the real Oscar. He's very humble, he's very realistic, he's polite but also very private. He's a very, very, intelligent young man. He's focused on the data, and working with the engineers has always been one of his strong points.

'When he first got in that BRDC F4 car, there was a little bit of vindication, for me, when what I'd seen in the kart and in the data transferred across to racing a car, because that doesn't always happen. What were his strengths through the period of time that I worked with him? He's super calm, super composed and he was able to see the big picture.'

Seeing that big-picture vision involved cutting ties with Alpine and moving to McLaren. It was also a smart move by McLaren to secure one of the sport's hottest prospects, even though, with Lando Norris, it gave them the youngest F1 pairing on the grid. For those of us in the media, McLaren's decision to sign Piastri seemed perfect, especially given their slump to fifth place in the

2022 constructors' championship. Ricciardo's promise had failed to yield results, and opting for a young talent like Piastri made total sense for the team's long-term strategy. Brown had identified that McLaren wouldn't be in a position to fight for titles until 2025, and this move provided the team with a runway to achieve that goal. The biggest question, however, would be: how long would it take Piastri to get up to speed, given he had been sitting on the sidelines as Alpine's reserve driver for the whole of the 2022 season? Would he be rusty? The other question was, how would he go up against Norris, who had comfortably beaten Ricciardo?

CHAPTER 12

BRUTAL HONESTY

At the end of 2022, McLaren announced that Andreas Seidl would leave his position as team principal to head up Audi's fledgling F1 programme. The German car giant had laid out plans that would see them come into the sport for 2026, taking over the Sauber team, and they had identified Seidl, then 46, as the man to lead the project. He'd had success at Porsche, taking them to three consecutive victories in the Le Mans 24 Hours and the drivers' and constructors' titles in the World Endurance Championship, before joining McLaren.

Seidl was a likeable figure. He frequently engaged with the media and always spoke honestly about McLaren's progress. In turn, he had received positive coverage for helping drag McLaren up from the bottom of the grid, where they had finished the 2017 season after a woeful campaign. Under Seidl's watch, McLaren had clambered to mid-table, were sitting behind the big three of Red Bull, Mercedes and Ferrari, as well as Alpine, and had won the 2021 Italian Grand Prix with Ricciardo.

His departure was seen by the media as a blow that threatened to derail McLaren's progress and the team's long-term plan to be in position to fight for world titles in 2025.

However, the picture internally was somewhat different. A new wind tunnel that would help the team's aerodynamics department with their modelling was in the pipeline and the team had an exciting and young driver line-up with Norris and Piastri. Also, Brown had been aware of Seidl's intention to leave the team, which had given him the opportunity to line up Andrea Stella for the role of team principal. The Italian had previously worked at Ferrari from 2000 and had been the race engineer for Michael Schumacher, Räikkönen and Alonso before he followed the Spaniard to McLaren for the 2015 season. Stella was first made McLaren's head of race operations before being promoted to performance director in 2018. The following year he was given the title racing director and had been identified as one of the pillars behind McLaren's turnaround in fortunes.

Speaking after Stella's appointment, Brown said: 'Andrea is a highly talented, experienced and respected member of our team with a strong track record of leadership and success in Formula 1. His move into this role is a great example of the strength in depth we have in our team, and I'm excited to be working more closely with him, with a joint focus on moving up the grid and winning races.'

Stella, who had never been in the limelight during his time at Ferrari or indeed McLaren, said he felt 'privileged' to be offered the role leading the team. He added: 'We are realistic about the amount of work ahead of us to move back up the grid, but I am excited and encouraged that I am on this journey together with a team full of talent, experience, racing spirit and dedication.'

Stella's first public speaking event in McLaren colours was at the launch of the 2023 car, the MCL60, which took place at the team's factory. Over time, I have attended numerous livery launches and, for the best part, they are almost pointless. The car is usually last year's model, painted differently and with new sponsors. The drivers haven't even driven it yet, so their thoughts on it don't hold much weight. It is, however, a good opportunity to assess the mood ahead of the first test. It is quickly apparent whether a team has confidence in the work done over the winter, and that all the calculations based on their scale models and wind-tunnel testing add up.

Yet, that unveiling at McLaren was like no other I had previously attended – or have been to since. Both Brown and Stella openly admitted that the car was not good enough and had fallen short of their expectations. There was no sugar-coating or pretending all was well. While some of my colleagues were interested in the shape of the sidepods (the airscoops on the side of the car), it was Stella's honesty and openness that struck me as the bigger story. He had just taken over the reins from Seidl and this was the first McLaren car launch under his watch, but he said: 'Assessing last year's performance, we identified multiple areas of opportunities [or areas to improve]. The good news is that pretty much all of them have been addressed, predominantly aerodynamics. There's some other areas of the car that will be improved by developments in the early stage of the season. So we are not entirely happy with the launch car, but optimistic that we will take a positive step soon.'

Asked when a step-up in actual performance was expected, he continued to be realistic: 'It is always difficult to translate what you see over the winter in terms of development to where you're going to be in terms of pecking order.'

In essence, McLaren had crunched the numbers and, using all the modelling software and wind-tunnel predictions, had come up with a design that it thought would work on the track. The only way to know for sure, however, was when the car would run for the first time. Even then, it was all relative to what their competitors had produced over the winter. Stella was effectively writing off his team's chances before a wheel had even turned.

At the time, it seemed as though McLaren might regress to the sluggish performance of 2018, or worse, to the unreliable early years with Honda. But, in hindsight, by managing expectations, Stella was also alleviating pressure in relation to his initial impact with the team. All of the work on the 2023 car had been overseen with Seidl as team principal and, while Stella was privy to the development, it was not wholly his concept. He had created breathing space for himself.

That was just as well, for at the preseason test in Bahrain, McLaren encountered teething problems, with some of the testing time cut short as the team made on-the-spot and somewhat rudimentary changes to certain car parts to reinforce them and avoid mechanical failures. It was also evident that neither Norris nor Piastri felt comfortable in the car, as their lap times were uncompetitive with the rest of the field. The mood had dropped even further since the livery launch. McLaren already suspected they would be playing catch-up but, after the opening run in Bahrain, they were looking at the realisation that they could be left trailing at the bottom of the timesheets, and this had now begun to weigh heavily on the team.

It was especially tough on Brown, who had overseen Stella's promotion and was ultimately accountable for how the team were performing on track. To be out of contention for race victories at this early stage of the season cranked up the pressure again. Speaking at the Bahrain test on Friday, Brown was upfront: 'We know we set some goals for development, which we didn't hit, and we felt it was better to be honest about that. Like everyone, we have a lot of development coming, so, we are encouraged by what we see around the corner. I think we will be going into the first race off of our projected targets, but it is hard to really know where that means we will be on the grid.'

The season had seen the introduction of new regulations that removed intricate front wings and changed the traditional concept of downforce. In previous years, the rules had been geared towards designing cars that would be pressed into the ground by the pressure of the air running over the bodywork. For this season, the philosophy was the reverse in that the bodywork underneath the car would cause it to be sucked closer to the ground to improve its handling. The concept, known as ground effect, meant that there would be less turbulent air in the wake of the F1 cars; consequently cars could run closer to each other and there could be more overtaking manoeuvres.

Piastri was not yet convinced by the new McLaren and, talking about his first runs in the car, he said: 'I would say a small step up from last year. We know we've got a few things in the pipeline for hopefully soon in the season. But so far, it's, I think, similar to what I remember from my limited experience in a ground-effect car.'

In conclusion, Brown admitted the team needed to improve its development rate: 'Our aspirations are to get back to the front,' he said. 'We know that will take a little bit more time. We have some good developments coming, but so does every other single team in F1. We need to pick up the pace.'

The sentiment was echoed by Stella, who also offered a reason to explain what had gone wrong in development. 'In terms of aerodynamic efficiency of the car, we are still shy of our target. But looking ahead to the season, we remain optimistic.'

• • •

There was little to be optimistic about in the opening GP, on 5 March 2023 in Bahrain, as Piastri, on his McLaren debut, became the first driver to retire from a race in the new season. He had climbed to 12th place before he suffered an electrical failure and, despite a steering-wheel change, was unable to cure the problem.

Norris, too, was not without mechanical problems and, while he did finish the race in 17th, two laps down, he had a pressure leak with the engine pneumatics that impacted the gearbox and required him to stop every ten laps so mechanics could top up the system by connecting an airline to the car. It really was quite ridiculous to watch.

In the McLaren press release that followed the disappointing opening race, Norris is quoted saying: 'We decided to stay in the race, and to try and stay at least within one lap from the leader, for the last ten laps. Then if there's a safety car, see if there was an opportunity. We did six stops. Then we had a pneumatic problem and various other issues, which just brought us out the race more and more.' Norris was later quizzed on whether there were any positives he could take from such a poor start and he joked: 'I think the best thing was the mechanics had a lot of pitstop practice!'

McLaren's result, coupled with the team's candid admission that they had plenty of work to do, had created a narrative in the media that the team was again in trouble. It was an easy assumption to make. But ahead of the following race in Saudi Arabia, Norris sounded more optimistic. It was not clear if he was just toeing the line or genuinely seeing signs of an improvement, but he insisted McLaren were 'far from' a crisis, while admitting the 'harsh criticism is acceptable' after their poor start to the 2023 season. 'Oscar's problem was an issue we'd only seen for the first time in years, so I'm confident that's fixed,' he said. 'And with my issue, Mercedes [who supplied McLaren's engine] are sure they fixed that and, again, it's something that hasn't happened for years and years. Everyone makes it sounds a lot worse than it is, calling it a crisis. It's far from that, it's not even close to it.'

Inevitably, despite Norris's loyal words, the negativity around the team had reopened debates about where his future lay in F1. In the past, he had been linked with a move to Red Bull, with boss Christian Horner known to be an admirer of the British driver's talent. The move made sense, for Norris was close friends with Red Bull's world champion Max Verstappen and would, on paper at least, be the perfect foil. Verstappen has a reputation for being somewhat of a team-mate killer, in the sense that any driver who competes alongside him is soundly beaten and the upshot is they end up leaving the team. Norris, however, offered more of a test and the fact he was friends with Verstappen in the first place meant the pairing had the potential to be low maintenance.

The proposal also gained traction because Verstappen's current team-mate Sergio Pérez was not delivering solid points on a regular basis – something Norris had been doing.

So despite having a deal until the end of 2025, Norris had found himself again facing questions about whether he would be willing to stay with the team and wait for the situation to improve, or decide to force through a move to Red Bull. Yet even with the rumour mill in overdrive, Norris was adamant that the links to Red Bull were 'fake stories' and again pledged his allegiance to McLaren.

While Norris was being probed by reporters about his future, the career of Brown was now the subject of debate within McLaren. The slow start to the year had not gone unmissed by the shareholders, and the pressure on Brown was mounting. This wasn't evident from the outside until the 2024 instalment of Netflix's *Drive to Survive* when he was grilled on camera by the McLaren Group's executive chairman Paul Walsh, and he revealed the scrutiny and strain he was under.

He also opened up about it when we spoke at the Canadian Grand Prix in 2024: 'The start of the 2023 season was the hardest, because that was on my watch and I saw how we got there. In 2016, '17 and '18, it was calm, because we were making progress. We were increasing sponsorship and morale was going up. But in 2023, when it was like we were as bad as we had been in 2016, it was a shock to the system. Fans went nuts, sponsors weren't happy. But I didn't allow anyone to see I was under pressure. I kept everyone rallied up, and made some moves quickly [such as promoting Stella].

'The team principal [Stella], the technical director [Neil Houldey] and the head of aero [Peter Prodromou] were all promoted. Everything else stayed the same. I was unhappy with what I saw after the upgrades we introduced at the 2022 French GP. While the failure of the upgrades was concerning, I was more troubled by the leadership team's response. Amidst the headlines about Daniel Ricciardo's contract, I was dissatisfied with the overall leadership at the highest level. Consequently, I decided that changes were necessary.'

Brown's honesty was an eye-opener and he was speaking candidly, which I appreciated. He continued: 'If you look back at the success we had in 2021, you can see that it can be traced back to the team we had in 2019, Andrea Stella, Peter Prodromou, Gil de Ferran [sporting director] and Pat Fry [engineering director]. They did the 2020 car. The '21 car was just a power unit change. The people that came in in 2020 reaped the benefits for 2021. They were on their own in 2022 and the car was average at best.'

You cannot disagree with Brown's assessment and the proof would come later on, but ultimately he deserves credit for sticking with his philosophy and making the switch to promote Stella at that time, backing the Italian and his leadership skills to help the team get back to the front.

There was a spike of optimism within the team at the Australian Grand Prix on 2 April 2023, when they scored a double points win, with Norris climbing from 13th on the grid to finish 6th, while Piastri, in his home race, went from 16th to 8th in an impressive showing. The fourth race in Azerbaijan saw the arrival of the much-anticipated upgrades. They brought a new floor, a crucial part of the ground-effect philosophy, plus a new rear wing and other components engineered to cut drag and increase speed.

The McLaren Technology Centre, or MTC as it is widely known, is the headquarters for McLaren's racing teams across all the championships they compete in and McLaren Automotive, their road-car division.

Race winner Fernando Alonso celebrates with second-placed team-mate Hamilton at the Malaysian Grand Prix in April 2007.

Alonso is chased down by Hamilton at the 2007 Monaco Grand Prix. The two drivers would eventually come into conflict, resulting in Alonso leaving the team.

In June 2007, Hamilton celebrates winning his first F1 grand prix in Montreal, Canada.

Hamilton poses following his maiden victory in Canada, with the team dressed in their 'rocket red' T-shirts. Hamilton's father Anthony, who worked multiple jobs to help fund his son's early career, is to his left.

Lewis Hamilton walks through the paddock with McLaren team principal Ron Dennis and the team's CEO Martin Whitmarsh at the 2008 Australian Grand Prix. Hamilton would go on to win the title that season.

Hamilton and Jenson Button are pictured either side of McLaren's communications director, Matt Bishop, after qualifying for the 2012 Chinese Grand Prix.

A young Lando Norris stands alongside McLaren's race drivers for 2018, Stoffel Vandoorne and Alonso. Norris is dressed in race overalls minus the team's sponsor, wine producers Chandon.

Carlos Sainz, in his blue race suit, celebrates on the podium after being awarded third place in the 2019 Brazilian Grand Prix. Hamilton had originally finished third but was issued a five-place post-race penalty that promoted Sainz to third. The team recreated the podium long after the crowds had dispersed.

Struggling to breathe, Norris removes his champagne-soaked facemask after celebrating his first podium at the 2020 Austrian Grand Prix. The race, where Norris finished third, marked the return of F1 after the pandemic.

Norris is third at the 2021 Monaco Grand Prix and takes to the podium sporting a different colour race suit as part of a change of livery with sponsors Gulf. He is joined by his close friends Sainz and Max Verstappen.

Daniel Ricciardo wins the Italian GP in 2021 while Norris comes second. Together they administer a 'shoey' celebration to the team's CEO Zak Brown. As part of a bet, Brown gets the Monza circuit tattooed on his arm after the race.

Norris looks over a broken trophy on the podium at the 2023 Hungarian GP. While celebrating, Norris accidentally knocked over Verstappen's winner's trophy, breaking it in two.

McLaren team principal Andrea Stella is flanked by Oscar Piastri and Norris at the 2023 Japanese Grand Prix in Suzuka. Norris came second and Piastri was third.

Norris and Verstappen make contact whilst battling for the lead at the 2024 Austrian GP. The flashpoint would spark a furious reaction from Norris, who was sent out of the race.

Norris achieves his maiden F1 victory in Miami, May 2024. He celebrates in style in front of the hospitality unit which is on the Miami Dolphins pitch.

In July 2024, Piastri wins the Hungarian Grand Prix, his first in F1. It comes after Norris is ordered to swap places with the Australian.

Norris delivers a fantastic performance at the 2024 Singapore Grand Prix, winning by a huge margin over Verstappen and keeping his drivers' championship hopes alive.

Zak Brown celebrates on the podium following Norris' win in the 2024 Abu Dhabi Grand Prix. The victory secures McLaren the constructors' championship.

The McLaren team celebrate their title in front of their garages in Abu Dhabi.

Both drivers responded with improved qualifying results, with Norris starting as high up as the second row, which he converted into a 9th-place finish. Piastri meanwhile was just out of the points in 11th, but it appeared there was some progress being made.

However, any hopes of an improvement were dashed at the inaugural Miami Grand Prix when Norris limped home in 17th after clashing with Alpha Tauri's Nyck de Vries. Piastri finished in 19th, struggling with overheating brakes. The result brought McLaren crashing back down to the reality that they still had issues to fix, as Stella observed post-race: 'The main takeaway is that after a decent weekend in Baku from a performance point of view, we had a reality check. The information we gained here helps us understand that some development directions still need to be pursued.'

The disappointment was evident and Norris was not as guarded with his comments as he had been earlier in the season, identifying his McLaren as one of the slowest cars, if not *the* slowest, in the race – a damning assessment.

In Monaco at the end of May, the team ran a special 'Triple Crown' papaya, white and black livery as part of their 60th anniversary celebrations, honouring their previous successes in the Monaco F1 GP, the Indy 500 at Indianapolis and the Le Mans 24 endurance race – a unique hattrick. But there was not much to celebrate on track, as Norris was 9th and Piastri 10th.

Things did not improve at the Spanish Grand Prix either, notwithstanding a positive qualifying session, which had put Norris in third place. But he had already spoken about not finishing in the points. Norris's habit of looking at things in a negative manner had now become commonplace, but his derision about even considering a points finish was baffling. It grabbed the headlines and wove into the narrative that McLaren had no chance of winning. Unfortunately, he turned out to be right after he made contact with Hamilton on the opening lap, breaking his front wing. A pitstop dropped him to last place and he would eventually come home in 17th, while Piastri was a lowly 13th.

Team morale was low, despite assurances that improved parts were in the pipeline. The drivers were unhappy and, so far, results reflected no sign of an uptick in performance. As the season switched across the Atlantic to Canada for the 18 June GP, McLaren were headed for another disappointing season. The pressure on Brown and Stella had intensified and now there was no hiding place. McLaren needed to find a way back, a much-needed lift in confidence and to stop the negativity that had infiltrated the team and the factory.

A boost did not arrive in Montreal, and the team left feeling flatter than ever. Norris was hit with a time penalty for what the panel described as 'unsportsmanlike behaviour' for driving slowly when a safety car was triggered after George Russell crashed. Norris had deliberately slowed, allowing his McLaren pit crew to perform a 'double-stack' – changing Piastri's tyres and then his immediately after, without them leaving the pit lane. The tactic is a bold move but means that both drivers are placed on the same race strategy, in that they both stop for fresh tyres on the same lap. Each team has already calculated their optimum strategy for the race and they often put the second driver on to an alternate strategy, so that they cover the second-best option. But putting both drivers on the same preferred tactic means a team is putting all their eggs in one basket.

If executed properly, the first comes in and pits and leaves his pit box just as the other car arrives, in one seamless move. Neither driver loses any time waiting for the other to finish their stop and both drivers are on the optimum strategy. It is not, however, a common tactic, as the likelihood of the pit crew making mistakes is increased when both cars are stopped within seconds of each other.

McLaren were exasperated when Norris was issued a five-second time penalty, which dropped him down to outside the points-paying positions in 13th, while Piastri finished two places ahead of him.

'An intense race,' said Norris afterwards. 'We were a little bit unlucky that I lost the position at the beginning but happy apart from that. I think the pace was OK. Of course, unfortunate we got the penalty but we'll review that as a team. Next up is Austria, one of my favourite tracks, so I'm looking forward to it. We'll give it our all and try to score some points.'

Unbeknown at the time, Norris's post-race comments in the McLaren press release would prove telling for what was about to come in the second half of the season.

CHAPTER 13

THE REVIVAL

Sometimes it can be challenging to identify the precise moment when a team turns its fortunes around, unless it is glaringly obvious, such as a decisive victory. Even then, though, there is always the suspicion that a single result could have been a flash in the pan. It is commonplace for a team desperate for an uptick in results to believe that the next set of parts off the production line will prove to be a silver bullet, and if the success comes after the introduction of a series of upgrades, then blind trust in the new parts could set them off on a pathway of limited returns.

The changes made to the car with the purpose of improving it are usually referred to as either 'updates' or 'upgrades'. These can be mechanical, to improve performance and reliability, or aerodynamic to assist handling and ultimately reduce lap times. The latter frequently get more attention because the parts are visible on the car, unlike the mechanics within the engine, which is hidden away under the bodywork. These parts are in development for months. What started out as a sketch on a notepad or computer would have been run through the computational fluid dynamics programs – highly sophisticated modelling software that predicts the airflow over a particular part.

An engineer will assess whether the new part will add performance in itself, and also whether it will complement the existing components. Teams frequently discuss design philosophy, theorising how each component works in harmony to channel airflow effectively. For instance, a series of winglets on the front wing can create a stream of air over the bodywork to generate downforce. Similarly, the endplates, the vertical sides of the front wings, redirect air around the tyres to enhance the car's stability.

McLaren's problem was that they had started 2023 with an evolution of the previous year's car, which had been conceived under Seidl, and also before several major improvements at the MTC. There had been an overhaul of the machine shop, the development of the team's wind tunnel, a new simulator, a new composites facility to assist with the production of parts, and also changes to the technical team, now headed up by Stella. His numerous positions since joining McLaren alongside Alonso at the end of 2014 had given him a comprehensive understanding of the production process and the requirements for enhancing the car's performance through updates. His insights contributed to the delivery of the first set of updates for the Austrian Grand Prix on 2 July 2023.

That Austrian GP marks a pivotal moment in McLaren's recent history, symbolising the team's turnaround on track, largely due to the new upgrades. After candidly addressing their issues at the beginning of the year, McLaren's performance in Austria provided a timely opportunity to evaluate the impact of these enhancements, even if it came slightly later than anticipated.

In pre-race build-up, the mood within the team was upbeat. Stella was making optimistic forecasts, backed up by what the data had been saying about the new parts. He now needed to see the changes work in real life on the track. Stella's pre-race confidence aroused Brown's curiosity, as he recalled in an interview he gave to the team's website. 'That was a bit unlike him. But he got it right. So, he's not afraid to lay it out there and make bold predictions, without going over the top. He just calls it as he sees it.'

At the Austrian GP, the parts, including a revised floor and significantly redesigned sidepods, were ready to be added to Norris's car only. Piastri would get them at the next race in Silverstone. While it can be unfortunate for the driver who didn't receive new parts and is not an ideal situation to improve his performance, running two different configurations allows for valuable data comparison between the drivers. McLaren's findings were supported by the results: Norris finished 4th, his best result of the season, while Piastri, with the old set-up, was placed 16th.

It was an outstanding result for Norris, and certainly no fluke. He topped the timesheets during the second qualifying session and ultimately secured fourth place on the grid for the race. In the sprint shootout, the qualifying session for the 30-minute sprint race, Norris again demonstrated his speed by qualifying in third place. Although he finished outside the points in the sprint race, he excelled in the main GP on Sunday, securing his fourth place after Ferrari's Carlos Sainz was hit with a ten-second time penalty for going off track.

As Norris returned to the team's hospitality following his debrief with the engineers, he was met with a round of applause from his McLaren team in honour of his achievement. The enthusiastic clapping interrupted Stella's media session just as the Italian was asked for his thoughts on his driver's performance. 'I think this round of applause answers your question,' he said with a smile. 'Normally in motorhomes and hospitality, you hear these noises when your driver comes from a podium or a victory. It is nice to see because this is a bit of a milestone in our journey to the front.'

Norris had admitted to feeling 'a bit nervous' that the pace would not be competitive enough but said it was 'better than I was expecting, which was a good surprise'. Meanwhile, Stella was not getting carried away, and typically called for 'prudence': 'Thanks to the upgrades we could move our competitiveness towards the top of the second group of cars, so we're effectively a bit surprised that we could compete with Mercedes, Aston Martin and even at times being near to a Ferrari. But I would again invoke prudence. This could just be Austria, conditions and kind of Lando-specific situation. Definitely need to look at Silverstone. That could possibly be more realistic.'

The British GP saw further upgrades, this time applied to both cars. The new parts significantly improved handling and resolved the porpoising issue, which had caused the cars to bounce up and down when they reached high speed. This aerodynamic effect occurred when the car was sucked so close to the ground it made contact, breaking the aerodynamic pull and causing the car to shoot upwards again. This cycle of suction into the asphalt followed by the loss of downforce made driving extremely challenging, leading to backache, headaches and even impaired vision for drivers as their heads bounced up and down in the cockpit.

McLaren's upgrades not only resolved the porpoising, but also enhanced tyre performance and increased their longevity, allowing McLaren drivers to run longer without needing a pitstop. While F1's rules require drivers to change tyre compounds during a race – such as switching from hard to soft – the extended tyre life provided McLaren's strategists flexibility in their race plans.

McLaren arrived at Silverstone with cautious optimism, tempered by a challenging start to the season. However, all doubts were swept aside when Norris qualified second and Piastri third, delivering a stunning result for the team. In the race, Norris seized the lead from pole-sitter Verstappen, thrilling the home crowd by leading for four precious laps. The sight of a McLaren at the front underscored a powerful message: 'McLaren was back in contention for victories.' Despite a wretched start to the campaign, they were now frontrunners. While Verstappen did regain P1 to win, Norris would cross the line in second place, securing McLaren's first podium at Silverstone in 13 years – since Hamilton finished runner-up to Mark Webber in 2010.

Piastri also impressed with a fourth-place finish, which would have been third had he not missed out to Hamilton, who made his pitstop during the safety-car period while the Australian had already pitted. That was hard on Piastri. 'It stings a little bit,' he said after the race. Nonetheless, he was now beginning to show some of the promise with which he had arrived at McLaren.

Hamilton hailed his former team's recovery, calling their car 'a rocket ship' in post-race interviews, and adding: 'It's great to see the McLaren back in competitive form. It's been such a long time. The most impressive part was at the end following [Norris]. Honestly, it was amazing to watch how good his car was at high speed. I know we have some work to do to catch up.'

For Norris, understated as ever, standing on the podium in his home race was 'pretty special'. He went on to reflect on his experience running at the front, albeit briefly before being reeled in by Verstappen, who would dominate the season in the Red Bull: 'It's an honour to be able to race with these drivers who have created history and are some of the best ever to come through F1. I want to be someone who can join in and create some of my own history. It's an honour and a privilege, and exciting at the same time.'

As for Stella, he had witnessed his developments validated in Austria and at Silverstone, but was reluctant to take the credit, and in his post-race interview he explained the changes in the wider team that had led to this sudden upward trajectory. He said: 'My focus is just doing the right things, focus on performance, focus on creating a vision for the team, making sure everyone understands what the vision and direction is. But the most important thing is you don't do these things alone. It is just a different way of working.' And it was working.

In the following race in Hungary, Norris secured another podium finish, taking second place, after moving up from third on the grid. Piastri, who had qualified in fourth, ended the race in fifth after a brush with Red Bull's Sergio Pérez forced him onto the grass, causing him to drop a position.

The race will be fondly remembered for Norris accidentally smashing Verstappen's first-place trophy, a handmade vase worth an estimated €40,000. Norris's champagne-spraying technique on the podium involves banging the bottle down hard, sending the fizz out of the top, but in doing so he knocked over the pricey pottery. Initially, Norris somewhat embarrassingly blamed Verstappen for 'placing it too close to the edge'. The organisers of the GP agreed to replace the trophy with a new version, and Norris joined Verstappen to collect it. Verstappen posted an image of the two of them and the new trophy with the words 'it's fixed', along with the Hungarian flag icon.

It was knockabout fun, and also testament to the friendship between the two. Over the year, the two had become close through their love of online gaming. Since Norris had not been anywhere near to competing directly against Verstappen, there was, at this point, no on-track rivalry and the two frequently travelled and socialised together.

At the Belgian GP, Piastri secured second place in the sprint race, while in the main race on Sunday, the Aussie collided with Sainz at the start, suffered suspension failure and was forced to retire. Norris, meanwhile, had looked quick in practice but was unable to take that form into the race and finished seventh. It was a similar story in Zandvoort for the Dutch GP on 27 August, where neither driver was able to capitalise on the car improvements. Norris qualified second but ended the race in seventh, while Piastri was placed in ninth.

In the post-race fallout in the media, it became clear that McLaren's pit strategy during the rain-hit race had been flawed. While the car had improved enough to compete at the front, the team's sharpness in other areas was still lacking. This phase of McLaren's development was revealing; the rapid progress of their car had exposed weaknesses that needed to be addressed, as Norris explained: 'If I start by looking at the final positions, we got some points, which is a good thing, but not as many as we should have got. We made some incorrect decisions and, on a day like today, that can win or lose you a lot of time. We were just on the losing end. We'll review it, we'll make sure we do a better job next time.'

There was further disappointment at the Italian GP, with Norris finishing in 8th place and Piastri failing to score points, ending up in 12th. The race would also provide the first signs of strain in the relationship between the two drivers. Norris had unsuccessfully requested to swap places with Piastri, feeling he should have been allowed past. The two ultimately banged wheels and were fortunate to not suffer damage to their cars. The incident was concerning for Stella, who made his disapproval clear.

'There should never ever be contact between two McLaren cars. There was a contact, which doesn't fit the way we go racing at McLaren.' Stella underlined the fact that there should be 'clear parameters as to what is acceptable' and went on to explain that no driver is bigger than the team they are driving for.

In much the same way that the British Grand Prix had validated McLaren's decision regarding upgrades, the team's overall strong performance as the F1 season left Europe reaffirmed that they were still on the right track. These results had significant implications, prompting the team to rethink their approach to races. McLaren was no longer merely aiming to consolidate points in the hope of climbing the constructors' championship; they were now serious contenders for podium finishes. While Verstappen's Red Bull remained too dominant for wins to be realistic, there was a growing sense that McLaren were best positioned to capitalise if the Dutchman made a mistake.

Furthermore, it was Norris who solidified his position within the F1 hierarchy. He was coming of age and had now firmly settled into the role as team leader. This development might not have been fully recognised at the time, given the fast-paced nature of the races and Verstappen's dominance, but in hindsight, McLaren's astonishing turnaround from that bleak start to the year was truly impressive. On 17 September in Singapore, one of the toughest tracks on the calendar due to its heat, humidity and challenging street circuit, where the slightest mistake could result in a race-ending crash, Norris finished second and Piastri seventh. George Russell's crash from second place on the final lap promoted Norris's position on the podium, highlighting McLaren's remarkable progress.

The Japanese GP marked another significant milestone in McLaren's revival, with Norris finishing second and Piastri third, securing the team a double podium behind Verstappen. It was stark contrast to the season opener in Bahrain, where both drivers failed to crack the top ten. Norris acknowledged that the improvement in performance exceeded expectations. 'The jumps we have made in terms of positions are probably more than we had been expecting,' said Norris following the result. 'I don't think at any point this season we were thinking, "Can we get close to qualifying on pole in certain places? Would we have certain podiums so early in the season?" It would have been a hard no in the beginning of the year. But we were very patient. We knew early on in we were not going to be great initially, but we also knew some good things were coming. To be quicker than Ferrari, quicker than Mercedes, from having a much worse car, I think that is what has been so impressive.'

Oscar Piastri now had his first podium finish under his belt, and his qualifying performance, where he had outpaced Norris to second place on the grid, stood out. The narrative of McLaren's remarkable revival had somewhat overshadowed the impressive nature of the Aussie's debut season. In his typically deadpan fashion, Piastri's reaction was to analyse and identify areas for improvement. 'It's nice to have that,' he said in the press conference when asked about his front-row start. 'There's not been that many Australians in F1, full stop. It's not a record I'm trying to chase, being the fifth Australian to start from the front row, but it's nice just to have that success, especially so early on in my F1 career. Some people don't get this opportunity in their entire career. So for me to have it in my first six or seven months is a privilege. But I want to try and be the next Australian to break some other records. So, a nice start, but of course, I want to be able to do more.'

Piastri would set a new record at the following race in Qatar, on the weekend of 7–8 October 2023, by becoming the first Australian driver to win an F1 sprint race. This short-race format, lasting 30 minutes with no requirement for pitstops, had been introduced in 2021 to spice up the action on Saturdays with a mini race. In Qatar, a rare mistake from Verstappen, when he went wide and had his qualifying lap times deleted, meant that Piastri started on pole for the sprint with Norris lining up in second. Piastri converted that P1 into a victory, while Verstappen's second place, ahead of Norris in third, was enough to secure the Dutchman his third world title. Although not an official grand prix, Piastri had nonetheless got a win for McLaren, coming before Norris had the chance to stand on the top step on the podium. While not publicly acknowledged, the fact that his team-mate had scored a win before him, just as Ricciardo had done in Monza, was notable. In the Qatar GP, Piastri again came out on top with second place, with Norris in third for another double podium.

Norris scored second-place finishes at both the US and São Paulo GPs, ultimately ending the year in sixth place in the drivers' championships. Notably, since the Austrian GP, he was the second-highest points scorer behind Verstappen. Piastri meanwhile was ninth in the standings. Before the race at the Red Bull Ring in Austria, McLaren had accumulated only 17 points. After the Austrian GP, they amassed an impressive 285 over the next 14 races.

At the 2023 season finale in Abu Dhabi, Zak Brown sat down in the McLaren hospitality unit to have brunch with a select group of journalists. He explained to us how he had restructured the technical department, with Stella at the top. 'He's very tough, he's very professional, very articulate in his delivery. He's not political. He's got no ego at all. And I'm pleasantly surprised, not just by what he's brought to the table, but how quickly it's had an impact. I think we all see that the turnaround has been pretty awesome'.

It was clear how enamoured Brown was with Stella's leadership: 'The impressive thing is, it's the same people but a different team because of the leadership of Andrea. His communication skills, his demand for performance. He has a great ability to look at commentary from his team through their lens. He sets clear direction, has high expectations and empowers individuals.'

A technical team principal, Stella worked with aerodynamics technical director Pete Prodromou and engineering technical director Neil Houldey, while Rob Marshall had arrived from Red Bull as chief designer and David Sanchez came from Ferrari as technical director of car concept and performance. Piers Thynne, the chief operating officer, also played a big role.

In the same interview, Brown addressed questions about his driver pairing. He expressed his admiration for both drivers, but also acknowledged how their relationship had been challenging at times, especially with McLaren's competitive standing and Norris's strong desire to secure that elusive first win. 'We know there will be a day where they are looking after their own interests but I feel Andrea and my strengths are around driver management, so I think we can get ahead of that and ensure it stays healthy.'

'I'm impressed,' said Brown when asked about Piastri. 'Surprised by how mature he is. His ability to learn has surprised me, as has his calmness for a driver of his age, and how he got rid of the rust he should have had [through not racing for a year at Alpine] pretty quickly. The speed hasn't surprised me, but I would have expected another shunt or two.

'A very experienced 24-year-old and an awesome rookie at 22 is a pretty awesome driver line-up. As I look at what we need to get back to winning world championships, it starts with two drivers who are capable of it, and I think we've got that.

Brown enthusiastically explained that the team's financial structure was robust, with 70 per cent of the F1 team owned by the McLaren Group and 30 per cent owned by MSP Sports Capital. He noted that cashflow was positive and the team was in a healthy, profitable state. He was clearly breathing a sigh of relief that the US firm MSP Sports Capital's investment had provided a crucial lifeline during the COVID shutdown, especially now that F1 was enjoying a boom in popularity and profitability.

As we finished our brunch, Brown left us with an invigorating assessment of a team on its way back from oblivion. It was in rude health financially, the driver line-up was exciting and delivering, and the management structure was also in place. The expectation level had been cranked up a couple of notches and Brown was keen to reflect this. He was adamant they had learned from the team's mistakes: 'I would rather us not have had the start of the season we had, but it's made us a better, stronger team and given us more momentum. There's a real "we can do this" energy in the team. They have started talking about taking more technical risk, being more aggressive.

'We knew we were going to be bad [at the start of 2023]. It would have been worse if we hadn't known. We were transparent about it, which gave Andrea a lot of credibility with everyone.

'The sport is tough and only getting tougher, but we are ready for it. I would be disappointed if we're not at the sharp end challenging for race wins next season.'

It was a bold prediction but one that was built on trusting the internal process that he had installed.

CHAPTER 14

OPTIMISTIC PREDICTIONS

If there had been any pessimism about McLaren's start to the 2023 season, the outlook for 2024 was decidedly different. I received an invitation to attend the MTC on Monday 15 January, an unusually early date for a season launch as teams typically spend this time refining their designs for the new season. The invitation was vague, leaving me uncertain of what to expect. Upon arrival, it was revealed that this event was a livery launch, showcasing the new colour scheme rather than the car itself. It was a confident move in the middle of the off-season, and the team had added to its workload with a media event. It would later transpire that the marketing team was also working on a special livery to celebrate Ayrton Senna's achievements as a McLaren driver.

Designing a team's livery is a complex process that involves multiple parties. First and foremost, the aerodynamics team play a crucial role. Ideally, they prefer an unpainted surface since paint adds weight. However, paint is favoured over stickers, because stickers create tiny ridges that, despite their small size, can impact the car's streamlined design. For instance, the Mercedes F1 team once used an embossed three-pointed star logo on the nose of their car but later replaced it with a painted motif to improve aerodynamics. The livery must also be approved by the paying sponsors to ensure satisfaction. Finally, the images need to be sanctioned by the FIA and Formula One Management (FOM) to ensure they work with the TV broadcasts and graphics.

The atmosphere in the MTC was incredibly laidback and a noticeable shift from 11 months earlier. Even at this early stage, there was a sense among my colleagues that this year would be a strong one for McLaren as they moved closer to their goal of challenging for the title in 2025.

Stella delivered an optimistic assessment of this year's challenger, shifting the focus of discussion away from the paintwork, which remained largely unchanged from previous versions.

'So far, I must say that we haven't observed any diminishing returns. Of course, this will need to be confirmed once we get the car on the track. However, based on our wind tunnel and CFD (computational fluid dynamics) development, the progress we made last year, which led to advancements in Austria and Singapore, appears to be sustainable. I expect this trend to continue at the start of the season. Additionally, we are already working on new developments that we hope to introduce soon, and they also look promising. Therefore, I believe that the linear progression in our development can be maintained.'

Stella was asked how this winter had been an improvement over the previous year, especially with the team's new wind tunnel now operational.

'At this time last year, we could see from the numbers – efficiency, downforce, drag – that we had hit a plateau. It was clear we needed to change our conceptual direction to regain development momentum. This year, we haven't experienced that plateau. New ideas have emerged from the technical department, forming the basis for upgrades that I expect to be implemented relatively early in the season. So, it's a completely different scenario. Not only is the organisational perception more positive, but we are also seeing significant numerical progress.'

Then attention switched to Red Bull, who had just completed the most dominant season in F1 history. Verstappen had won a record 19 of 22 races and the team had triumphed in all but one of the GPs in 2023. Such a commanding performance led to speculation that Red Bull, being so far ahead of their rivals, had shifted their focus to developing the 2024 car much earlier. Those additional weeks – or even months – of development could significantly impact their start to the 2024 campaign, potentially giving Red Bull a supremely quick car from the opening race in Bahrain. While McLaren's strong finish to 2023 had bolstered their confidence in challenging Red Bull's dominance and securing more victories, Verstappen's team remained the favourites for the title given their recent success.

Stella elaborated on some radical thinking behind his management structure, which empowered his colleagues to generate fresh ideas. Unlike most F1 teams, where the technical team is solely responsible for developing new designs to enhance the car's performance, Stella was advocating for a more collaborative approach: 'This initiative began last year, and it's crucial that we equip the team with the capability and capacity to continuously generate new ideas. We are meticulously ensuring that we can capitalise on these performance opportunities that appear to be available. While this is evident in our numbers, it is a different story when it comes to actual competitiveness on track, as that depends on what our competitors have achieved. Specifically regarding Red Bull, there's an element of uncertainty about 2024 because they didn't develop their car significantly in 2023.'

Brown also identified Red Bull as the team's biggest rivals but expressed concerns about the energy drink owning two teams on the grid: Red Bull and their sister team, RB (previously known as Alpha Tauri and before that Toro Rosso). Brown was wary of reports suggesting that RB could move from their base in Italy to the UK, potentially allowing Red Bull to pool resources and share insights from their sister team. This would violate F1's cost-cap rules, which prevent teams from spending more than a stipulated amount on car development during the season.

Brown had been outspoken about Red Bull breaching the cost cap in 2021. When the team exceeded the $145 million budget by a figure of $2.3 million, the McLaren boss called for a strict penalty. Red Bull were fined $7 million and hit with a 10 per cent reduction in their permitted allocation of aerodynamic testing time – the latter penalty was designed to hit the team hardest, for it prevented them from developing their car the following season to the same degree as the previous version. Red Bull begrudgingly accepted the penalty for the 'minor breach' in the regulations, while the FIA report stated that the bulk of that overspend was a result of the team failing to understand various exclusions, including social security benefits, sick pay and even team catering. Had Red Bull reallocated those costs in budgetary terms, they would have overspent by $550,000. This was still a significant amount when you consider that a whole new front wing, development, testing and assembly costs around $350,000. Brown's fear that Red Bull would be able to hide such breaches has so far been unfounded, given Red Bull have not violated the cap for a second time and, in the meantime, the sister team remains based in Italy, rather than moving to the UK.

Of course, McLaren's driver pairing was also a hot topic for discussions. The dynamic between Norris and Piastri was intriguing, as two evenly matched drivers of roughly the same age. This gave McLaren a vibrancy that was missing from their competitors such as Aston Martin and Mercedes, who had experienced campaigners in their squads, Alonso and Hamilton, respectively. Meanwhile, Ferrari's pairing of Charles Leclerc and Carlos Sainz lacked the colour and freshness offered by Piastri and Norris. Norris had been actively engaging on social media, amassing a new army of fans, while Piastri was more reserved, preferring to maintain his privacy. The relationship between the two was entirely different to the big-brother-style friendship Norris had enjoyed with Sainz, but it was friendlier and more complementary that the pairing of Norris and Ricciardo.

Stella was asked about his pairing, seeking an assessment of Piastri's positive debut season. He said: 'The relationship between Lando and Oscar is a point of strength in our team. I would like to recognise and acknowledge how much Lando contributes to creating the conditions for a fruitful relationship that supports the team and the growth of both drivers. When we signed Oscar, he brought similar characteristics. Through the natural process of getting to know each other, we can now see that this has led to a very, very functional collaboration between the two drivers.'

Stella explained that Norris and Piastri's driving styles allow them to interpret each other's data to assess where the other driver was stronger. This is a considerable benefit when teams need to dial in a car in a short amount of time. For instance, in the sprint races where there is only one practice session, as opposed to three during a regular race weekend, getting the practice session right is crucial. Having two drivers who prefer the same set-up in terms of car performance makes refining that set-up that much easier. This contrasts with Mercedes around this time, for example, as Hamilton preferred to brake as late as possible into corners, whereas Russell favoured a more balanced approach.

However, some of my colleagues had also detected an underlying tension between Norris and Piastri. While their relationship was an undoubted strength for the team in advancing car development, there was a steely determination behind Piastri that belied his lack of experience. Rob McIntyre describes Piastri as someone who did not reveal many emotions, making him incredibly difficult to read and second-guess.

During Button and Hamilton's time at McLaren, where they were evenly matched drivers in terms of results, Button often sought a psychological edge over his team-mate. Although he did not play practical jokes on Hamilton, he and his team capitalised on any weaknesses he displayed.

Norris, however, faced a different challenge as Piastri was unlikely to wear his heart on his sleeve and be affected by the same sort of minor psychological play. There was little in the way of emotion for him to pick up on from the Australian, should Norris seek to exploit it. By contrast, both Ricciardo and Sainz had been uncomplicated to have as fellow team drivers, in the sense that they were easy to read.

The question was put to Stella as to whether Piastri's potential would cause him a headache in the form of managing his two drivers as they competed for victories, given that Piastri already had won one sprint race. So far, the Norris and Piastri relationship had been largely harmonious and cooperative, and Stella felt there was no reason why it would change. He said: 'When you asked about Oscar winning, and you talked about the headache, my reaction wasn't headache! I look forward to it! It would be an incredible result considering what we have seen last year with Red Bull where there wasn't really much space for anybody else.'

Stella went on to explain how he hoped that his two drivers would share in their respective successes, which seemed to have rather a healthy dollop of wishful thinking. He went on to explain that, if he were to imagine Norris's response to the thought of Piastri winning a race, then he hoped Norris would use that as motivation. A win from Piastri would give assurance that the car was now quick enough to win races and he should use it to establish what he needs to do to better his team-mate and his own performance.

'This game is not only about how good you are today; this game is about how much you improve every day,' he said. 'If you look at champions in F1, Verstappen is not the same driver as he was last year or 2021 and certainly not the driver he was when he started. It's all about continuous improvement. This is definitely the way I see how Lando could process that situation. The message to the drivers has always been, what can you do to improve every day?'

The questions continued to focus on Norris and his failure to win his first F1 race. In fairness, the opportunities had been slim given Verstappen's dominance but nonetheless there had been chances. His last victory had come in the F2 season opener in Bahrain in 2018 and by now he had amassed 12 podiums without reaching the top step. Would he be able to end that wait in 2024? Ricciardo had done so in that decisive moment in Monza in 2021, but the consensus was that Norris lacked the same killer instinct and had been guilty of some mistakes in 2023. That said, Stella pointed out that his driver was the second-highest scorer after Verstappen from the Austrian GP onwards. He may not have had the victory, but he was proving extremely consistent in terms of podiums.

Stella was keen to focus on the development Norris needed to unlock his potential when it came to fighting at the very front. He explained how 'Lando is unexplored as to how good he is. Sometimes he surprises us with some of the performances he can put together.' But, crucially, he added, 'Consistency in this kind of delivery, this is what makes the difference, so that's the ethos and the top objective for 2024'.

Stella knew his driver was good enough to end that drought but required him to adjust his focus in order to capitalise when the opportunity came up. As well as wanting to see a change in Norris, Stella also felt the team had let their drivers down. He opened up about the focus on McLaren's mentality, as being in a position to fight for wins was alien for much of the team. From a management point of view, Stella was being protective but it also showed he felt there was still plenty of work to do within his team. He said: 'The first victory is always the most important because you get some confidence with it. But, at the moment, I would say the main reason why this has not been possible is because we haven't put Lando in contention to consistently compete for the victory. So, when Lando wins his first race, it will be a beautiful moment ... So we look forward to it and hopefully we'll have the opportunity in 2024.'

Things had significantly improved off track as the results improved on it and McLaren was now on solid financial footing. Memories of furloughing staff during COVID were still relatively fresh but as the sport continued to grow, F1 teams rode the wave of popularity into rude financial health. The boom in popularity showed no sign of slowing down and the 2024 season would see F1 embark on its longest ever season, taking in a record 24 GPs – two more races than the previous record.

The lengthy calendar and the sold-out races were not the only metric for measuring F1's popularity, for the sponsors on McLaren's car were noticeable. Brands such as Chrome, Android, Cisco, Dell, Monster Energy, Jack Daniel's, Lego and Coca-Cola all held sponsorship deals related to the McLaren car in a portfolio that contained over 50 partners. Brown's words about the financial health of the team were largely unreported but nonetheless significant, given that the Bahrain Mumtalakat Holding Company, the Bahrain sovereign wealth fund which had been an investor since 2007 and boosted its shareholding in 2020, would later take full ownership of the McLaren Group in March 2024.

'For the Formula One team, we're fiscally very healthy,' said Brown. 'We turned a profit last year for the first time in quite some time, and anticipate continuing to do so. We're 70 per cent owned by McLaren Group, 30 per cent MSP Sports Capital and UBS, so we're a separate entity [from the McLaren Group]. Obviously we share a brand with McLaren Automotive. The stronger they are, the better. We work very closely together, but that is a separate entity, so what happens there, it is good news for Automotive, it gives them the resources and the commitment they need, much like Mumtalakat provided us when they brought in the investment, that was to give us the resources we needed to get back to where we are now, challenging for podiums and being fiscally healthy, and being able to invest in drivers like Lando and Oscar.'

Just ten days after launching the MCL38, McLaren confirmed that Norris had signed a new multi-year deal with the team. The announcement was made on 26 January 2024, a month ahead of preseason testing in Bahrain and ahead of the season-opening Bahrain Grand Prix on 2 March. Norris already had a contract running until the end of 2025, having signed it in 2022, but his impressive performances in 2023 prompted McLaren to secure his services for a longer period. Although the specific details were not disclosed, it was widely believed that the new deal would extend beyond 2026 and into 2027.

Norris had already attracted interest from other top teams, including Red Bull, particularly with doubts over Sergio Pérez's future. Mercedes was another potential suitor – but with Charles Leclerc signing a new deal a day before Norris's announcement and Lewis Hamilton's move to Ferrari for 2025 announced on 1 February, Norris was not considered an option for the Italian team. German car giant Audi, however, which planned to acquire the Sauber team from 2026, would likely have had Norris high on their wish list.

So why did Norris decide to stay with McLaren, especially when the team had yet to provide him with a car capable of winning races regularly?

'I'm convinced, as a team, we have everything we need to achieve both the team's goals and my personal goal of winning titles. Am I convinced I'm capable of doing it? Yes. And I'm convinced the team is capable of doing it. Yes. It's everything that happens day to day: the people here, the work ethic, the mentality, the approach to everything. The atmosphere, the camaraderie we've built over the years. I enjoy being part of all of that. I want to be part of this story of turning things around, going from the struggles at the beginning of my F1 career, going through the ups and downs, and sticking with the team. I love racing, and I love to have fun and enjoy it. For me, that's the number one thing at the end of the day – doing what I love with a team that I love and enjoy every moment with. When you factor these things together, the improvements we've made, it was definitely an easy decision.'

When asked about interest from other teams given his six second-place finishes in 2023, Norris explained that he felt a sense of loyalty to McLaren for giving him his initial break in F1, although he admitted to enjoying the rumours in the press about driver movements now that he was off the market.

'I've always enjoyed seeing what you guys write every now and then. I'm always focused on what I need to be focused on. For the whole team, that's really the most important thing. I'm sure when one of your drivers is linked to other teams, it's probably not easy to see. So from my side, giving everyone at McLaren that bit more confidence in me and showing my confidence in the team was important. I'm committed to the team and staying.'

This commitment proved to be a massive boost for everyone at McLaren heading into the new campaign.

CHAPTER 15
THE CONTENDER

Preseason testing in Bahrain was dominated by one topic alone, and it had nothing to do with McLaren or indeed F1. The talk was all about Red Bull boss Christian Horner, who was the subject of an internal investigation by the team's parent company, the energy drink maker based in Austria. Little was known about the investigation or the accusation of inappropriate behaviour, and Horner has always denied the allegations.

The paddock gossip went into overdrive and the speculation was rampant. There was a growing sentiment that Horner might not be able to retain his position within the team, and could either step down or be removed as team principal. It seemed unthinkable that this team, which had won all but one of the 22 races in 2023, was facing such a predicament and so much uncertainty. If Horner were to leave, considering he had been with the team since January 2005, what impact would it have on the reigning champions? Would it lead to Adrian Newey also departing? And what about Max Verstappen? Would he too leave the team in the wake of the allegations? There were so many questions.

One thing was certain: the situation was unsettling for Red Bull and presented an opportunity for their rivals to take full advantage and keep the pressure up on Horner. As brutal as it sounds, there is little room for friendship within F1. It is a ruthless mix of entertainment, business and sport, and any show of weakness is immediately exploited by rival teams for maximum gain.

Despite the media storm, Horner vowed to attend the preseason test – and did – insisting it was business as usual. However, the debacle raised many questions about the team's management and structure, while gossip swirled around who was supporting Horner and, crucially, who wasn't. There was also a real sense this could be the end for the all-conquering team, depending on the outcome of the internal investigation.

But if Red Bull's rivals were hoping that the off-track drama would impact their preseason testing programme, they were in for a disappointment. On the opening day, Verstappen posted the quickest time. The Red Bull driver's fastest lap around Bahrain's Sakhir circuit was 1.1 seconds ahead of Norris's McLaren – a considerable margin given McLaren's pre-test optimism. Verstappen had also shaved 1.5 seconds off his best lap time during the 2023 test.

Brown and Stella's fears that the RB20 car would be the result of months of work, given Red Bull hadn't needed to spend time developing the dominant RB19 to stay ahead of their competitors, proved correct. Despite already having the most successful car in F1 history, Red Bull had moved on with a new design concept, featuring a sculptured sidepod arrangement with various slits cut into the bodywork to assist its aerodynamic performance, which had their rivals scratching their heads.

For McLaren, the focus was on ensuring that their efforts developing the MCL38 over the winter would come to fruition once the car was running on track. There was nothing the team could do about Verstappen's place at the top of the timing screens. Instead, Norris's best was good enough for second. He was pleased with his opening 73 laps and said, 'First of all, I'm really happy to be back behind the wheel. Our first test with the new car felt very enjoyable and it was reliable, so all in all, a positive day.'

For Piastri, who managed to put in 57 laps on the opening day of the test, the focus was also on the way the day had gone without a hitch, as he described his first timed run of the season as a 'pretty solid day', and echoed Norris's sentiment that the new car was an improvement on the last edition.

On day two, Norris again looked the quicker of the two McLarens, although a fuel system problem had curtailed some of his track time, and he also identified some refinement requirements in how the car handled. He notched up 52 laps and admitted to running 'into some small issues', but feedback from the team suggested that, despite not being totally problem-free, it was shaping up to be a solid test for the team.

A clutch issue on the third day proved more troublesome for Norris, who only put in 20 laps during his final half-day of testing, before he handed over to Piastri. While Norris struck a less optimistic tone, reflecting on the 'one or two setbacks here and there', Piastri was able to recover from the clutch issue, and the Aussie racked up 90-odd laps around the circuit.

Revealingly, both drivers identified Ferrari and Red Bull as the teams to beat, noting that they had enjoyed trouble-free runs and had looked quick during the test, and the McLaren duo were concerned that they would be third in the pecking order – at best. Mercedes, too, looked to have made improvements over the winter. On day one, it was Verstappen who led Norris and then Ferrari's Sainz. Day two, it was Sainz's time at the top of the timesheets while Pérez was second quickest in his Red Bull, Hamilton occupied third spot in his Mercedes, and Norris was fourth. And on the final day, it was again a Ferrari that was quickest, with Leclerc setting the pace ahead of Russell's Mercedes and Piastri down in seventh place.

Norris said: 'We're definitely quite a chunk behind Ferrari and quite a chunk behind Red Bull – I think they're clearly a long way ahead. Apart from that, we're still not in a bad position. We're probably just around that next pack. Those two teams definitely seem to have a decent advantage over everyone else.'

It looked like McLaren's solid end to 2023 would not be carried forward into 2024, with some media outlets predicting a mid-table result at this early stage of the year.

In summing up, Norris added: 'It was not the end of the world, definitely, but you always want a perfect day ... but still plenty of things learned and a lot of stuff that I wanted to get done. I was happy for the most part, but [there are] a couple little things that I wish I could have done more.'

Norris's comments were understandable, and were probably prompted by his frustration at realising he would not be starting the season with the quickest car. Piastri echoed the views of his team-mate, identifying Ferrari and Red Bull as favourites.

The drivers' assessment was fair and perhaps reflected a feeling of deflation after such a strong end to the previous campaign and a positive winter. That said, of course, this was only testing and the real challenge would come in the season-opening Bahrain Grand Prix.

Stella adopted a pragmatic approach and in his media session presented an alternative view. The Italian spoke about improving the car's weaknesses from the previous year, highlighting rear grip as a particular area of progress. He said: 'From a performance point of view, the car delivers what we expected. No big surprises, which in itself is good news, because there are some elements of innovation. I think the MCL38 is a good foundation for development, and is a step forward compared to last year's car.'

So, McLaren had improved, but their rivals had not stood still, and it was clear that all the turmoil surrounding Red Bull internally had not affected the team's performance in testing. Stella added: 'Overall, I can see that many cars have made the step forward, which is normal. Everyone finds performance in every week of development. There's one car that seemed to have found a big step. Unfortunately, the car that was already the quickest last year. I would say the [chasing] group was already quite compact last year, and to me it looks like even more compact this year.'

Ultimately, in summary, Stella was pleased with the way the three-day test had gone and the team were heading into the opening race of the year very well prepared. He too would admit to being 'prudent' given Ferrari and Red Bull's obvious form, but nonetheless, there was a positive feeling as the team approached the new season.

• • •

Ahead of the 2024 season, it was clear that Norris was on manoeuvres to challenge Verstappen for the title. He ended the 2023 season reflecting on what he could have done better, as he analysed a near-perfect run of results for Verstappen. Yet, as we have seen, thanks to those McLaren upgrades, he had finished the second half of the season as the second-highest scoring driver, taking 193 points from the Austrian GP onwards, outscoring Red Bull's Sergio Pérez by 34 points and Hamilton by 71 points during that period. Pérez and Hamilton had finished second and third in the championship, respectively.

Verstappen had been dominant most of the season, but there were moments when Norris could have been more aggressive in his battles with the world champion, particularly as he fought his way through the field at the US GP in Austin and in Brazil. In Brazil, Norris surged from P6 to P2 off the start line, and briefly challenged Verstappen for the lead. After the race, Verstappen acknowledged Norris's effort, saying his opponent 'gave it a good go', and expressing his belief that Norris would be contending for more wins in the future. 'I know how good Lando is and it's nice to see him up there,' Verstappen remarked after the São Paulo race. 'He deserves that as well, McLaren deserves that. Hopefully we'll have many more battles.'

Over the years, within the media, we've seen how Norris's relationship with Verstappen has developed. It was as close as any driver had got to being friends with Verstappen, who typically keeps himself to himself. On top of their shared fondness for gaming, they were fellow residents of Monaco and would sometimes socialise together.

During the preseason interviews, Stella urged Norris to become more consistent, like Verstappen, a challenge that would inevitably put him on collision course with the Red Bull driver. Stella, having worked with Michael Schumacher, Kimi Räikkönen and Fernando Alonso, was essentially asking Norris to adopt a more ruthless approach. Consequently, we were eager to see if Norris could not only deliver the consistency that Stella demanded, but also evolve as a driver to stand up to a competitor as formidable as Verstappen. Would he be able to outmuscle possibly the most aggressive driver on the grid?

Another aspect was mental toughness. The anguish Norris displayed when he fell short or made a mistake in 2023 was evident. How would this change when those errors were costing him wins, rather than simply points?

A third element, as we headed into the 2024 season, was how he would contend with Piastri. We had seen how the Australian had made an excellent start to his F1 career, taking the victory, and the team's first pole of the season, at the Qatar sprint race. Later in the season, Norris had taken pole himself for the sprint race in Brazil, where he went on to finish second to Verstappen in the short-race format. And in the actual São Paulo GP on Sunday, despite lining up in sixth on the grid, he also finished up on the second step of the podium behind Verstappen. The head-to-head comparison with his team-mate in 2023 was all in Norris's favour. He'd scored 205 points to Piastri's 97 and edged their qualifying battle 15 to 7. As much as Stella wanted to detract from talk about the tension between his two drivers, it was inevitable that if they continued to fight for wins, then it would ultimately put a strain on their relationship and it was going to take some managing. Even the most optimistic F1 team principals understood that having two high-performing drivers on the same team could lead to jealousy and competition between them. Stella's wish for them to act as motivation for each other was a noble sentiment, but it was not realistic. The Norris vs Piastri subplot was intriguing and would be another storyline to watch alongside the primary Norris vs Verstappen battle.

Norris, meanwhile, was content. He had his new contract and was adamant that he was right to sign it before learning of Hamilton's switch to Ferrari. He was asked by Sky F1 about whether he regretted putting pen to paper so early in the season given that, at least in theory, Mercedes would have offered him a good shot at winning a world title. Also, if he had entered discussions with a rival team, that in turn could also have driven up the value of his McLaren contract. But Norris was unwavering. 'I'm very happy,' he said. 'I could have waited. I had the choice. I knew opportunities were potentially coming my way. I'm confident in my team, I'm confident in what we've been able to achieve and what we can achieve going into the future.'

• • •

As McLaren entered the 2024 season, it was tinged with sadness following the sudden death of Gil de Ferran. The Brazilian former racing driver, who won the Indianapolis 500 and was two-time IndyCar champion, was a respected and admired figure within motorsport. He died at the age of 56 in late December 2023. De Ferran had been instrumental in much of McLaren's recent improvements, and he was the man McLaren turned to in order to help Fernando Alonso's bid to win the Indy 500 in 2017, when the Spaniard took part in the famed race for the first time.

De Ferran and Alonso struck up a friendship that ultimately led to him becoming McLaren's sporting director from 2018 to 2021. Although he remained in the background, those inside the team knew how valuable his contribution was. None more so than Stella and Brown, who to this day continue to pay tribute to his memory and acknowledge the significant role he had in guiding McLaren during their rebuilding phase.

De Ferran's initial relationship with McLaren came to an end in 2021, but after a poor season in 2022, Brown persuaded him to return in an advisory role, as Stella set about refining his management processes in the wake of Seidl's departure. In an interview with the BBC following de Ferran's death, Stella said: 'Most people know Gil as a champion in IndyCar and so on, but personally I know him for being somebody incredibly competent in motorsport, Formula One, strategic approach, people coaching. When somebody in the team has a conversation with Gil, they always come out quite inspired and like: "Ah, I think I better understand what I have to do now."' As we will come to see, de Ferran's impact would be remembered at the end of 2024.

There were also changes behind the scenes to McLaren's ownership. Over the winter, the group's shareholders unanimously approved a full recapitalisation of the business, which would provide a 'simplified' and 'streamlined' governance process. It was a restructuring that was required as the team was starting to pull itself out of the red and into the black. The group had propped up its financial situation in 2020 in the form of a £150 million loan from the National Bank of Bahrain, and had sold a stake of its F1 team and agreed a sale and leaseback of the MTC to unlock more capital.

The restructure would see the Bahrain Mumtalakat Holding Company take full control of the business. In the accompanying press release, Paul Walsh, McLaren Group executive chairman, said: 'We are delighted at Mumtalakat's continued commitment to McLaren through this deal, which strengthens our ownership and governance structure. This will further enable us to focus on delivering our long-term business plan, including investment in new products and technologies, whilst continuing to explore potential technical partnerships with industry partners.'

It marked an advancing relationship with Mumtalakat, which first acquired a 30 per cent stake in McLaren in 2007 from former chairman Ron Dennis and Mansour Ojjeh. Mumtalakat was now the owner of the whole McLaren Group, which consisted of the supercar business, known as McLaren Automotive, the technological arm of the business, called McLaren Applied, plus McLaren Racing, of which the F1 team was just one part. It also included the team's IndyCar, Formula E and Extreme E teams.

The takeover was a huge boost, given the uncertainty over McLaren's overall financial status. For while the F1 team was turning a profit, the road-car division was making heavy losses after production stopped during the COVID pandemic. McLaren had also experienced problems with its Artura hybrid sports car. The takeover assured the company's short-term future.

There was further good news in the form of a new contract for Brown, who signed to stay on until 2030. In the same way that

Norris's commitment had buoyed the team, Brown's new long-term deal was seen as significant and another building block in McLaren's progress. He said: 'I am thrilled to continue leading McLaren Racing and to be a part of such a historic race team. It is a privilege to work alongside the talented men and women across McLaren Racing's different race series. Together, we will continue to push the boundaries of motorsport and strive for the highest performance on and off the track.' Paul Walsh hailed Brown's impact, saying he has 'demonstrated exceptional leadership qualities and has been instrumental in driving McLaren Racing forward'.

Operationally, McLaren were in good shape with key staff and their drivers under long-term deals and the automotive business now being placed on a solid footing. While the winter test had not gone totally to plan, there were plenty of optimistic faces in the team on the flight to the season opener in Bahrain.

CHAPTER 16

READY FOR PODIUMS

By 2 March 2024, the season opener in Bahrain, the furore surrounding Red Bull and the internal investigation into boss Christian Horner had escalated even further. Horner continued to deny any wrongdoing, but rival team bosses, including Brown, were calling on F1's governing body, the FIA, to intervene, seeking transparency and clarity over the accusations and how they had been handled.

Brown's role in the intervention had particularly riled Horner, coming after the American's persistent pestering of the FIA to punish Red Bull for breaching the cost cap in 2022. He had even written an open letter to the FIA and Formula One Management to complain about the overspend during the 2021 season, urging Mohammed Ben Sulayem, the FIA president, and Stefano Domenicali, CEO of the Formula One Group (FOM is an operating company of the Formula One Group), to take the breach seriously. The letter was leaked to the press and said: 'The overspend breach, and possibly the procedural breaches, constitute cheating by offering a significant advantage across technical, sporting and financial regulations.'

Brown's letter, implying cheating, was naturally dimly viewed by Red Bull, especially as the American explicitly stated, 'the bottom line is any team who has overspent has gained an unfair advantage'. While the letter had angered Horner, he was no stranger to being shot at by rival teams, but it was intriguing to watch Brown once again attempt to increase the pressure on the embattled Red Bull boss.

The initial grievance raised against Horner in early 2024 was extremely serious and it would be logical for the opposing teams to be kept informed of the accusations. However, as the matter was being handled internally by Red Bull – and crucially not Red Bull Racing – there was a sense that the FIA's jurisdiction did not extend into the wider corporate structure of the business. Nonetheless, Horner's position at this point seemed untenable.

All that changed with a press release issued from Austria on Wednesday 28 February. It said: 'The independent investigation into the allegations made against Mr Horner is complete, and Red Bull can confirm that the grievance has been dismissed.' It added: 'The investigation report is confidential and contains the private information of the parties and third parties who assisted in the investigation, and therefore we will not be commenting further out of respect for all concerned.'

Horner was in the clear. But, almost 24 hours later, I, along with a select group of people in F1, received an anonymous email claiming to be evidence of WhatsApp exchanges between Horner and the complainant. The email, its contents and distribution list seemed to have been designed to have maximum impact and eliminate Horner's presence in F1. Horner would not comment on the contents of the email, but it had plunged his future at Red Bull back into doubt.

A combustible Jos Verstappen, Max Verstappen's father, told the media 'the team is in danger of being torn apart. It can't go on the way it is. It will explode. He [Horner] is playing the victim, when he is the one causing the problems.' His comments inadvertently pulled his son into the conflict, leading to uncomfortable questions about his future with the team.

Meanwhile, a broader power struggle emerged within the Red Bull team, driven by the energy drink company's internal dynamics. The conflict was framed as a battle between Red Bull GmbH, based in Austria, and the Thai majority shareholder of the Red Bull parent company, Chalerm Yoovidhya. Chalerm, the son of co-founder Chaleo Yoovidhya, who died in 2012, holds a controlling 51 per cent share of the Red Bull company. The struggle for control intensified, following the death of Red Bull's co-founder, Dietrich Mateschitz, in 2022.

This power struggle had again shifted all attention onto Red Bull until qualifying, when the focus returned to the F1 cars.

• • •

In the lead-up to the Bahrain Grand Prix, Norris had time to reflect on the three-day preseason test. Although he had left the Middle East with a slightly pessimistic mindset, he returned the following week with a different perspective. His philosophy was that the opening race would not determine the outcome of the long season. Despite the team's increased ties with the tiny island of Bahrain through the takeover of the McLaren Group by Mumtalakat

Holding Company, the Sakhir Circuit had always proved to be tricky for the team, as Norris admitted. 'Bahrain has never been a good circuit for us. We've never had one of our strongest races here,' he said. 'But I think it's way too early to judge and say, "OK, we're not going to be great here in Bahrain, that's the end of the season for us."'

Norris's prediction proved to be accurate, as he qualified down in seventh place for the race – much to his frustration. He felt the MCL38 had the potential to challenge Verstappen for pole, but was left ruing his mistake during the final qualifying session, which had cost him a spot on the front row of the grid. 'I messed up sector one,' he said. I just had a little oversteer as I came on the throttle. It easily cost me one and a half tenths, and one and a half tenths today was easily P2. Then I felt like I wanted to push a bit more. That was the wrong thing to do and I paid the price again in turn four, another couple of mistakes. But honestly the car was easily good enough for a front row, so I'm disappointed I didn't deliver it.'

It was a bittersweet moment for the team to realise that the car was quick enough but driver error had proved to be decisive. Norris was joined on the fourth row of the grid by Piastri, who had qualified in eighth place. The Aussie was also optimistic, though, noting glimpses of pace and that Verstappen was not as far ahead as initially feared, saying that it 'hopefully sets up an interesting year'.

As for the opening race, both Norris and Piastri were unable to make much progress from their starting positions, with the former coming home in sixth while Piastri was eighth. Verstappen, despite the turmoil at Red Bull, won the race.

It had proved to be a solid, if not spectacular, opening weekend and a decided improvement on the previous year. Perhaps the biggest concern was continued weakness in the low-speed corners. These corners have a larger turning angle where the cars require harder braking than normal to bring the car's speed down without it losing traction, as opposed to fast corners where a driver would simply lift off the throttle and allow aerodynamic downforce to slow the car to make the corner. Norris's frank assessment was that it was 'no different to last year', in that the car was still a handful under braking, adding: 'It's clear there's a lot of areas we need to focus on still, and to improve on, if we want to be more consistent and challenge.'

But putting a positive spin on it, he pointed out that the fact the track exposed a well-known, inherent weakness in the car was not a shock, and also that the result was not a true reflection of the pace of the car, as both drivers had been able to do battle with Mercedes's Hamilton and Russell.

Stella was equally pragmatic and, instead of reflecting of the missed opportunity in qualifying, listed the positives from the opening race: 'It's good to begin the season with a strong performance here in Bahrain. We've been reliable, we were quick enough to fight the Mercedes, and this allowed us to score good points at a track we know isn't the best for the characteristics of our car. It's a good foundation for the further improvements we plan to introduce as soon as possible.'

At the Saudi Grand Prix, which came the following week, McLaren looked solid but were lacking the pace to rival Red Bull and Ferrari, who again had the quicker cars. There was a slight anomaly in the proceedings when Sainz suffered from appendicitis, prompting Ferrari to call up 18-year-old Brit Oliver Bearman as his replacement for qualifying and the race. Bearman, who was enrolled in the Ferrari young driver academy and had been taking part in Formula Two events, impressed by qualifying in eleventh place, narrowly missing out on reaching the top ten, while Piastri qualified in fifth and Norris was in sixth.

In the race, Piastri quickly passed Alonso to move into fourth place. Following Lance Stroll's crash, the safety car was deployed, allowing Piastri to stop for hard tyres. While the rest of the field also took the opportunity to switch to fresh tyres, Norris stayed out and took the lead in P1. However, at the restart he couldn't hold off Verstappen, who was on fresh tyres, and was subsequently passed by Pérez and Leclerc as well. Norris eventually pitted on lap 37, rejoining the track in eighth place where he managed to fend off a challenge from Hamilton. Meanwhile, Piastri maintained the fourth place he had gained at the start in what was an impressive performance.

Norris was ambivalent about the result, which had seen him drop back two places from where he had qualified, but he praised the team for rolling the dice during the safety-car period. 'You never know at the time,' he said afterwards, 'and we wanted to try something different, and not just stay behind. We could have gained a lot of points, or we could have lost a few. And in the end, we lost a few. But that's just the way it is sometimes. So it was a good try, I think it was the correct call to make. Sometimes I feel like we're a little bit safe. It's nice to be a little bit more aggressive, and try something different. So I'm happy with our decision. It wasn't the best one, or let's say the correct one. But that's in hindsight.'

The media also took note of this shift in McLaren's strategy. The team, which had been overly cautious at times in 2023, demonstrated a newfound willingness to gamble on the possibility of another safety car, a common occurrence on the high-speed Saudi circuit. Had there been another safety car or indeed a red flag situation while Norris was leading, the outcome would have been significantly different. For Piastri, however, his fourth-place finish was the best the team could have realistically hoped for.

After the first two races of the season, there was a short break before the Australian GP, which allowed McLaren to regroup and assess the start of their campaign. The team was undoubtedly in a stronger position than it had been 12 months earlier, competing with Mercedes for the title of the third-fastest team behind Red Bull and Ferrari, but the Italian team's form had prevented McLaren from securing a podium. While the overall assessment was positive, some inherent problems remained, particularly in those slow-speed corners and comparatively poor top speed. However, McLaren was aware of these challenges and Stella had already initiated plans for considerable upgrades, though the extent of these changes was kept under wraps. The updates were expected to be available around races six or seven, likely Miami or Imola. Until then, there was still performance to be found in the upcoming races.

The Australian Grand Prix on 24 March proved to be a seminal moment in the 2024 season for several reasons, partly because it featured the use of team orders from the McLaren pit wall, a subject that would spark considerable debate throughout the season. Additionally, the race in Melbourne provided another opportunity for Piastri to impress, following his solid showing there in 2023 in front of his home fans.

From the outset, Norris had looked especially quick and he topped the timesheets for first practice as the team experimented with a different set-up for Piastri. Meanwhile, Verstappen and the two Ferrari drivers edged the second and third sessions. However, in qualifying, Norris and Piastri performed much better, taking fourth and sixth place respectively.

A penalty from the stewards for Pérez, who was found guilty of blocking Nico Hulkenberg, saw the Mexican demoted three places on the grid. As a result, Pérez lined up in sixth place on the grid for Sunday's race. This meant the McLaren duo both benefitted, with Norris inheriting P3 and Piastri starting in fifth.

Verstappen, who had won the opening two races and taken pole in Melbourne, was soon overtaken by Sainz and started radioing his team about brake issues. He retired the car on the fourth lap, marking a rare moment of poor reliability from Red Bull. The upshot was that Norris found himself in second, while Piastri had made his way to third.

In the hope of preserving their positions, McLaren called in Piastri for hard tyres on lap nine. By stopping before his teammate, Piastri returned to the track on fresher tyres and was able to eat into Norris's advantage. When Norris made his stop on lap 14, he returned to the track behind Piastri, who had executed what is commonly known as the undercut. This strategy, although fairly common, requires precise calculations. Teams employ mathematicians to work out the permutations of when to pit a driver, optimising the strategy for the correct call. On this occasion, it allowed Piastri to make up two places, now running in third place, which he had inherited from Norris.

The downside of making an early pitstop is that tyres wear out sooner than those of other drivers with fresher rubber. When Piastri started to struggle with tyre wear and Norris was catching him up, McLaren issued the order for the two drivers to swap positions. It was hard on Piastri, especially since Verstappen and Hamilton's retirements had eliminated two of his podium rivals, making a top-three finish in his home race a real possibility. However, there was no doubt that Norris was the quicker, so McLaren delivered the order for Piastri to allow Norris to pass. Norris went on to secure a third-place finish, while Piastri had to settle for fourth.

Piastri said he had no hard feelings about the team's call and instead admitted he felt he had let himself down with 'too many mistakes' on his final lap in qualifying, which could have seen him start further up the grid. 'For me, it was completely fair. Norris qualified in front of me yesterday, went a bit longer on the first stop and he was catching me and was quicker at that point of the race. I was keeping with Leclerc and Lando was catching both of us, so I was honestly kind of hoping he'd be past me and go and get Charles. Of course, at home, I would have loved to be able to stay in third. But for me, that was completely fair.'

Norris was delighted with the podium, but, typically, couldn't help reflecting on the missed opportunity for a second-place finish, noting how Leclerc had benefitted from an early pitstop, similar to Piastri. Norris said afterwards. 'I'm very happy and proud of the team as P3 and P4 are a lot of points in the championship, so that's the first thing,' Norris said afterwards. 'We missed out on Charles

[Leclerc]. I think our pace was a little bit better. He undercut us in the first stint so there was maybe a little bit of hope for second place. Our pace was strong enough today but Ferrari and Carlos [Sainz, who won the race] did a very good job, so hats off to them. They've been fast all weekend. I probably wasn't expecting to be on the podium so I'm very happy.'

It was increasingly evident that McLaren were getting closer to competing for wins but the team order had become a point of interest. Norris had expressed his feelings over the radio, and while Piastri said he understood McLaren's decision, it did not sit well with the Australian crowd. Stella maintained that the decision was not part of a broader team strategy, but rather driver management to improve both drivers' chances of making it on to the podium.

In his post-race media session, Stella painted a positive picture, saying: 'I would say that swap wasn't even strategic. That was executional. The swap would have happened naturally because Lando had much fresher tyres. Lando was always going to overtake Oscar. We called the swap to avoid that this comes to unnecessary racing, unfair racing – Lando had much, much fresher tyres.'

Confrontation was averted, at least for the time being, but Norris's assertiveness was something of which Piastri was now acutely aware.

By the Japanese Grand Prix on 7 April, McLaren had found their rhythm and, much like in the second half of 2023, were proving to be quick from the outset of each GP weekend. While some teams struggled to hone their cars' performance over the practice sessions, McLaren seemed to start with a solid benchmark at each race. This trend continued at Suzuka, where Piastri topped the second qualifying session. Unfortunately, he was unable to replicate this form in final qualifying and had to settle for sixth on the grid. Norris, however, managed to secure third place and spoke afterwards about making 'some good steps forward'.

Sadly, he was unable to capitalise on the second-row start, and finished in fifth place while Piastri ended up in eighth. Verstappen's victory in Japan extended his lead in the drivers' championship to 77 points, placing him 40 points ahead of Norris, who was in fifth place. The constructors' championship showed a similar picture, with Red Bull accumulating 141 points in the opening four races while McLaren, in third behind Ferrari, had 69 points.

• • •

In the days after the Japanese Grand Prix, the team announced changes to its management structure, revealing that David Sanchez had left the team. On paper, this appeared to be a bizarre situation. Sanchez had left Ferrari in March 2023 but had been placed on gardening leave until 1 January 2024 before he was allowed to join up with McLaren, so he would be unable to pass on any information about Ferrari's challenge. Now, just four months later, he was leaving McLaren.

The reason for his sudden departure was that the role he had intended to take up no longer existed within the team. As Stella explained, the position they had initially discussed 12 months earlier had evolved, mainly because of McLaren's dramatic improvements on track. The new structure placed Stella at the top as team principal, while also holding the role as technical director of performance.

As we have seen, Rob Marshall had taken up the role of chief designer, effectively becoming responsible for developing the car concept, with Neil Houldey as technical director of engineering and Peter Prodromou remaining as technical director of aerodynamics. By keeping the team to three key individuals – plus Stella – decision making became much quicker, allowing parts to be pushed through to development more efficiently. There no longer seemed such a need for Sanchez's role as director of car concept and performance. A few weeks later, Sanchez joined Alpine as executive technical director.

McLaren's strong start to the season, particularly by Norris, continued in Shanghai with the return of the Chinese GP for the first time since 2019 due to the COVID pandemic.

The race itself was a thriller and punctuated by safety-car deployments but Norris managed to keep his head, moving up from fourth ultimately to finish second behind Verstappen, with an exceptional drive. After the race, Norris quipped: 'Whenever I finish behind Max, I feel like it's a win!' This result, understated at the time, proved to be of great significance. Notably, Norris had earlier taken a brilliant pole position for the sprint race, only to run wide under pressure from Hamilton and finish sixth, just ahead of Piastri. In qualifying, the McLaren duo again demonstrated evenly matched performances, lining up in fourth and fifth on the grid.

The significance of the Chinese Grand Prix result was that it confirmed the team's progress with the development of their car, and this improvement had come earlier than expected. Norris and Piastri now knew they had the tools to fight for podiums consistently, not just at tracks that suited the car's set-up. This realisation had lifted the spirits of the entire team.

For Norris, the result established him as the nearest challenger to Verstappen, who remained untroubled out in front. It also demonstrated a mental fortitude, proving he could overcome the frustration and disappointment of mucking up in the sprint race.

Despite his second-place finish in the grand prix, Norris was still lamenting the missed opportunity in the sprint. He had performed excellently in sprint qualifying and his inability to capitalise on it still irked him. When asked about the podium finish, he laughed and said, 'I didn't make a mistake in turn one and go off!' referring to his error 24 hours earlier. He added, 'A great day, really a surprise, so very happy for myself and for the whole team, more importantly. Definitely exceeded our expectations but a lot of things went our way.'

Norris's response embodied his honesty, delight and relief at McLaren's progress, while also stopping short of overblowing the result and his own achievement. His half-joking comment about his 'mistake' was endearing, showing he was still hard on himself and striving for perfection by focusing on the weekend's negative aspect.

Such was his pessimism that it later emerged he had a bet with his McLaren mechanics that he would cross the line 35 seconds behind Leclerc's Ferrari in the main race – even though the Frenchman was starting in seventh place, three places behind Norris. 'Happy to be wrong with myself,' Norris said. The reality was that Ferrari no longer had the pace to match McLaren, who had the second-quickest car.

For Stella, seeing Piastri finish eighth after a challenging race in which he sustained damage from Daniel Ricciardo, it was the first time he publicly expressed confidence in catching Red Bull. The result was a shot in the arm and further proof that his process and the technical restructuring were yielding results. With ongoing uncertainty surrounding Red Bull and the long-term impact from their internal investigation still unknown, Stella hailed the team's 'strong trajectory', adding, 'If we keep this strong trajectory for the next 12 months, why not? We may reach Red Bull.'

Meanwhile, Norris's performance provided Stella with further confirmation that he was now progressing as a driver. Having previously challenged Norris to show the same level of consistency as Verstappen, Stella was pleased to see him driving at a higher level, aside from the sprint-race error. He was consistently quick and his race craft was now mighty impressive. In Shanghai, he had carefully managed his tyre life, making it easier for the team's strategists to determine the optimum pitstop strategy. Stella revealed in the post-race media sessions how Norris had worked with the team over the winter to analyse his weaknesses, such as his errors in qualifying, and focused on how to make improvements.

Still, though, a win eluded him. When asked on Sky F1 whether he believed he would finally secure his maiden victory in a GP, Norris was unequivocal. He sensed it was coming. 'Max is doing a good job,' he said, 'Red Bull are doing an amazing job. I can't fault them and I can't be too annoyed at that. But I feel like I am getting a lot out of the car, especially on Sundays. So I have to be happy with the job I'm doing and one day, I think, it's coming. I think we can get a win this year.' Norris had said 'year', but deep down he knew the pressure was building on him to get that victory sooner rather than later, now that McLaren again had a competitive car.

CHAPTER 17
THE TIDE TURNS?

'Woooooo! Woooooo! About fucking time ... I love you all. I love you all. Thank you so much. We did it! We did it!'

Norris's radio message to his team after winning the Miami Grand Prix on 5 May 2024 still brings a smile to my face.

'Thanks, Mum, thanks, Dad. This one's for my grandma. Thank you very much.'

It was his 110th F1 race and, finally, he'd managed to win one. During my time in Formula One, I don't remember a more popular winner of a Grand Prix. The press room has no view of the track, so we saw him cross the finish line on the TV monitors, and the usually divided and partisan press corps burst into a spontaneous round of applause. For those of us who had followed Norris's ascendency to F1, the difficult early years in a below-strength car and the pain of those missed opportunities, this was the moment we had been waiting for.

• • •

The Miami weekend had started with some good news for McLaren. One full upgrade had been produced and delivered ahead of time, and it was added to Norris's car. Piastri received only a partial upgrade. The results were promising, with Piastri clocking the second-fastest time behind Verstappen in the sole practice session of the sprint-race weekend. During sprint qualifying, Norris topped the first and second sessions, finding more pace than any other driver. However, in the third session he couldn't match his previous best and qualified in ninth, while Piastri was sixth.

The sprint race saw Piastri consolidate his sixth place, while Norris was caught up in an accident that involved Hamilton, Alonso and Lance Stroll, and was forced to retire. As he made his way back to the pits, he walked across a live race track without permission from the stewards, earning himself a €50,000 fine, half of which was suspended. Norris had not come close to being struck by a passing car, but the fine was issued to send a message to the lower levels of motorsport that drivers cannot cross a live track until told to do so by a marshal acting under instructions from race control.

Qualifying for the main race had also been unspectacular, with Norris lining up fifth on the grid and Piastri in sixth, behind the two Ferraris of Leclerc and Sainz, and the Red Bulls of Pérez and Verstappen. But in the race, an early lock-up by Pérez nearly took out Verstappen, Sainz and Leclerc, forcing them to take evasive action. This allowed Piastri to jump to second behind Verstappen. For the first 28 laps, it seemed like the Aussie might be McLaren's top finisher. Then Verstappen pitted on lap 23, due to a damaged front wing, allowing Piastri to inherit P1. Piastri then pitted from the lead along with Sainz on lap 27, dropping them both behind Verstappen. However, Norris had preserved his tyres and when a safety car came out a lap later, it turned the race on its head. Norris pitted on lap 29, effectively getting a free pitstop, and rejoined ahead of Verstappen in the lead. When the safety car returned to the pit lane, Norris was forced to defend his lead from Verstappen. He did so with aplomb, maintaining a good pace and holding off the Red Bull man, who couldn't match his speed. As Norris ran out in front, in clean air, it looked like he would finally secure his first victory.

The weather was consistently warm and dry and, barring any mistakes or further safety cars, he was poised to be crowned the winner. The final few laps were certainly nerve-wracking as he navigated the Miami circuit to take the chequered flag 7.612 seconds ahead of Verstappen, with Leclerc finishing third. Piastri would end the race in 13th.

After the race, a clearly jubilant Norris paid tribute to the team: 'I'm just proud, really. I mean, a lot of people doubted me along the way. I've made a lot of mistakes over my last five years, but today we put it all together, so this is all for the team. I stuck with McLaren because I could believe in them, and I did believe in them, and today proved exactly that.'

Norris's father Adam attends most of his races but, as bad luck would have it, he was not there in Miami to witness his son's maiden win. 'My family are the ones who got me into racing, supported me, and allowed me to get to Formula One to reach my dream and do what I've loved to do since I was a kid. I literally remember now being at the race track for the very first time in my life. My brother, my dad and me just standing there and watching and just seeing the cars go by. Today, being on top of the podium, you think of those moments.'

When I asked about his message for his grandma, he added: 'She's not been so well lately. I saw her last week and I told her that I was going to win a race and I didn't say when. I didn't think it would be coming this soon, so I'm just very happy that I was able to as quickly as I did.' It was a touching moment.

He continued: 'A lot of people doubted that McLaren could win races. They doubted that I could win races. But I was confident. Deep down I knew that our time was coming. We've chipped away, especially the last couple of months. A win today would have been a lot less likely without these upgrades, so, I would like to say it's the start. And now I'm already hungry for more.'

Reporters wanted to know if during the race he was haunted by memories of Russia 2021, when he slid off the track while leading from Hamilton in the wet, which seemed to strike a nerve: 'Russia '21 was a very, very different situation to today. A lot of people talk crap about Sochi and the things which went on, and say they doubted I could go out and win races, and perform under the pressure of leading, especially with Max behind. But this year I've been much better at keeping my mind focused. I'm doing a good job. I'm fast and I'm executing things exactly how I want to do. I've improved on a lot of my weaknesses and all that hard work has paid off. So no, I wasn't thinking of [Russia]. I was smiling. And I was thinking, "How am I going to celebrate?"'

Norris was clearly relieved finally to prove people wrong after years of pressure and self-expectation. Norris added that he had always held respect for the people he raced against so when he got out of his McLaren, it meant a lot to him to have Alonso, Hamilton, Verstappen, Sainz and Leclerc congratulate him.

It was a joy to witness the McLaren team celebrate. All the engineers and mechanics, the marketing and communications teams and the catering and hospitality staff gathered together for the photographers. Eventually, Norris turned up and the champagne was cracked open, sending papaya-clad staff running in all directions. Ferrari's team principal Fred Vasseur was among them, congratulating his friend Brown, who had tossed him a McLaren hat to wear. It was unusual to see a rival team boss celebrating another team's win so publicly – usually it would be an exchange of WhatsApp messages – but this felt like a big moment. Not only had Norris's win broken new ground for the driver, but it had also set McLaren up to compete with, and even surpass, Red Bull. There was a palpable sense that the tide was turning.

• • •

The win for Norris was another moment for Brown to reevaluate the team's progress under his stewardship. They had come a long way since those dreadful days with Honda when the team struggled to finish races. As ever, he took time publicly to thank everybody for their input. In the weeks that followed back in the MTC, it was clear that there was a lot of respect for the American, and the way he was running the team with Stella.

Expectation levels shot up after Miami and there was almost a feeling that Norris would go on and win the next race in Imola. His first win could open the floodgates, positioning McLaren as strong challengers to Red Bull in the constructors' championship. And the Brit could also now take the fight to Verstappen, who was still facing questions about his future in the team. These uncertainties were exacerbated by relentless overtures from Mercedes boss Toto Wolff, who had made it abundantly clear he wanted Verstappen to replace the departing Hamilton.

McLaren's pace in Miami proved to be no fluke and, after looking strong in practice at Imola, Piastri qualified in second place while Norris was third. It was incredibly close, however. Verstappen had struggled for performance and was down the timesheets on all three practice sessions, but he found form in qualifying, taking pole ahead of Piastri, who was then dealt a blow when he was penalised for impeding Kevin Magnussen. The grid drop that moved Piastri down to fifth inadvertently moved Norris up to second, alongside Verstappen in P1.

It left the situation deliciously poised as Norris prepared to go head-to-head with Verstappen, now armed with a newfound level of confidence after breaking his duck. In the press room at Imola there was a sense that, for the first time since facing Hamilton's challenge at the tail end of the 2021 season, Verstappen was no longer entirely sure of his ability to win a race.

The race would prove to be a slow burner for McLaren. Norris, who was biding his time and preserving his hard tyres, eventually picked up the pace and started hunting down Verstappen. He closed the gap to just 1.6 seconds with five laps to go, and the spectators were treated to a grandstand finish. In the tiny press room, for the second consecutive weekend, there was a shared desire for Norris to get past the world champion and take the win. But on this occasion, he ran out of time. With one or two more laps, he would have caught and passed Verstappen.

Norris's drive had caught the eye of Red Bull boss Horner, who admitted his driver had been placed under 'massive pressure' by Norris and stated that McLaren's upgrades had clearly worked, adding: 'The cars are converging after the latest upgrades, they are looking very similar. McLaren were very quick at this circuit and Ferrari as well.' Piastri finished fourth, having started fifth owing to the penalty.

At the Monaco GP, McLaren ran a special livery as a tribute to Ayrton Senna, the team's most revered driver, who died at Imola 30 years earlier. The team had decided to swap out the papaya orange in place of a yellow and green colour scheme that paid homage to the Brazilian's national flag. This is by no means a comparison between the two drivers, but it felt poignant coming after Norris's victory, for it invoked memories of the team at its peak. McLaren were buoyed by the success and they could start dreaming again.

This time it was Piastri who set the pace. He qualified in second behind Leclerc, while Norris was fourth alongside the other Ferrari of Sainz. Crucially, Verstappen was down in sixth and his team-mate, Pérez, would start the race in sixteenth.

Overtaking opportunities in Monaco, however, are scarce, and in Sunday's race the top ten finished the race in the order in which they had started. It was a dull procession, only livened up by Leclerc finally winning his home race after a number of missed opportunities.

Piastri's brilliant second place and Norris's fourth, with Verstappen down in sixth, meant McLaren had claimed a huge chunk of points in the constructors' championship. The team left Monaco with 184 points, while Red Bull had 276. Norris was also up to third in the drivers' championship, behind Verstappen and Leclerc. The world champion was not happy, claiming that after last year's dominance Red Bull were now getting 'found out' by their rivals.

In Montreal on 9 June, McLaren again looked quick, but came away feeling that another victory had slipped through the team's grasp. Norris and Piastri had qualified in third and fourth respectively, but an ill-timed safety car during the race stopped Norris from taking the win. The incident occurred after Norris had overtaken both Verstappen and pole-sitter George Russell. Norris appeared comfortable, extending his lead by two seconds per lap over his rivals until Logan Sargeant crashed out in his Williams, prompting the release of the safety car. The timing of the safety car meant that by the time McLaren instructed Norris to pit for his tyre change, he had missed the entrance to the pit lane, so was unable to get into the pits. As he was subsequently forced to complete another lap, other drivers behind took advantage of the race being suspended behind the safety car. It meant that when he made his pitstop and returned to the track, he had fallen behind both Verstappen and Russell and was running in third. In his post-race comments, Norris stated that he had ample time to make the stop, blaming his team for making 'the wrong call'. He felt that the fact he took an extra lap before pitting had cost him the win: 'We should have won the race today and we didn't,' he said afterwards, clearly taking a dim view of the runner-up spot. 'We didn't do a good enough job as a team to box when we should have done, and not get stuck behind the safety car. So I don't think it was a lucky or unlucky kind of thing. This was just making a wrong call. It's on me and it's on the team and it's something we'll discuss after. We're at a level now where we're not satisfied with the second. The target is to win and we didn't do that.'

It was an interesting shift in dynamic. Now, finishing second was a disappointment.

Norris's frustration was evident while Verstappen's win was fortuitous. The Dutchman joked afterwards that it was payback for Norris's victory in Miami, where he of course had benefitted from the timing of the safety car. Verstappen said: 'It sometimes works for you and sometimes it works against you. So this time, it was working for us. I guess in that sense, it's 1–1 now this year. But that's racing.'

There was now a growing sense that this was shaping up to be a battle between the two for the title, increasing the tensions between the two teams in the process. Despite seeing Leclerc in second place in the drivers' championship, Norris now had the pace each weekend, while Verstappen's form was inconsistent. Norris knew he could catch the world champion, but couldn't afford to drop any points to the Red Bull man.

Norris responded brilliantly to the frustration he felt in Canada with a scintillating pole at the Spanish GP. What made it more remarkable was that just a few hours earlier, he had been sent scrambling out of McLaren's hospitality in his socks as fire ripped through the unit. He stood there in the paddock looking up at the building while smoke poured out of the back. Dressed in a T-shirt and black trousers, he'd forgotten his shoes in the rush to get out. Moments before, I had been sitting in the downstairs section enjoying a morning coffee, while both Piastri and Norris relaxed in their respective drivers' rooms. The lights went out and an order came from the kitchen staff to vacate the building, which incidentally had just undergone a refurbishment.

The Barcelona paddock was closed off as emergency services arrived on the scene to tackle the blaze. Pirelli Motorsport chief Mario Isola, who is a part-time paramedic in his native Italy, also bravely ran into the hospitality unit armed with a fire extinguisher from the neighbouring Pirelli hospitality. The building was put out of use, and Norris and Piastri were forced to take sanctuary in the team's engineering buildings as their pre-qualifying preparation was thrown into chaos, making Lando's second-ever pole position even more impressive.

Speaking after qualifying, he said with a smile: 'A bit more of a stressful day than I would have liked! I lost my shoes. That was probably as bad as it got for me. I've not been in my normal room. I've not been able to relax and chill out as much as what I normally do but I've had a lot of offers from people, so it's been great. A lot of the teams have been very, very nice to us.' He obviously appreciated the rare moment of camaraderie with their rivals in the paddock.

At Sunday's race, all eyes were on the British driver to see if he could convert his pole position into a win. However, a poor start saw him drop two places and, while he was able to recover to take second spot plus a bonus point for the fastest lap time, it was again Verstappen who ended up on the top step of the podium, albeit with a slender 2.219-second lead. Hamilton was third and Russell fourth. Piastri was seventh and now struggling to match his team-mate.

For Norris, it was yet more potential points dropped, but this time there was no team to blame for a poor tactical decision. His failure at the start had ultimately cost him yet another win, and he lost more ground in the championship to Verstappen. In typical self-critical fashion, he said: 'Today we were the quickest, we had the best car, and I didn't maximise it. The start is down to me and doing what I got told, and executing that. With a good start, we easily should have won.' Norris was dejected and fed up, despite leapfrogging Leclerc to second in the drivers' championship, sitting 69 points behind Verstappen with 14 races still to go.

CHAPTER 18

AUSTRO-HUNGARIAN BATTLES

There is something special about the Austrian Grand Prix. Whether it is the beautiful setting in the Styrian mountains, the clean air or the old-fashioned race-track layout with modern facilities, the race usually delivers. The 2024 instalment was no exception, principally down to the fact that we saw a distinct and unexpected change in attitude from Norris in the way he competed against Verstappen.

We arrived in Austria for the 30 June 2024 grand prix with questions still surrounding Verstappen's future. Mercedes boss Toto Wolff had continued to float the idea of signing the Dutchman, despite his team's decision to select the then 17-year-old Italian driver, Andrea Kimi Antonelli, from their driver programme as Hamilton's replacement.

Verstappen had become the story in Austria. Norris's poor start in Barcelona, which had cost him a shot at the win and his second place in the championship, had become a footnote. As

Norris admitted, the 69-point gap between the two meant that he needed 'something more' to turn the tide again in the title race.

The Austrian GP was another of F1's sprint weekends, shaking up the usual format with reduced practice sessions and an additional short race. During practice, Verstappen had set the pace ahead of Piastri in second. However, Norris outperformed the Australian to secure second place in sprint qualifying, with the other McLaren in third, both trailing behind Verstappen's Red Bull.

In the sprint race itself, Verstappen battled with the two McLarens, with Norris overtaking the pole-sitter to take the lead. But Verstappen regained his position, and then Norris was blind-sided by Piastri, who passed him into second place. The sprint race finished with Verstappen in P1, Piastri second and Norris in third. In the post-race media conference, Norris looked disconsolate. He'd thrown away more championship points and, to make matters worse, his team-mate had finished ahead of him. Norris was livid with himself.

However, one of the remarkable aspects of Norris in 2024 – which went largely under the radar – was his ability to bounce back from adversity. Though disheartened by the sprint race, he responded with a brilliant performance in qualifying for the main Austrian GP, securing second place. But he was still behind Verstappen. Something needed to change.

The Austrian GP then proved to be a defining moment in Norris's season. He would go head-to-head with Verstappen and prove to be no pushover. The drama unfolded in the final stages of the race, as the two tussled for the lead over the course of a handful of laps. The incident was triggered after Verstappen, who had led for much of the race, made a slow pitstop, putting him under pressure from a fired-up Norris. At turn three, a sharp right-hander at the top of the hill, Verstappen's block forced Norris wide while Verstappen continued to move to the left, causing them to collide. The collision caused terminal damage to the McLaren, and Norris, who had been the quicker of the two drivers, was forced to retire from the race. Verstappen, for his part, picked up a left-rear puncture and fell to fifth. The stewards blamed him for the collision and dished out a ten-second time penalty. Ironically, the penalty was insignificant as Verstappen had such a lead over Nico Hulkenberg's Haas that it did not affect his fifth-place finish. Verstappen picked up ten points, while Norris's retirement after 64 laps meant he scored zero.

Norris was seething. After the race, he lashed out at Verstappen, calling him 'reckless' and 'desperate'. It was fighting talk. 'He was doing things you're not allowed to do.'

Incidentally, Piastri had secured a brilliant second place but Norris and Verstappen's clash was the big story.

Then it was Stella's turn to hold court, as Norris sat there looking despondent. Unusually for someone so cautious, he also took aim at Verstappen, insinuating that he had driven in such an aggressive manner because similar tactics had gone unpunished by the FIA in 2021 when he battled Hamilton for the title. The incident had clearly driven a wedge between the two drivers, who were friends off track, and Stella suggested that an apology from Verstappen might help to keep the relationship intact.

'I don't give a shit about that,' said Verstappen in typical blunt fashion ahead of the British GP at Silverstone when asked about apologising and, perhaps more meaningfully, the public perception of his aggressive defence against Norris in the Austrian GP. 'I go home, I live my life. And the only thing that I care about is just my relationship to Lando.' Uncharacteristically Verstappen had reached out to Norris in the hours following their collision to clear the air. While it is unlikely he apologised, the two did discuss the incident.

Verstappen was bullish. 'I think we came to the conclusion that we actually really enjoyed our battle,' he said. 'We looked at the incident, and it was a silly little touch that had, of course, great consequence for both of us. But we like to race hard. We've done this for many years, not only in F1, even like online racing, where we had a lot of fun together.'

By the time the next race, at Silverstone on 7 July, came round, Norris had cooled down, and Verstappen mentioned that the two 'agree on 99 per cent of everything', adding, 'I always said to Lando, when you go for moves at the inside, the outside, you can trust me that I'm not there to try and crash you out of the way. It is the same the other way around, because we spoke about that as well. Naturally, there's always a human reaction when someone drives on the inside or outside. But I felt that I didn't do anything massively over the top.' When asked if he would change his approach in the future, he was conclusive: 'We go at it flat out. That's what we agreed to. Because that's what we like to do. And that's what's good for F1 as well.'

Norris was now also playing down the feud: 'I think it's clear, it's not something I need to talk about,' he said ahead of his home race. 'It's tough, it's on the limit. I think it's what we love. I thoroughly enjoyed the whole fight I had with him. Of course, it was a shame things ended the way they did but, apart from that, things are clear from what you see on TV and I'm excited to go racing again this weekend.'

There was a sense of disappointment that he didn't continue to stand up to Verstappen. The sport had become too chummy. F1 has experienced a number of close friendships in the past. In the late 1950s, Mike Hawthorn and Peter Collins formed an allegiance at Ferrari. Graham Hill and Jackie Stewart bonded after Jim Clark's death in 1968, and in the next decade, Mario Andretti and Ronnie Peterson were close mates at Lotus. More recently, Vettel and Räikkönen were close, along with Norris and Sainz. Yet there had always been a sense of edgy competition between the leading drivers in the sport. Verstappen's unchallenged titles in 2022 and 2023 had seen him placed in a class on his own and, as such, there was no pressure on him or need to fight with any other driver. He was winning week in and week out. Now Norris was on his tail, surely it was naive to think the friendship would remain intact as they continued to fight for wins.

One friendship that was developing was that between Zak Brown and Ferrari team principal Fred Vasseur. The two had revelled in each other's success and it was interesting to see how their relationship had developed over the first half of the season, given the turbulent history of McLaren and Ferrari, most notably surrounding Spygate. In an interview I did for *Autosport*, Brown suggested it was because the two shared the same 'ethical boundaries'. He explained how Vasseur's teams competed with the same principles he held in his team, and he assured me that they would 'fight hard on and off the track but we are going to race each other cleanly'.

He went on to talk about his own driver line-up and managing their careers, offering a pragmatic approach: 'When – and not if – they tangle at some point, there is mutual respect and we will sit down and talk it through, and never let it elevate and learn from it. I am not on the inside in other teams, but we have seen tensions brewing and I am not sure team bosses step in early enough. That is one of my strengths. I have plenty of weaknesses, but that is a strength because I have raced and understand the psychology of a driver.'

• • •

Brown had some explaining to do after a disappointing end to the British GP. Although Hamilton's victory marked an emotional end to his winless streak at Mercedes, the sentiment at McLaren – and in the press room – was that this was yet another missed opportunity. By lap 20, racing in mixed weather conditions, Norris and Piastri were running in first and second at Silverstone. When it got too wet for slicks, instead of opting for the double-stack and calling in both drivers for a tyre change, Norris went first and Piastri was called in a lap later. As a result, the Australian lost a lot of lap time and, with it, McLaren's strategic advantage of running in first and second.

Things got worse when Norris, who had maintained his lead, was instructed to pit for slick tyres after the rain had stopped. Unfortunately, the call from the McLaren pit wall came a lap later than the one from Mercedes, allowing Hamilton to gain the advantage with the quicker tyres and ultimately seize first place. Adding to McLaren's woes, Verstappen overtook Norris late in the race to secure second. Norris ended up in third, with Piastri finishing fourth, in what should have been a historic one–two finish for McLaren.

'It was tough,' said Brown afterwards. 'Hindsight's 20/20, as they say. I think we ultimately got it wrong. I think both our drivers could have won. When you're leading the race, you also have to be the first with decisions ... We'll have to do a debrief. We had a slow stop and [Norris] came out a couple of seconds behind Lewis.'

It should have been a crowning moment marking the team's resurrection in front of the UK crowd, but they had fluffed their lines.

Norris took the result hard, as expected given his tendency to focus on weaknesses. He remarked, 'There were so many things good, but a few too many letdowns. As a team, I don't think we did quite the job we should have done, but still lovely to be on the podium here ...' It was painful to watch the driver express the rawness of defeat and the significance of missing out on winning his home GP.

• • •

As McLaren continued to run at the front and take a chunk of points at each race, their push for the constructors' championship gained momentum. This effort was bolstered by a dip in form from Verstappen, a resurgence in Mercedes's speed and some woeful performances from Verstappen's Red Bull team-mate Sergio Pérez. Consequently, the scrutiny on McLaren intensified, reaching new heights at the Hungarian Grand Prix on 21 July.

After weeks of bungled chances they finally achieved success. Piastri secured his maiden victory, with Norris finishing in second place. However, the win felt bittersweet. Despite this being the team's first maximum-points finish since the 2021 Italian Grand Prix when Norris was runner-up, that time to Ricciardo, instead of an all-out celebration, Stella and Brown once again found themselves sifting through the pieces of another investigation into what went wrong,

Norris, who had started on pole, made yet another poor getaway and fell behind Piastri. However, he was promoted to first place during his pitstop, as McLaren chose to pit him first on lap 45 to prevent a rival team from undercutting their drivers. This strategy allowed Norris to undercut his team-mate, who pitted two laps later, and take the lead. McLaren then attempted to rectify the situation caused by their earlier strategy call by instructing Norris to swap positions and return the lead to Piastri. Norris did not comply. As the laps dwindled, Norris's race engineer, Will Joseph, repeatedly urged him to relinquish the position. 'OK, Lando,' Joseph radioed,'ten laps to go. Just remember every Sunday morning meeting we have.' Joseph was referencing the pre-race strategy meeting where the drivers are reminded they are racing for the team, not just for themselves.

The situation grew increasingly desperate. 'Lando, he can't catch you up,' said an exasperated Joseph as Norris continued to push hard. 'You've proved your point and it really doesn't matter.' Norris hit back with: 'He's on much quicker tyres. I mean, I would have tried to undercut anyway. If I didn't I would have gotten …' Joseph interrupted: 'I'm trying to protect you, mate. I'm trying to protect you … Lando, there are five laps to go. The way to win a championship is not by yourself. You're going to need Oscar and you're going to need the team.' This exchange was uncomfortable to witness and highlighted not only flaws in the team's strategy, once again, but also in its ability to manage its drivers.

Brown, who had proudly proclaimed that, as a former driver, he could spot any building tensions, had been blindsided by this scenario, even though Norris had clearly grown frustrated by the mistakes and missed opportunities. The Englishman eventually conceded his position on lap 68, allowing Piastri to retake the lead. But it was too late. The damage had been done.

Norris's actions sparked a debate. Some argued that multiple world champions, like Schumacher, Senna and Vettel, would have been more ruthless and not conceded position, asserting that such a mentality is required at the top level. Others felt he should have respected the team's orders and not taken matters into his own hands. Much of McLaren's recent development had been a consequence of a steady management team working harmoniously together. Norris had now jeopardised that relationship. He'd undermined the team's instruction from Stella, embarrassed his race engineer and, more significantly, he'd revealed his hand to Piastri. Norris had been grappling with a dichotomy: 'You've got to be selfish in this sport at times. You've got to think of yourself. That's priority number one – think of yourself. I'm also a team player, so my mind was going pretty crazy at the time. I know what we've done in the past between Oscar and myself. He's helped me plenty of times. But I think this is a different situation.'

It would be unfair to suggest that Piastri's first GP win was simply handed to him by team orders. He earned his victory by qualifying in second place, and making a better start to pass Norris.

The win was fully deserved, and it was unfortunate that the subsequent team orders overshadowed it. Piastri's triumph cemented his reputation as a talented driver with a measured approach, and it seemed that Norris's actions did not faze him. While Norris's radio exchanges with his race engineer were charged with emotion, Piastri maintained calm communication. Unflustered, he now matched Norris on one win each, despite trailing his more experienced team-mate in the drivers' championship. Quietly, Piastri – a driver with equal machinery and growing confidence – was becoming a challenge for Norris.

When Norris was asked how difficult it was to allow Piastri through, he acknowledged that he might have ignored the team's instruction. He said: 'It was tough. I think it would be tough for anyone when you're leading the race to give it up. I was obviously put in the position – they made me box first which gave me the chance to lead the race and to pull away quite comfortably. I did what I was supposed to do, but it also gave me the opportunity to lead. So, I think it was fair just to give the position back. I don't want to come across like a guy who's not fair.' He admitted that Piastri 'drove a better race than I did, you know, he got a good start, a better start and mine sucked. He deserved it and it was the right thing to do.'

Norris also reflected on the missed points in the championship, noting that title rival Verstappen, despite finishing fifth at the Hungaroring, still had a 76-point lead. 'When you're leading the race and have to give it back, it hurts. Especially because every point will help in the drivers' championship. I know I'm a hell of a long way behind Max, I get that. I threw or gave away seven points today, not because of switching positions, just because of a bad start again. And that's where I lost my race.'

Stella's assessment of the incident was different. The Italian claimed he knew Norris would eventually hand the position back, and summed up by promising that the team would continue to learn from its handling of the race, and just how the undercut had cost the leading driver his position.

By the time the Belgian GP at Spa had come around on 28 July, just ahead of the summer break, Norris's mood had shifted. He had spent a few days reflecting on the outcome of the race in Hungary and admitted it could have been handled much better. He felt embarrassed for overshadowing Piastri's debut GP victory, and regretted there were hardly any headlines celebrating the team's one–two finish, admitting it was something he did 'not feel too proud about'. When asked whether he would do anything different if he could turn the clock back, Norris was to the point. 'I'd just let him pass straight away,' he said.

Norris had again backed down or, more accurately, performed a U-turn. It was genuine, from the heart, but it raised questions about whether he was too soft.

There was now a growing sense that McLaren were wrong to ask him to swap places with Piastri. With Verstappen no longer dominating races and McLaren having the quicker car, the team should have prioritised Norris's season, as he still had a chance to catch the world champion. In the constructors' championship, McLaren had been making significant progress and, partly due to Pérez's poor form, they were closing in on the world champions. However, the constructors' title race would take care of itself. What was needed was Piastri's support and subservience to ensure that Norris could score maximum points each weekend.

Piastri's laidback nature meant he remained largely unaffected by the hullabaloo. 'It's been nice to chill out and kind of let it soak in a little bit,' he said when asked about being an F1 winner for the first time. 'I feel like I deserved it. I certainly don't feel like it was given to me or anything like that. That's not to say there's not things I could still do better.'

At the Belgian GP, Verstappen faced a ten-place grid penalty due to an unscheduled engine change, starting him in 11th place. This presented Norris with the opportunity to close the gap in the championship standings. However, Verstappen's impressive drive to finish fourth showcased his skill in damage limitation. In contrast, Norris had a subpar race, finishing fifth. Meanwhile, Piastri secured second place behind Hamilton after Russell, who initially crossed the line first, was disqualified for having an underweight car. With no team orders to blame, Norris had blown another chance to gain ground and failed, while Piastri was beginning to outscore his team-mate.

Norris needed a strong comeback and it came at the Dutch GP in late August, the first week back after the summer break. It was Verstappen's home race, a track he had dominated since it had returned to the F1 calendar in 2021. However, Norris stepped up, securing pole position by nearly half a second. This time he converted it into a victory – despite another poor start. And this time his dad, Adam, was there to savour the moment.

Norris delivered a calculated drive, explaining that he was 'surprisingly calm' at losing first place on the opening lap to

Verstappen, adding, 'Maybe because I'm a bit used to going backwards at the start! I'm very prepared for those kind of scenarios.' He kept Verstappen in his sights and, when he noticed the Red Bull's rear tyres losing grip, seized his opportunity. Passing Verstappen, Norris claimed victory and the bonus point for the fastest lap. After missing out in Hungary and in Spa, Zandvoort delivered the maximum points available. He reduced Verstappen's lead to 70 points, with 234 still up for grabs. And Piastri's fourth-place finish, narrowly missing a third consecutive podium, helped McLaren close the gap to Red Bull in the constructors' championship to just 30 points.

CHAPTER 19

PAPAYA RULES

After a reassuring and welcome result at the Dutch GP, the internal conflict that had surfaced during the Hungarian GP reemerged at the Italian GP on 1 September 2024. This was, in some ways, inevitable. Piastri's form had improved, bringing him much closer to competing with Norris. The two were separated by the smallest of margins – in fact, the top six in qualifying were within a couple of tenths of a second. Norris secured pole, with Piastri in second place, extending McLaren's excellent spell of dominance. Meanwhile, Verstappen only managed to qualify in seventh place as Red Bull continued to struggle for pace.

The race was set for an explosive start between the two McLaren drivers. Yet another poor getaway from Norris opened the door for Piastri, and the two battled wheel-to-wheel on the opening lap. It made for some uncomfortable viewing from the McLaren garage as they ran each other so close, but ice-cool Piastri prevailed, managing to squeeze past Norris at turn four and take the lead. In the scuffle, Norris also lost another place to Leclerc, who had started fourth. After the round of pitstops, Norris set about working his way back up to the front. By lap 20, Norris was 1.8 seconds behind race-leader Piastri when his race engineer told him over the radio: 'You are allowed to race Oscar,' before adding 'Papaya rules.'

Both parts of the message from Will Joseph were crucial. Firstly, Norris was free to compete against Piastri. There would be no team instructions or orders that had previously seen the two swap positions in Hungary, surprising many, given Norris's position in the championship and need to take points from Verstappen. The second part – 'papaya rules' – was a shorthand term intended to remind Norris to keep it clean, with 'papaya' referencing the team's iconic orange colour.

However, Norris was unable to catch his team-mate, and was overtaken by Leclerc, who powered back into second place. The Ferrari man was then put into the lead when Piastri made his second pitstop. Leclerc did not make a second stop and he nursed his Ferrari home on ageing tyres to take the win.

By allowing the drivers to battle for track position, and ultimately failing to restore the starting order, this 'papaya rules' saga quickly began to look like a missed opportunity for another one–two finish, with Norris closing in on Verstappen in the championship standings. Verstappen, incidentally, finished sixth. Norris finished third and Piastri second, earning valuable points for the team, but not the maximum.

Asked if Piastri's move on Norris at such an early stage of the race was within the papaya rules, Stella said: 'We will have to review it, together with the drivers, look at the videos, understand their point of view, and then assess whether they were fully compliant or not.

'We will take the learning, if there is any, and adjust the papaya rules to best pursue both the constructors' championship and the drivers' championship.'

It was a familiar story of promising to learn from an unexpected event without effectively managing the situation. McLaren faced a steep learning curve as they dealt with the kind of driver conflict that Brown, as a former racing driver himself, had hoped he would be able to anticipate. However, no one could have foreseen Piastri's bold manoeuvre that had caught Norris off guard. Brown commented: 'Their start was great and we had discussed them getting behind each other and fanning out to ensure nobody else could get by. I think Lando was probably caught by surprise, expecting to tuck into a one–two and pull a gap.

'Papaya rules are, it's your team-mate, race him hard, race him clean, don't touch. It was an aggressive pass so that's a conversation we'll have.'

Brown was asked whether the simmering tension between his drivers was a result of the team not prioritising one over the other. 'They are both young drivers who want to win,' he said. 'We have always believed in having two number ones. That's always been McLaren's way. It can be difficult to manage – we've seen it with Senna and Prost. They [Norris and Piastri] get along great; they race each other clean. It's philosophical – are you a one-car team or a two-car team backing both drivers? But Andrea and I are taking it one race at a time.'

Understandably, given his recent run of good form, Piastri was adamant that he did not want team orders clouding the results of races. He had positioned himself to challenge Norris, both for pole position and during Sundays' grands prix. He approached each weekend with the mindset of winning – focusing on supporting the team's position in the constructors' championship rather than prioritising his team-mate's championship ambitions. However, it was clear that if asked to play a supporting role in the final stages of the campaign, he would be willing to do so. 'The gap is still very big between Lando and Max, and it's even bigger for myself,' he said. 'But it's not impossible. So, yes, we'll take it on a case-by-case basis every weekend. Of course, if the gap gets significantly smaller, and I'm not so much in the picture, then I'm aware I could be called upon to try and help out. But I think with the gap how it is at the moment, it's still very, very early for that. And ultimately, I want to go out and win races as well.'

Somewhat surprisingly, given all the reaction to what happened in Monza, McLaren announced in the run-up to the Azerbaijan GP that it would now consider favouring Norris over Piastri on '50–50 calls' to boost his title challenge. It was good leadership. The move was needed to preserve the relationship between its drivers and their respective garages, while also ensuring that any rift, derived from internal competitiveness, did not ruin their chances of winning the constructors' championship. With eight rounds to go, the gap between Norris and Verstappen stood at 62 points, still a considerable margin that should have been reduced, given the speed of Norris's McLaren versus the problems Verstappen was encountering with his Red Bull, struggling with handling and lack of pace.

In an interview for Sky Sports F1, Stella delicately explained why the team had decided to change their approach, after initially making it clear they wouldn't. 'After Monza, we took a look at the first lap with Lando and Oscar. We checked what we could have done better,' he said. 'If you enter a chicane in the first lap P1 and P2 and exit P1 and P3, I'm not sure if we acted in the best interests of the team, and that's our main objective and principle. It was a very constructive conversation. Each of us, myself included, raised our hands and said, "We could have done this better." We put all these learnings together and they will form the foundations for the final part of the season.'

Piastri was 44 points behind Norris in the drivers' standings. The numbers had been enough to persuade Stella to change the team's approach, but the feeling in the paddock was that, although it was the right move, it had been done too late in the season.

Nonetheless, this was the boost that Norris needed and it was crucial for him to capitalise on it. However, just as we were eagerly anticipating McLaren's strategy in action, with both drivers working together to close Verstappen's lead, Norris found himself starting the Azerbaijan GP in a disappointing 15th position on the grid – 11 places behind the Red Bull man. During qualifying, Norris experienced a slide on his final flying lap, losing him valuable time, before being forced to slow down due to Esteban Ocon's slow-moving Alpine. Meanwhile, Piastri qualified in second place behind Leclerc.

When asked about his chances of making up places in the race due to the circuit's long straights, Norris adopted the 'glass-half-empty' approach, explaining how cars struggle in the turbulent air they create, which pretty much rules out running close behind the car in front. 'I don't even think it's as easy as that, honestly,' he said. 'Following is pretty much impossible around here and overtaking is a lot worse than everyone thinks. I hope I'm wrong, of course. I hope there's plenty of chances, but I'm not expecting that.'

Ironically, Norris did get chances to overtake and was up to fifth by the 14th lap, having made a breathtaking start to the race. Coming into the weekend with the support of his team-mate, it was then actually Norris who would assist Piastri for the Aussie's second win of the year.

Norris had found himself running ahead of Pérez, who was hunting down Piastri. Although Norris was a pitstop down on the Mexican and his tyres needed changing, after a request from the pit wall to hold up the Mexican, he duly obliged. Slowing down Pérez's progress meant the Red Bull driver was unable to undercut Piastri when he made his pitstop from the lead. This smart tactic from McLaren marked an improvement in their decision-making. While Pérez was ultimately taken out of the race in a collision with Sainz, Norris's role in stalling Pérez for two laps was critical in helping Piastri remain ahead.

Incredibly, the papaya rules, after the endless debates, resulted in victory for Piastri, a win that he labelled the best of his career. This victory came despite the wishes of his race engineer Tom Stallard, who had warned him against attempting his race-winning pass on Leclerc on lap 20 to put himself into the lead. In the cooldown room before the podium ceremony, Piastri admitted to Leclerc he feared his late lunge into turn one would result in a crash into the wall, and that it was a case of now or never. 'I felt a bit sorry for my race engineer because I basically tried to do that in the first stint and completely cooked my tyres. So, he came on the radio and said, "Let's not do that again," basically. And I completely ignored him the next lap and sent it down the inside … It was a high-risk, high-commitment move, but that's what I needed to do to try and win the race.'

There was no denying this, or suggesting it had been gifted to him. He'd not only won the race but the points he'd scored helped McLaren usurp Red Bull at the top of the constructors' championship table for the first time in over a decade. Stella hailed the achievement as a milestone but maintained that their job was not yet done – they still had to win it.

• • •

At the Singapore GP weekend, I caught up with Brown ahead of qualifying for the 22 September race, and we discussed the progress of the team over the year. McLaren had built upon their results in 2023 and, while there had been mistakes, both operationally and from the drivers, Brown had every reason to be pleased with the development and clearly placed his faith in Stella and the management team, which was paying off handsomely. Yes, there was now a rivalry between his drivers, but due to their respective good natures and tendency to remain level-headed, it had not caused any internal rift.

When we speak in the McLaren hospitality unit in the paddock, I ask Brown if he's already exceeded his expectations, having delivered McLaren back to the top of the constructors' standings. 'We've exceeded our timeline,' he corrects me. 'I thought we would get to where we are now, or in this ballpark. It could never be like "we're going to be number one" because the wind tunnel still wasn't fully online by the time we had planned this car. So we got to where we are now while only at 92 per cent full strength. And given how competitive the sport is, I thought we would need everything to get to this point. We are now at 100 per cent, and we have to maintain that. We can never sit still. We know the minute we back off the throttle, we would drop down to 95 per cent. We need to keep the momentum, which is staying state-of-the-art in technology and never falling behind. It's about just making sure we don't slow down.'

I ask Brown about the relief he must feel at seeing the team's improvement, given he had come under pressure from the McLaren board to stop their slide to the back of the grid, and start moving in the right direction. 'I'm still scarred and hopefully permanently scarred,' he says, reflecting upon the strains of winter 2023, when he realised they would not start the season with a competitive car. 'It's interesting, there's two types of people in this world, those that are motivated by the thrill of victory and those that are motivated by the fear of defeat. I'm motivated by the fear of defeat, which gets me out of bed every day. It's probably unhealthier, more stressful, and probably explains why I had ulcers a year and a half ago!

'I'm never relaxed. I'm never comfortable, and I think being uncomfortable is a good thing. Yes, we're very financially healthy right now, but if we never landed another sponsor deal again, and people didn't renew in five years, we're in trouble. It means that you've got to be hustling.'

I thought it was interesting that he picked 2023 as the low point in his tenure at McLaren, rather than the Honda debacle when he first arrived, which was obviously when the team were at their lowest ebb. 'I felt like 2016 and 2017 were a disaster, but I kind of inherited that and I needed to clean it up,' he said. 'But I definitely felt like I owned 2023. That happened on my watch. It was like: "You've got great drivers. You've got the budget. What's your excuse?"'

We switch our attention to how well Stella is doing leading the team. He'd impressed us in the media with his management, and when speaking to the team's drivers and staff, it quickly becomes clear he is universally liked and well respected. Tales of him bringing pastries to meetings all feed into the feeling that he is building some great team spirit within the organisation, that is missing at some of their rivals.

Brown continues enthusiastically, 'Andrea loves McLaren. He loves his job. You can see his level of engagement is off the charts. I call him the swan … My feet are above the water, but his are going just as fast below. So he's more elegant about how quickly he's moving.'

In terms of keeping staff, he says that you lose people, not that teams steal people. In the same way, teams don't steal sponsors, you lose them. He says he has got only one person to blame if a team member is poached – himself. The subject of what helps to maintain a healthy environment within a team challenging at the front brings Brown back to Stella.

'Andrea's got a great phrase; "Don't eat the poison biscuit." I've got to insulate the team from all the "incoming". Everyone's going to be trying to stir it in the media, and with the FIA. That's what we all do! I've got to protect the team, because if you look at one team in particular, where there's lots of poison, lots of "incoming" poison, look what's happening …'

Brown stops short of naming any team here but the presumption from my reading of the situation is that he is speaking about Red Bull, who over the course of the season have seen Adrian Newey decide to join Aston Martin, while long-serving sporting director, Jonathan Wheatley, has announced he will be joining Audi when the German team takes over from Sauber ahead of their 2026 campaign. He continues: 'That is an unbelievably great team which, at the moment, is going in the wrong direction because of culture. People are leaving, there's lots of noise. What's changed? The culture or the people?'

• • •

The Singapore GP is widely regarded as one of the toughest on the F1 calendar, primarily because of the humidity, which can reach 90 per cent, and the temperature inside the F1 cars, which can soar to 60 degrees Celsius. Furthermore, the challenging nature of competing on street circuits, where the walls are close and the run-off areas are minimal, adds to the difficulty. If a driver does make a mistake, he usually ends up crashing into a wall and it is race over.

The ease with which Norris triumphed in this demanding race was staggering. Not only had he secured a scintillating pole position, but he also won by an impressive 21-second margin over Verstappen, who finished second ahead of Piastri. Norris's victory was a landslide, keeping his title aspirations alive. He'd have taken the bonus point too for setting the fastest lap had Daniel Ricciardo not pitted on the penultimate lap to set a quicker time in what proved to be his final race for Red Bull's sister team, RB.

Norris broke his pattern of poor starts to lead the race and masterfully controlled the pace. In fact, he was so calm and kept pushing so hard – despite being urged to slow down by his team – that he almost hit the wall twice in an otherwise brilliant drive.

'It was an amazing race,' he said afterwards. 'A few too many close calls, a couple of little moments in the middle, but it was well controlled, I think, otherwise. The car was mega. I could push. We were flying the whole race and at the end could just chill.' The fact he was chilling out while leading arguably the toughest race of the year got a chuckle from the assembled press. He continued: 'I didn't want to have a one-second lead. I wanted to have the biggest lead possible.'

Piastri's climb from fifth on the grid to third – and another bad finish for Pérez in tenth – meant that McLaren increased their advantage in the constructors' standings over Red Bull, much to Brown's delight. After the race, Horner joked that McLaren were 'taking the piss' in their radio message to Norris, asking him to open up a five-second gap to Verstappen, which Norris obliged within three laps. 'Although I shouldn't say that in any official capacity,' Horner added, making light of the fact that Verstappen had been slapped with a community service order by the FIA for swearing during a press conference earlier in the week.

This was a seminal moment in the title race. McLaren had not only caught up to Red Bull, but they were now pulling ahead in the constructors' championship. It felt that Horner could see the writing on the wall. Despite this, Verstappen was still digging in, doing enough to ensure that, even on his bad weekends, he was not haemorrhaging points to Norris. The battle was far from over.

Interestingly, on the way back to the UK, Brown posted an image on social media of himself and Horner dressed in pyjamas for the overnight flight, with the caption 'Peace in F1 has been restored on flight home (where's Netflix when you need them!) – but the battle will continue on track. What an awesome sport!'

CHAPTER 20

ADVANTAGE VERSTAPPEN

As the 2024 season ran into the final six races, Norris trailed Verstappen by 52 points, while McLaren led Red Bull in the team competition by 41 points. At the United States Grand Prix in Austin on 19–20 October, there were extra points available, given it was another sprint-race weekend.

There were still 180 points available to Norris, but Verstappen's lead meant that even if the McLaren man won all the remaining six races, he would not win the title if Verstappen finished second in each of those races and the sprint races. Verstappen would have to drop points or, looking at it in another way, Norris had to outscore him by just under nine points in every race.

However, it was Verstappen who dominated the sprint qualifying to take pole, with Norris down in fourth. In the short race, Norris was able to make up one spot to third, behind Sainz. Verstappen maintained his lead to take the victory and a further eight points, while Norris's result earned him six points.

Norris responded impressively by securing pole position for the US GP. He had been 0.031 seconds quicker than Verstappen on their first laps and, just as the Dutchman had started putting together his final lap, an accident involving Russell brought out the yellow flags, forcing him to abort what would have been his flying lap. Norris had been fortunate, but it was a welcome boost after Verstappen's win in the sprint.

It was Norris's fourth pole in five races, and he had also clinched victories in two of the previous four races, Singapore and Zandvoort, while Piastri had won in Azerbaijan. A crucial radio message from his race engineer had played a key role ahead of his pole lap. Sensing a dip in his driver's confidence, Joseph advised Norris to 'trust the car and the lap time will come'.

'He knows I don't like that kind of stuff normally, but I'd said after Q2 I was not confident at all in the car,' Norris revealed. 'I was bouncing everywhere, and I just lacked confidence, at that point, to put a good lap together. Whether what I did was because of Will's comments, I'd probably say no, otherwise I'll boost his ego too much! ... But I probably needed it. A little kick doesn't hurt, sometimes.'

However, Norris's unwelcome habit of making poor starts resurfaced in Austin. Verstappen seized upon his slow getaway, and he was also leapfrogged by the two Ferrari drivers in the opening lap, dropping him down to fourth place. Norris battled back. In the final stages of the race, as he and Verstappen fought for third position with the Dutchman running behind the two leading Ferraris, Verstappen forced Norris wide causing the two cars to go off track. Leclerc took advantage of the scuffle, and swooped past them both to win the race, with Sainz taking second place.

The stewards penalised the McLaren driver with a five-second penalty, dropping him back to fourth place, crucially, behind Verstappen. The decision to punish Norris and not Verstappen was controversial, as it was Verstappen who had forced Norris wide in his defensive manoeuvre. McLaren asked the FIA for a right of review into the penalty, hoping for it to be overturned.

While McLaren felt that their driver had nowhere else to go, Red Bull felt that Norris should have been forced to surrender the place because he left the track and gained an advantage by cutting the corner.

Verstappen hit back and accused McLaren of 'complaining a lot recently', and the Dutchman had no sympathy for Norris, saying, 'It's very clear in the rules: outside the white line you cannot pass. I have been done for it as well in the past. I think in 2017, or whenever it was. I lost my podium like that. I just remained calm, trying to do the best I could.'

In the run-up to the Mexico City GP the following week, Norris was adamant that he should not be forced to change the way he raced. He was still fuming about being the only one penalised, despite both running wide. The FIA rulebook had been checked, and it sided with the defending driver, not the one attacking. However, McLaren argued that since Norris was ahead at the apex, he was no longer the attacking driver as he was in the lead at the point both cars went off. They felt that the decision should be reversed.

A 25-minute meeting took place with the race stewards, Stella and McLaren's racing director Randeep Singh, plus Red Bull's Jonathan Wheatley and senior race engineer Stephen Knowles.

McLaren presented new evidence, arguing that the stewards had made an error. Their case hinged on the point that Norris was ahead, not level with Verstappen, as stated by the FIA. However, five hours after the hearing, the stewards ruled that McLaren's new reasoning was 'not sustainable and is therefore rejected' and, consequently, they did not overturn the verdict. Begrudgingly, McLaren accepted the decision. A statement from the team confirmed they 'acknowledge the stewards' decision to reject our petition requesting a right of review' but 'disagree with the interpretation' that an FIA document with inaccuracies could be deemed an admissible element of the decision.

Norris said: 'I've not spoken to Max at all because he did what he thought was right and I did what I thought was right. I still disagree, and as a team we disagree. I was completely ahead of Max, I was over a car length ahead of him. I was no longer the attacking car. He was. Effectively, he had gone in too hard and overtaken off the track.' McLaren felt that Verstappen's aggressive driving style needed to change. It rekindled memories of their battle in Austria where Verstappen's defensive driving had taken Norris out of the race. Norris added: 'Do I need to make some changes? Yes. And adapt a little bit more. But is everything I am doing wrong? Also no.'

Norris and Verstappen clashed again during the Mexico City Grand Prix, with Norris still reeling from the disappointment of being penalised in Austin and believing that Verstappen's driving had contributed to the incident that led to his penalty. This time, however, it was the Red Bull man who was sanctioned: two ten-second time penalties. First, Norris was pushed off track while attempting to overtake Verstappen on the outside at turn four. Although Verstappen stayed on track, he was ruled to have forced Norris off. He received a second penalty four corners later, where he ran Norris wide again, and gained an advantage by going off the circuit. As Verstappen served his penalties, he finished in sixth place, while Norris was second, unable to surpass Sainz.

Norris again could not hide his frustration at what had happened. 'Max knows what he has to do. He knows he did wrong, deep down he does. And it's for him to change, not me. Max is one of the most capable drivers on the grid, if not the most. He knows what he can and can't do and what the limits are.'

Verstappen's driving was also criticised in the media. The 1996 world champion Damon Hill was openly scathing about the Dutchman, who wasn't unduly fazed: 'I don't listen to those individuals. I just do my thing. I am a three-time world champion. I think I know what I'm doing. Some people are just being very annoying. I know who these people are and I don't really pay a lot of attention to them. I have got this far in my career. Some people are just a bit biased.'

The ongoing battle between McLaren and Red Bull had reignited the war of words between Brown and Horner, with Brown expressing disappointment that the gap between the two drivers remained significantly in Verstappen's favour at 47 points. When asked after the race if he felt the penalties were suitable, Brown responded: 'Probably not enough. I mean, it's getting a bit ridiculous. But I do applaud the FIA stewards – enough's enough. Let's just have some good clean racing moving forward. Lando drove brilliantly.'

Sainz's win in Mexico, combined with Leclerc's third place, Norris finishing second and Piastri in eighth, propelled Ferrari into second place in the contractors' championship, now trailing McLaren by just 29 points. 'It's a lot tighter than I'd like it to be,' Brown said, 'but it's great for F1. Great to see Ferrari and McLaren are going at it for the world championship. We certainly can't rule out Red Bull, they're not far behind. It's going to be an exciting finish to the season.'

At the São Paulo GP on 3 November, Verstappen took aim at those who had criticised him, saying 'it was nothing new' and adding that the previous year, when everything was so 'perfect' for him, 'it must have hurt a lot for many people that they couldn't say anything negative'. He said that he felt he was being targeted because he was not British. 'Now they've got the chance to say something, so they're all coming out of the woodwork. At the end of the day, I've got the wrong passport for this paddock,' he snapped.

Verstappen ventured that he felt he was being targeted by the FIA, as well. After all, he was fined €40,000 and given a community service order for using the 'F word' during an official press conference in Singapore. While Leclerc, who had used it during the Mexico GP, was only given a €10,000 fine, half of which was suspended. Verstappen remarked: 'I can't say the word, and apparently that only counts for me.'

Norris had led the only practice session for the São Paulo GP, another sprint weekend. However, it was Piastri who shone in sprint qualifying, taking pole ahead of Norris by 0.029 seconds. The Australian led for most of the 24-lap race, before being instructed to let his team-mate pass, allowing Norris to score more points. Verstappen initially finished third, but received a post-race penalty for driving too slowly during a virtual safety-car period, adding five seconds to his time, dropping him to fourth behind Leclerc. Though he had technically breached the rules, the penalty seemed pernickety and wound him up still further. He later confessed to wanting to smash up his team's garage in frustration, feeling targeted by the stewards after recent penalties in Singapore, Austin and Mexico.

Norris's sprint win, although boosting his title hopes, felt hollow as it was truly Piastri's victory. When congratulated, he replied: 'Not proud about it but we worked well together as a team. Today was the result that we wanted. Oscar deserved it but we're doing what we have to do, so I thank him and the team.'

Stella echoed this sentiment, 'It was well done by the team, and it would not be possible without both drivers working so cohesively. We are definitely very happy with the conversations that are happening right now and with the support that Oscar is giving Lando. This is the best result we could ever have for both championships.' Verstappen's advantage was now 44 points while McLaren were 34 points clear of Ferrari.

A heavy thunderstorm in the afternoon caused qualifying for the race to be postponed to Sunday morning, setting the stage for a thrilling race day. The downpour continued, wreaking havoc on the rescheduled qualifying session, resulting in five red flags as Franco Colapinto, Sainz, Lance Stroll, Alonso and Alex Albon all crashed out. Amid the chaos, Norris held his nerve and delivered a brilliant qualifying performance to secure pole ahead of

Russell. Verstappen, facing a five-place grid penalty for taking a new engine, could only manage 12th in qualifying, placing him 17th on the grid.

Once again, it was advantage Norris, just as it had been in Spain, Hungary, Zandvoort, Monza, Singapore and Austin, consistently securing poles. Verstappen ultimately started in 15th – as Albon and Stroll did not start. This presented a significant opportunity for Norris to reduce that gap and keep the title race alive.

However, it was yet another poor start from Norris as Russell passed him off the line and took the lead. While most of the field carefully navigated their way around the wet track, Verstappen embarked on one of the most impressive recovery drives in wet conditions in F1 history. By lap 12, he had gained 11 places and was up to sixth. As conditions worsened, all eyes were on whether Norris and Verstappen could keep their cars on track.

Safety-car deployments following crashes for Colapinto and then Sainz shuffled the order as teams gambled with pitstops. When the safety car came in on lap 42, and the race resumed on lap 43, Verstappen, who had climbed up to second behind Esteban Ocon, surged into the lead. Meanwhile Norris, who had lost out by making an early pitstop just before a red flag and been undercut by Verstappen and Ocon, slid off track at turn one.

That moment on lap 43 of the São Paulo Grand Prix proved to be a pivotal shift in the title race. Norris, who had been excellent all weekend in the mixed conditions, locked up and he dropped to seventh place. Verstappen, under immense pressure from recent weeks, went on to set the fastest lap 17 times over in a wet-weather masterclass. With Piastri's assistance, Norris moved up to sixth, but was now 62 points behind Verstappen with only 86 points remaining in the final three rounds.

Norris expressed his frustration over making his pitstop just before the red flag, which allowed Verstappen to make his tyre swap without losing track position. According to F1 rules, drivers can change tyres when the race is stopped, a regulation that disadvantages those who have already pitted, as Norris experienced. 'It was the right time to box ... So no regrets, just unlucky,' he remarked. 'It's a silly rule that no one agrees with, except when it benefits them. You win some, you lose some. It benefitted them today. So, well done to them. I did all I could today, that's all.'

• • •

Verstappen headed to the Las Vegas Grand Prix on 23 November with the opportunity to secure his fourth consecutive F1 world crown. He qualified in fifth while Norris would start the race in sixth. Russell took pole followed by Sainz, Pierre Gasly and Leclerc. Hopes for a competitive title race had been extinguished and Norris was resigned to seeing Verstappen clinch the championship. 'Whether he wins or not tomorrow, for me it's not going to change anything,' Norris said after qualifying. 'He's pretty likely to win the championship, but I'm here to do my best in every single race I can. Whether Max finishes ahead or not, that's life.'

Norris's comments reflected his acceptance of the situation, but he could take pride in being the only driver to challenge Verstappen for as long as he did, especially given McLaren's slow start to the season. 'I'm proud. I'm happy we've brought it this far. And it's us, no one else.'

Norris also explained that he initially did not feel ready to challenge Verstappen at the start of the campaign, but had developed significantly through the season. After their encounters in Austria, Austin and Mexico City, he felt more comfortable going up against him. 'But it was probably too late. Max is one of the best drivers ever in F1. And to go up against someone so good takes a bit more than what I have done this season. But since the summer break, it was close to what it should be. It is the first time we've had a chance to fight at the front. We've not been able to do that for the past six years.

'I feel I've done a very good job and performed very well, some of my best performances by far. I am not completely happy with what I've done but, for the first time, I feel I have got what it takes to fight for the championship. It doesn't mean I'm complete and, when you are competing against drivers like Max, you have to be close to perfect.'

Norris had already begun his debrief and assessment of the campaign, identifying the São Paulo GP as a 'defining moment of the season'. He knew that mistakes – both his own and in the wider team – had cost him valuable points. 'There have been plenty of races where we didn't do as good a job as we could,' he admitted. 'At Silverstone, we could have had a one–two finish, but we didn't get it. There were plenty of times when we did not perform as a championship-winning team, and plenty when I haven't performed at the level of a championship-winning driver.'

As the Las Vegas Grand Prix approached, there was a sense of inevitability that Verstappen would be crowned world champion for the fourth consecutive time. The mood in the paddock was that, while it would have been good to see the title race extended, it was fitting for such a thrilling season, filled with off- and on-track drama, to culminate in Vegas, rather than at a sprint race in front of a sparse crowd in Qatar.

The organisers of the Vegas race had invested heavily to ensure its success. The second instalment was crucial, after mixed reviews in 2023 due to lengthy delays caused by a loose drain cover. Also, an exciting race, where a driver could be crowned world champion, provided an opportunity to attract audiences in the US, a market F1 is keen to continue to nurture.

Qualifying was dominated by Mercedes, with their car well suited to the cool conditions, as Russell took pole position. Verstappen qualified in fifth and Norris in sixth, with little separating the two title rivals. The race itself saw a measured drive from Verstappen who, aware of his points advantage, delivered a controlled performance to come home in fifth, one place ahead of Norris. In doing so, he won the title and Norris's challenge came to an end.

'Massive congrats to him,' Norris said after the race. 'He deserved it.' It was difficult to disagree as this felt like the best championship win in Verstappen's career. He had faced internal conflict within the team, which placed him and his father at the centre of a row. He had also faced questions about his future at Red Bull, especially after Adrian Newey announced his departure from the team. Additionally, Verstappen had to contend with Norris and Piastri, who had a quicker car for much of the season. Another significant factor was that he had single-handedly carried Red Bull's challenge in the constructors' championship as his team-mate Pérez was simply not delivering the results expected from him.

Norris could, however, take solace in the fact he was actually in a title fight, a testament to McLaren's rapid development. He was even able to be the last man standing, albeit seeing his challenge end two races before the final grand prix of the year. Assessing the world champion, Norris added: 'Max has no downsides. He has no negatives. When he's had the quickest car, he dominated races. When he's not in the quickest car, he's still been just behind us and almost winning the races anyway. He's not had any bad races the whole year. He just drove as Max has always driven, which is perfectly.'

Heading to the penultimate race in Qatar, the weekend after Vegas, it was going to be telling to see how Norris responded, now the title race was officially over. It was also crucial for Piastri, as his form had dipped and Ferrari looked resurgent in the constructors' championship. Would McLaren now blow the team title? Surely not. They could win the title in Qatar, another sprint weekend, if they outscored Ferrari by 20 points and if Red Bull did not outscore McLaren by 9 points.

Norris made the perfect start by qualifying on pole for the sprint, with Piastri in third behind Russell. In the race, Norris maintained the lead from Piastri, after a good start. He led the race until the final lap, when he pulled over and allowed Piastri to pass. This was payback for Piastri sacrificing his likely win in São Paulo to prolong Norris's title challenge. Norris, who had slowed considerably to the point of nearly losing second place to Russell, said: 'It was probably a bit closer than what I was wanting, but I'd planned to do it since Brazil. It's just what I thought was best. It's probably a little bit sketchy. The team told me not to do it, but I thought I could get away with it, and we did.'

Norris's defiance of team orders – Joseph had told him three times not to relinquish the lead – was a nice touch. It also showed he was over the disappointment of seeing Verstappen crowned the previous weekend. Norris's behaviour perhaps indicated that he was already preparing for 2025, and making sure that his relationship with Piastri was on a good footing if he needed his support next season.

Just as McLaren had given themselves some breathing space in their battle with Ferrari, it was soon wiped out in the Qatar GP. Verstappen, who started on pole, complained to the race stewards that Norris, running in second place for much of the race, had failed to slow significantly for waved yellow flags due to debris on track. Norris protested his innocence, but once Verstappen had grassed him up to the race officials, he was hit with a ten-second stop/go penalty. This sanction, often regarded as the strictest penalty in F1 bar disqualification, caused Norris to tumble down the order, returning to the track in 15th place. It was a harsh penalty that cost him some decent points and the chance to fight Verstappen for the win. But Norris, who ended up in tenth, took the punishment on the chin. The saving grace for the team was Piastri finishing in third place, behind Ferrari's Leclerc. It had been a disappointing result for McLaren and meant the outcome of the constructors' championship would be decided at the season finale in Abu Dhabi.

CHAPTER 21

RETURN TO THE SUMMIT

'It would be the most McLaren thing ever if they lost the constructors' title this season,' said a fellow journalist as we headed to the season finale in Abu Dhabi on 8 December 2024. They had a point, given McLaren's pattern of rise before a fall. In truth, you would have been hard pushed to find anyone in the press room who did not want to see them succeed as the constructors' champions. They had entertained us all season with some remarkable performances – and given us plenty of compelling stories to follow up. We had witnessed the ups and downs, the emotions of Norris and Piastri's wins, and the moments when they had squandered valuable points. It truly had been a fantastic season, now coming down to the wire for the team title, which is the one they all really want to win.

Given what was at stake, there was understandably a sense of nervous anticipation within McLaren's hospitality unit in the Abu Dhabi paddock. The team had kindly invited a select group of journalists along to a brunch with Brown, ahead of practice. A colleague bluntly put to him: 'it would be soul-crushing if you lose …' Brown replied: 'We're trying to do what got us here and not race any differently or think about the championship. I won't be calculating the championship permutations every lap: "He's in that position. Where are we?" I've spoken to a lot of other athletes that have been in this situation – Mark Messier, Anže Kopitar [both multiple Stanley Cup-winning ice-hockey stars] – and they're all like, "If you're not nervous, you're lying." So of course, there's adrenaline and nervousness. We'll be massively disappointed to not win it, but if that happens, we need to quickly shift our focus to what we've achieved this year. We've come from the brink of insolvency to five race wins, the second most consecutive podiums in McLaren's history, and we've gone down to the last race against Ferrari, beating Red Bull and Mercedes along the way. So if you offered me, at the beginning of '23, finishing second in the championship, winning five races, fourteen podiums in a row, I would have bitten your hand off. Of course, we'll be disappointed, but we'll need to quickly reflect on what we have accomplished, and be pretty damn proud.'

Brown's perspective was uplifting. He was asked too about whether he had any regrets about not using team orders earlier in the season to benefit Norris's own title bid. 'I don't tend to regret things,' he said. 'I tend to learn and go, "I could have done that differently." Otherwise you'd live in a series of regrets.'

Then the conversation turned to Norris and how much he had evolved as a driver over the past 12 months. Brown explained that was the ethos behind the whole team's development. 'I think Lando has learned a lot on how to race Max,' he said. 'Max has been transparent on how he races. I think Lando put up a great fight in Mexico, but also kept them out of an accident.

'In any sports team, you can go hire all the big names, but they don't always work. When I joined McLaren, there was friction between the leadership. It was all new to me, but I could see a lack of respect among some of the senior leaders. They blamed each other. But we're all working on the same race car, so let's all work together to fix it. Now we have a really good atmosphere. My job now is to keep that.'

Another job currently in hand was winning the constructors' title in Abu Dhabi. And once our interview had finished and the journalists had left the McLaren hospitality unit, I don't think there was anyone who believed they would not see out the task.

• • •

During his press conference after qualifying on pole, Norris was assured and confident, expressing his determination to finish the season with a victory. He wasn't content with merely securing the constructors' title; he wanted to win the race. Piastri had qualified second, with Ferrari's Sainz in third. Leclerc's Ferrari, however, would start from 19th on the grid having had a poor qualifying session and a ten-place grid penalty for an unscheduled engine component change. This situation heavily favoured McLaren, who had a 21-point lead. Yet, Norris was not interested in playing it safe. He stated: 'We've got to beat Ferrari, that's the aim, but we want to do it in style, and we want to win. I want to win.'

It was crucial that both drivers understood their responsibilities to the team: to bring the cars home and score maximum points, avoiding any internal conflicts. Any contact could eliminate both cars from the race, and Sainz would be ready to capitalise in his final race for Ferrari. Piastri echoed Norris's sentiments, adding: 'We'll do whatever we can to make sure we win the championship, and that's by far the biggest goal tomorrow. I'm sure we'd both love to win the race, but everyone would love to win the championship even more. So we'll make sure that happens.'

Both McLarens made a good start to the race, so too did Verstappen, who then tagged the back of Piastri's McLaren, sending both cars into a spin at turn one. It was a significant blow to the Aussie's race and McLaren's prospects, as he ended up facing the wrong direction and had to turn around after the rest of the field had passed. He found himself running dead last. Verstappen, who had caused the accident, also spun but completed a full 360-degree turn and rejoined the race in the right direction. Piastri remained composed and sarcastically labelled the Dutchman's bungled overtake as 'the move of a world champion'. Verstappen received a ten-second time penalty, but it was little consolation to McLaren. Piastri then made contact with Franco Colapinto's Williams in an eventful opening few laps, earning a ten-second penalty himself.

Piastri's incidents removed him from contention and left Norris as the sole McLaren driver in the points, and he maintained his position at the front. Sainz pitted on lap 25 in an attempt to undercut Norris, but McLaren responded a lap later by pitting Norris for fresh tyres, allowing him to hold his lead. As the laps counted down, Sainz was joined by Leclerc's Ferrari and the two red cars loomed behind the papaya McLaren. Any mistake or mechanical failure now would have been devastating for McLaren. The pressure was immense. Norris, who had been accused by some sections of the media of lacking mental toughness and branded 'Lando No-wins', was on course to deliver McLaren the constructors' title.

When he crossed the finish line to win the race, the Abu Dhabi sky lit up with fireworks as Norris, with Piastri coming home in tenth to score a point, clinched McLaren's first constructors' title in 26 years. Norris had led from start to finish and held his nerve in the most stressful of situations. Sainz was second and Leclerc was a brilliant third – having started in nineteenth on the grid. The victory also ensured that Norris would finish second in the drivers' championship to Verstappen. Norris whooped over his team's radio before declaring: 'Next year's going to be my year, too!' It had been a thrilling end to a fantastic season.

Wild celebrations erupted in the McLaren garage and hospitality, champagne corks popping, cigars being lit and congratulations all round. In the middle of all the festivities were Stella, Brown and McLaren's board members and the owners, including Shaikh Salman bin Khalifa Al Khalifa, the board chairman of Mumtalakat plus a member of the Bahrain royal family.

While the revelries continued at McLaren, Leclerc lamented on how much it had 'hurt' for Ferrari to fall short of their goal. He blamed a slow start to the campaign, saying in the opening races they 'were nowhere near being in the fight for the constructors' title'. For Sainz, who was now leaving the Italian team, his second-place finish was a 'bittersweet moment'. He'd done what he could, but it simply was not enough to overcome McLaren's advantage.

When Norris was interviewed afterwards, he thanked the team before proclaiming: 'Me and Zak already said we're going to get absolutely hammered tonight, so I'm excited. This is a historic moment for the team. They're going to want to celebrate, and I want to celebrate with them, so it's going to be a good night!'

It later emerged that as part of the exuberant celebrations, the team's owners chartered planes to fly McLaren's staff to Bahrain for a party, before flying them back to Abu Dhabi the following day. I'd discover that there were some disgruntled teams in the paddock who had tentatively suggested such celebrations contravened the cost cap. It was typical F1 politics, and nothing was going to stop McLaren from enjoying the moment.

When Stella made his way back to hospitality he had come back down to earth. He stood around a table with dictaphones spread out in front of him. I asked him how he was going to ensure that the team maintained its place at the top, drawing him to Brown's interview in Singapore where he had revealed Stella's 'don't eat the poisoned biscuit' motto. 'How has the poison biscuit leaked outside of McLaren? I have learned that the journalists are too smart or I am too naive!' he exclaimed, before continuing: 'Refusing the poison biscuit is one of the fundamental elements of checking and validating that the culture we have created not only works, but exists in real life. We will always have poison biscuits dropped in our cup in an attempt to create division, to break the cohesion that we have in the team. But we say every day that we are not going to pick the poison biscuit. It would be very naive and arrogant to think that we are perfect and now we can relax because we are world champions. The best philosophy is that you start again, as if you had lost. That is what we are going to do in preparation for next season.'

Stella had done an incredible job turning the team around, and incidentally I had voted for him in *Autosport*'s end-of-season awards ceremony as my person of the year, which he won. He added: 'From the time I joined McLaren to now, end of the season, celebrating a championship, means that we've gone through a circle. I often mention to the team that at the first race in 2015 in Australia, there was five seconds between our lap in Q1 and pole position. We have gone all the way thanks to great resilience, thanks to great belief. I would like to thank in particular Zak and Paul Walsh, and also all our shareholders for their faith in the change that they have implemented. The final bit of this circle came through the people. I am not sure if [others] can appreciate what it means to see such rapid progress of a thousand people, if they did not see it for themselves, but that is what has happened. That's what we've gone through at McLaren and hopefully this is not the end point, but the starting point for the future.'

Stella was wearing a distinctive pin badge on his shirt, depicting a crash helmet. When asked about it, he explained it was the image of Gil de Ferran's race helmet. Paying tribute to the Brazilian, he said: 'Gil was the first person I talked to when the proposal to become team principal came about. Because of his friendship, because of his wisdom and intelligence, because of his incredible qualities at a human level and because he was and had always been a great racer, he was the first person that I consulted. To me it was very clear that whatever I was going to build, I was going to build it with Gil. He has always been on my side. He was my advisor, my personal consultant. If we implemented a culture, if we created the belief, if we increased the standards to the required level, it was because Gil was also part of the process. It was straightforward to dedicate our first victory in Miami to Gil. He was always with us. I wear this pin all the time when I am at the factory. And for the final race, I needed to give a clear message to myself and to everyone that Gil was with us throughout the season.' It was an emotional and heartfelt tribute.

• • •

A few days after McLaren were crowned champions, I spoke to Louise McEwen, chief marketing officer at McLaren Racing, about the impact the success has had on the team's brand. McEwen had started working with McLaren as a consultant in 2014 and had previously worked for the team's title sponsor, the Vodafone group, for nine years. I felt that in order to quantify the team's success, other than in the form of on-track victories and the balance sheet, it was important to understand the significance of the team's brand. There was no doubt that Norris's popularity had rocketed, as too had Piastri's during his time in F1, but the team's marketability was incredibly different as it transitioned from the negativity of 2015.

McEwen tells me: 'There's this real image of our car that I sometimes use when I'm talking about the evolution of our brand. It's a shot of the McLaren MP4-30, from 2015 – pretty much a black car with a red line on it. There are very few partners on it. It was a DNF, and there's smoke billowing out the back. If I was to show a modern [new] fan that picture, they probably wouldn't even recognise the car as a McLaren. We'd got to the point where we were without a powertrain, without a title partner. The brand had lost its way, for various reasons. The only way to go was up. And one of our late shareholders, Mansour [Ojjeh], said to me, "Lou, we need to be more Luke Skywalker right now not Darth Vader." It was a really good analogy and I've often remembered it.

'What then happened was a process of rediscovering who we were. We kind of had to look inside a bit. We no longer had the wins to dine out on, we no longer had the drivers, we no longer had the powertrain or the partners. So we went right back to our roots and that incredible DNA and heritage.'

It is worth remembering McEwen is talking about an era before F1 benefitted from the huge swell in popularity generated by Netflix's *Drive to Survive*, which captivated audiences during the pandemic. Back then, the McLaren team turned to founder Bruce McLaren for inspiration. McEwen continues: 'We're second to Ferrari on the grid in terms of that long legacy and heritage. The papaya colour came back to the car again. Bruce had chosen papaya, astutely acknowledging that it stood out really well, even on black and white TV. Also, as he was driving his car, other drivers would see the bright papaya car in their wing mirrors. It was really distinctive. In those early days, there were a couple of sludgy versions. It took a little bit of time to get the fire right and bright, but now it makes me incredibly proud to see it. It really stands out on the TV screens, and when you have the helicopter view down the pit lane, the papaya just screams out.'

McLaren's brand has grown incredibly strong, however, like Stella, McEwen knows the team cannot afford to stand still.

'We're world champions for a year, which is very exciting,' she says. 'But there's also that feeling already, after the [Abu Dhabi] debrief this morning, that we've done it, but our margin of winning was 2 per cent – just 16 points over Ferrari. If we do it again, we've got to increase that. Our ambitions are to set the standard for high performance in sport, not even just F1. We're in a really solid position, but we've got everything to lose if we don't keep it up. So now is not the time for complacency. It's really about pushing the boundaries even more. You can't take your foot off the accelerator, otherwise you go backwards.'

• • •

As McLaren's return to the summit of the F1 standings settled in, the season concluded with the final analysis of the drivers' championship. Norris had finished in second place, 63 points behind Verstappen. Piastri was fourth, a further 82 points back. They had come up short but it had proved to be a valuable season for the two drivers. Norris felt the campaign had been his most educational yet and would help in his aspirations to become a future F1 world champion. 'I have probably learned more this year than I've learned probably in like the last three years,' he told me in an interview for *Autosport*. 'I learned more about how to win races and how to be in a position of fighting for a championship. I was the one who had the chance to put [Verstappen] under pressure. I'm proud that it was us at McLaren. No one else was doing that. The last few years have been about learning how to drive the car. This year, I've learned what I need to be, to be a champion. It is a different mentality.'

Norris explained how self-scrutiny had served to propel him forward. He had thrived on the pressure he had placed on himself to win. He spoke about how victory in the constructors' championship had forced the team to adopt a front-running mentality.

Initially, like himself, they had not been ready to fight Red Bull or Verstappen. However, both the team and Norris individually had grown stronger as a result of this learning and evolution.

Norris's words echoed the same message that had come from Brown, Stella and McEwan, about the unwavering continuation of McLaren. The team's perpetual narrative of success following adversity is part of its very DNA. This resilience stems from the people who work for and support the team. A fitting quote from Bruce McLaren in his autobiography captures this spirit: 'First comes natural ability. There are hundreds with it, but there must always be the dedication to want to apply it, continue applying it, and keep improving it.' It perfectly encapsulates the team's motto: 'Forever forward.'

ACKNOWLEDGEMENTS

To my children, Ted and Rose, for their love and for making me appreciate every day I spend in their company. This book has been written across 17 countries, on flights, train journeys – and family holidays!

To Mum and Dad, Dave, Maggie, Lucy and Sim for your backing – and for being there whenever I am not.

To all those who kindly gave up their time to speak to me as part of this book, for providing your knowledge, wisdom and anecdotes.

In fact, I'd also like to thank all those people I have spoken to over the past 13 seasons working in F1, who have helped shape *Forever Forward*.

The interviews, the off-record discussions over a beer; all of the insight into this special team has been invaluable!

To my work colleagues at *Autosport*; Rebecca, MMB, Alex, JBL, Haydn, Ed, Codders, Fil & Eli and the countless other people who help with the day job!

To all my friends on the circuit, for your jokes, kindness, encouragement and your questions in press conferences, something I feel incredibly strongly about.

To Lorna and all the team at Penguin Random House, for making this book such a pleasure to write and backing the vision I had 12 months earlier.

And to Melanie, my agent, for starting this journey in the first place.

Finally, to those at McLaren who have helped me tell this story. To Harry and Steve, Lando, Oscar, Andrea and Zak. It was a pleasure to tell McLaren's story and culminated in the most spectacular of endings.

IMAGE CREDITS

Rainer Schlegelmilch / Stringer / Getty Images (Images 1 & 6)
LAT Images / Stringer / Getty Images (Images 2, 9 & 13)
David Phipps / Staff / Getty Images (Images 3, 7, 8, 10 & 11)
JimSchwabel / Alamy Stock Photo (Image 4)
Heritage Image Partnership Ltd / Alamy Stock Photo (Image 5)
Ercole Colombo / Stringer / Getty Images (Image 12)
Sutton Images / Stringer / Getty Images (Images 14, 15 & 21)
UTA TOCHTERMANN / Contributor / Getty Images (Image 16)
David Goddard / Contributor / Getty Images (Image 17)
Mark Thompson / Staff / Getty Images (Images 18, 20 & 23)
Paul Gilham / Staff / Getty Images (Image 19)
dpa picture alliance archive / Alamy Stock Photo (Image 22)
Steven Tee / Staff / Getty Images (Image 24)
Getty Images / Stringer / Getty Images (Image 25)
MARK THOMPSON / Contributor / Getty Images (Image 26)
GONZALO FUENTES / Contributor / Getty Images (Image 27)
Mark Sutton / Staff / Getty Images (Image 28)
James Moy / Alamy Stock Photo (Image 29)
corleve / Alamy Stock Photo (Image 30)
Andy Hone / Stringer / Getty Images (Image 31)
NurPhoto / Contributor / Getty Images (Images 32, 33, 35 & 36)
Clive Rose - Formula 1 / Contributor / Getty Images (Image 34)

INDEX